François Mitterrand

IN MEMORIAM
David Bell

1921–1992

François Mitterrand

A Political Biography

DAVID S. BELL

polity

First published in 2005 by Polity Press

Polity Press
65 Bridge Street
Cambridge CB2 1UR, UK

Polity Press
350 Main Street
Malden, MA 02148, USA

ISBN: 0-7456-3104-5
ISBN: 0-7456-3105-3 (pb)

A catalogue record for this book is available from the British Library and has been applied for from the Library of Congress.

Typeset in 11.25 on 13pt Dante
by SNP Best-set Typesetter Ltd, Hong Kong
Printed and bound in Great Britain by TJ International Ltd, Padstow, Cornwall

For further information on Polity, visit our website: www.polity.co.uk

Contents

Acknowledgements

My thanks are due to the many people who have spoken to me about the subject and who have read the manuscript or parts of it before publication. I am particularly grateful to Dr Guiat, Professor Kuhn, Professor B. D. Graham and Dr D. B. Goldey for their scholarly comments. I wish to thank the National Archives of France, the Institut François Mitterrand and the private archives of Guy Mollet as well as the Socialist Party whose documents I was able to consult. Grateful thanks are also due to the Nuffield Foundation without whose help this work would have been impossible. For my part as a biographer I just about meet Dr Johnson's stipulation that you should have broken bread with your subject and, for the record, I, personally, see the Socialist Party's record as globally positive. I am also grateful to the many people who have given their time to talk to me about this biography and I am aware that their interpretation of Mitterrand's political career will not be the same as mine. I am responsible of course for any errors that persist.

D. S. Bell

Preface

This is a study of the politics of François Mitterrand. Mitterrand's career is an important one both for France and for Europe. He was in power in key positions through the Fourth Republic and became de facto leader of the Opposition in the Fifth before winning two presidential elections in 1981 and 1988. It was a career which covered decolonization, the crucial moment of the end of the Cold War, the collapse of the Soviet Union, German reunification, the opening out of French society and the building of European institutions. As the President, Mitterrand left an enduring domestic legacy, freeing up broadcasting and changing France's economy; and in foreign policy, the contemporary situations of the Euro and of European institutions are in part at least a result of his activity. Mitterrand, it should be remembered, took the route of European integration when the experiment in 'socialism in one country' failed in 1983 and then took those opportunities that arose to push it with vigour. In this choice he was more like de Gaulle's successors than like de Gaulle himself, but the enlarged Europe of the Euro and of Franco-German partnership are part of Mitterrand's legacy.

Thus Mitterrand is not a political figure who can be ignored, either as an actor on the French domestic scene or in European and international affairs. Mitterrand realized that the institution of the presidency presented an opportunity and, by including the Communists (who seemed excluded from power) and dominating the Socialist Party in coalition, he enabled the left to exercise power in the Fifth Republic for ten years. In this process, whether consciously or not, Mitterrand created a governmental left, pragmatic, capable of competing for office and effecting significant social change.

There is one key feature of Mitterrand's political life: its longevity. His political career, broadly understood, spans three Republics and one dictatorship, service of the Vichy regime as well as the Resistance, and a trajectory that moves from the conservative right to the radical left. Mitterrand was an eminent ministerial figure in the Fourth Republic who, had the regime survived a few more years (or perhaps months), might have been nominated Prime Minister. His tenure as President, elected twice, was an unprecedented fourteen years; for ten of those he held a majority in the Assembly and his hold on real power among Fifth Republic presidents comes second only to that of de Gaulle.

This book is an examination of how he achieved his political leadership and the techniques he used in attaining and wielding political power, of what has been called the structuring of politics so that he will win.[1] Mitterrand's political career (broadly understood) has to be set in context for the nature of his path to be seen properly. Thus the aim here has been to show where Mitterrand took one route rather than another and to show something of the nature of those decisions by investigating his way of structuring choices.[2] Mitterrand is therefore treated in this work as a political leader who took opportunities as they arose and who, like F. E. Smith (a nineteenth-century Conservative grandee), 'gloried in the endless adventure of governing men'.[3] Seen in this way, Mitterrand emerges from his long career as less enigmatic than is sometimes portrayed, and as one political figure amongst many others; the manifold paradoxes of a sinuous ascent are less puzzling than is often assumed. Mitterrand can be seen as a tough and single-minded professional at home with power and driven by a *libido dominandi*.

There are many biographies of the fourth of the Fifth Republic's presidents; there are many personal memoirs by collaborators, and Mitterrand's private life has been extensively examined, as has his early career. This is not an attempt to compete with those, nor is it a psychological or character analysis. Still less is this a 'balance sheet' setting out the lists of achievements and mistakes (though judgements of that sort cannot be avoided in places) and it is certainly neither the case for the prosecution nor for the defence. Perhaps it is like the old saying about making laws and making sausages: if you like them, it is inadvisable to look too closely at either process. François Mauriac, one of Mitterrand's supporters and a long-time friend, put it this way in his '*bloc-notes*' column: 'I ever took him for a little saint.'[4] There are many works, particularly on the first septennate, that offer differing accounts of Mitterrand's achievements. Moreover, the technical evaluation of Mitterrand's policies has spawned a sub-genre of its own and this book is not an addition to it.

Mitterrand was an advocate of colonialism, a decolonizer, an opponent of the Fifth Republic as well as one of its stalwarts. Over a long career he adopted many positions, some of them contradictory, and wrote copiously on most aspects of political controversy. He was also a lawyer and, briefly, practised at the Paris Bar when he lost his seat in the Assembly in 1958 until 1962. There is certainly evidence in Mitterrand's career of his ability to master a brief and to set out a case with forensic skill. His ability to re-invent himself is part of this talent and he did so on several occasions with no qualms.

None of this is exceptional. To take his changes of position: French pol-itics would be denuded of some of its principal figures if youthful alle-giances of the extreme right and the extreme left were held against them. At home in the UK, the New Labour front bench would be deprived of its leading modernizers if the former Trotskyites, Marxists, nationalizers and anti-Europeans were to be judged by their student (and sometimes not so ancient) allegiances. Mitterrand's wartime itinerary, from support for Pétain to support for the Resistance, is not without its parallels. Unlike his rival Alain Savary, few people joined de Gaulle in London in 1940. For example, de Gaulle's own entourage included people like Couve de Murville and Michel Debré, whose initial support for Pétain was white-washed out by their subsequent devotion to the General. Mitterrand retained the friendship and the help of many of the people from the various milieux in which he had mixed over the years. This did not deter-mine the shape of his career any more than did the acceptance of money from reactionary Texan business leaders prevent President Johnson from promoting and then implementing the most far-reaching civil rights legis-lation in the United States.[5]

But Mitterrand, showing a lawyer's facility, vigorously defended the positions he espoused: whatever the cause he took up, piano was not his forte. Over his long political life, this gave rise to a number of positions vigorously adopted, advocated and then dropped with something of the effrontery of a carnival shill. This is not unusual in politics and Mitterrand's case only stands out because of its sometimes strident tone and his lengthy career. His earlier commitments were forgotten over time but were exhumed as opponents sought to discredit his new stances. Mitterrand is unusual in that his move was from right to left, becoming more radical and less Catholic with age, whereas the usual path is from youthful marxism to an elderly conservatism in the bosom of the Church. But none of this could be held against a working politician even though, as happens on the left, a constant political philosophy is usually expected. Mitterrand was fond of good living and good books, but although his literary and histori-cal culture is often cited, he proved an unremarkable writer and certainly no philosopher. But then, in different circumstances, to quote Mauriac again, 'He could have been like me . . . a writer . . . rather than living his stories.'[6]

Mitterrand mastered the art of selling himself to the world while keeping everybody at arm's length. Most political motives are complicated but the argument here is that the search for the solution to the enigma puts far too elaborate a face on matters: François Mitterrand's politics were not paradoxical and did not follow a 'great melody'.[7] It was what Sidney Hook calls an 'eventful' political career. His was a career of ambition and that forms the mainspring of political conduct in any age and at any time. Seen in this way, the enigma and the contradiction dissolve and the portrait of a persistent and working politician emerges, more nuanced perhaps, but also less overbearing. And, of course, a politician determined to get to the top with the 'bullet and automatic purpose' that Ted Hughes identified in certain creatures. But there is a political artist at work here, brilliant (if morally peccant). Mitterrand's politics recalls Gore Vidal's description of Roosevelt's 'inspired, patternless arabesques . . . artfully dodging this way and that'.[8] France is the only country to have a Pantheon dedicated to the great figures of its history. It is, however, not until much later that it is decided whether a politician should be within it.

Abbreviations

AF	Action française
ARS	Action républicaine et sociale
CERES	Centre d'études de recherches et d'éducation socialistes
CFDT	Confédération française démocratique du travail
CFLN	Comité français de libération nationale
CGT	Confédération générale du travail
CIR	Convention des institutions républicaines
CNIP	Centre national des indépendants paysans
CNR	Conseil national de la Résistance
CSAR	Comité secret d'action révolutionnaire ('Cagoule')
CSG	Contribution sociale généralisée
EDC	European Defence Community
EEC	European Economic Community
EMS	European Monetary System
EMU	Economic and Monetary Union
ENA	Ecole nationale d'administration
EU	European Union
FGDS	Fédération de la gauche démocratique et socialiste
FLN	Front de libération nationale
FLNKS	Front de Libération Nationale Kanake et Socialiste
FN	Front national
GATT	General Agreement on Tariffs and Trade
GDR	German Democratic Republic
IEP	Institut d'études politiques
IHEDN	Institut des hautes études de défense
IMF	International Monetary Fund
JCR	Jeunesse communiste révolutionnaire
LVF	Légion des volontaires français
MCAs	Monetary Compensatory Amounts
MNPGD	Mouvement national des prisonniers de guerre et déportés
MRG	Mouvement des radicaux de gauche

MRP	Mouvement républicain populaire
NATO	North Atlantic Treaty Organization
OAS	Organisation de l'armée secrète
OPEC	Organization of Petrol Exporting Countries
ORA	Organisation de résistance de l'armée
PACA	Provence Alpes Côte d'Azur
PCF	Parti communiste français
PDM	Progrès et démocratie moderne
PLO	Palestinian Liberation Organisation
POW	Prisoner of War
PPF	Parti populaire français
PRL	Parti républicain de la liberté
PS	Parti socialiste
PSA	Parti socialiste autonome
PSF	Parti social français
PSU	Parti socialiste unifié
RCPR	Rassemblement pour la Calédonie dans la République
RDA	Rassemblement démocratique africain
RGR	Rassemblement des gauches républicaines
RMI	Revenu minimum d'insertion
RNPG	Rassemblement national des prisonniers de guerre
RPF	Rassemblement du peuple français
RPR	Rassemblement pour la République
SDI	Strategic Defence Initiative
SFIO	Section française de l'internationale ouvrière
Sofres	Société française d'enquêtes par sondage
SOL	Service d'ordre légionnaire
SPD	Sozialdemokratische Partei Deutschlands
STO	Service du travail obligatoire
UDF	Union pour la démocratie française
UDR	Union des démocrates pour la république
UDSR	Union démocratique et socialiste de la résistance
UGSD	Union de la gauche socialiste et démocrate
USSR	Union of Socialist Soviet Republics
WEU	West European Union

1

1916–1944

As Francis Bacon noted, all rising to a great place is by a winding path. Mitterrand's early years are controversial because of the accusations, widely reproduced, that he was active on the extreme right as a student and then deeply implicated with the wartime Vichy regime. It was a past that was dragged up on numerous occasions[1] to attempt to discredit Mitterrand, and it became a fraught topic on the publication of Péan's biography about those years in 1994.[2] Lurid rumours were given impetus by the inconsistent accounts Mitterrand gave of his time as a young student in Marshal Philippe Pétain's Vichy government working as a minor clerk.

Mitterrand himself has not helped clarify matters. He followed Gracian, who advised 'without lying, do not tell the whole truth', and whose writings are honeycombed with evasions, misdirections and contradictions.[3] Gracian was a seventeenth-century Spanish Jesuit aphorist with a mordently misanthropic view of human life. Mitterrand's statement that, 'back in France, I became a Resistant, without great problems', is *suppressio veri*.[4] This propensity to mislead is linked with his journey from the conservative right to the centre, then to head the Socialist Party in alliance with the Communist Party and with his desire to retell his own history to suit the needs of the time. For example, he implausibly claimed to have attended the anti-fascist meetings of Benda, Malraux and Chamson, to have been hostile to Franco, to have supported the university left on occasion[5] and to have sympathized with the socialist-communist-radical Popular Front in the 1930s.[6]

Early Life

For Mitterrand, the main formative political experience seems to have been the Second World War. In point of fact, his years at school and then at university were those of a middle-class, provincial Catholic with the attitudes of the time, who was comfortably off with servants and most of the amenities, including a Chenard-Walker car.[7] What does emerge, from testimony about Mitterrand's childhood, is the picture of a very religious (not to say devout), confident, determined, self-assured, but at the same time shy and aloof, individual who read voraciously. Mitterrand was reported, at various junctures until leaving university, as having a religious vocation (though also a political leaning). It is unlikely that the springs of his politics are to be found in his childhood or family circumstances, although his grandfather is credited with the remark: 'this little one will get himself talked about'.[8] In the Charente region where his family lived, there had been religious clashes between Protestants and Catholics. Although it was essentially rural, there does seem to have been a provincial snobbery of Brahmamic complexity separating the mainly Protestant and socialist or radical cognac producers from the rest of regional society and separate from the middle-class Catholics who were on the conservative right.

François Maurice Adrien Marie Mitterrand was born on 26 October 1916 in the family home at 22 rue Abel-Guy near the centre of the small town of Jarnac, Charente. François was the fifth of eight children and had three brothers: Robert, the eldest, went to L'Ecole polytechnique, Jacques entered the elite military school of Saint Cyr, and Philippe, the youngest, was conscripted onto Service du travail obligatoire (STO) and, on his return, became a farmer. There were also four sisters: Marie-Antoinette, Marie-Josèphe, Colette and Geneviève. Joseph, his father, was a well-educated man and railway employee who rose to become the stationmaster in Angoulême. He left the railway company at the age of 56, but he later inherited a vinegar-making business from his father-in-law. He was, however, cold and austere with a pronounced preference for long solitary walks. In the depression he became a supporter of the conservative Colonel François de La Rocque (leader of the militant Croix de feu right-wing party). Yvonne, Mitterrand's mother, was also a pious Catholic who gave time to social work and who read the classics of French literature and encouraged her children in that interest. In politics, she had been a supporter of the extreme right-wingers Paul Déroulède and General Boulanger.[9] She was of weak health and died at the age of 58 in January 1936. Mitterrand was only 19 at the time, but – unlike his father – she is rarely mentioned in his writings.

There were other influential family figures, including his maternal grandfather Jules Lorrain, who owned the vinegar works, and was a minor conservative Republican politician who had been elected to the municipal council. Jules Lorrain, who seems to have been an attractive and gregarious man, took the young Mitterrand in hand during long walks in the country in which he learned about the flowers and shrubs. There was also his son, Robert Lorrain, who was influential in Marc Sangnier's newspaper *Le Sillon* (a precursor of Christian democracy), but who died at the age of 20. Robert Lorrain was a friend of the author François Mauriac and the distinguished author was in consequence well-disposed to the young Mitterrand.

At the age of 9 Mitterrand went to the Collège Saint-Paul in Angoulême as a boarder. This was a religiously oriented school and Mitterrand's outlook was reinforced by the diocesan priests who ran it. It is not rare in France for politicians to have this religious background, but on the left it is unusual and his move leftward was accompanied by a loss of faith.[10] Mitterrand was a good but not an outstanding student (he failed the oral for the *baccalauréat* at first attempt), but he did well enough to go to university.

At the age of 17, in October 1934, Mitterrand went up to Paris (looking more like Tintin than Tonton) to study law, a subject which, as Burke observed, does more to strengthen the mind than to liberalize it. He was a student at both the Sorbonne and the Ecole libre des sciences politiques, and was, along with one hundred or so other provincial middle-class students, a resident in the modestly provided Marist student residence at 104 rue de Vaugirard. Here he made lifelong friendships with other students (Marot, Bénet, Dalle, Bettencourt, Fontanet and others), but the residence did not force them into a religious pattern. Mitterrand, however, was one of the faithful: a member of the Jeunesse Etudiante Chrétienne, his devout Catholicism impressed the Marists of the residence and some of his contemporary writings are of a soupy religiosity. His faith did not seem attenuated by his assiduous frequentation of student cafés and the availability of cinema, theatre, music and books. Mitterrand wrote a good deal on literature for student publications and joined the charity Saint-Vincent-de-Paul (of which his father was a supporter) and he became the president of his student section in 1937. This was when the student world (small and numbering about 30,000 in Paris at the time) and political life were in one of their most turbulent phases. The residence would have been affected by the politics of the time: it was a relatively conservative – not extreme – setting that would have strongly disapproved of the Popular Front, but where the extreme-right monarchist movement Action française's eponymous newspaper would have been read and appreciated.

In the wake of the Stavisky scandal there had been riots in Paris in February 1934 that had pitted the extreme right and the communists against the police and there were then clashes with the socialist left as the Popular Front alliance began to consolidate. (Serge Stavisky was a petty swindler who had pulled a number of politicians into his network and this, when he was unmasked, added to the discredit of the Third Republic political class.) Germany was rearming, civil war was brewing in Spain and the first bow waves of the Popular Front were arriving. There were violent confrontations between left and right in the Latin Quarter and the student body was torn between the two. It is probable that Mitterrand participated with de La Rocque's supporters (the Croix de feu) in the demonstration of 11 November 1934, which ended in front of Gaston Doumergue's house on the Avenue Foch.[11] Doumergue, supported by de La Rocque and a popular figure on the conservative right, returned to power after the riots of February 1934 but his government of National Union, including Marshal Pétain but excluding the PCF and SFIO, had fallen in early November.[12]

Mitterrand asserted that his passage through de La Rocque's movement was no more than a brief two weeks and that he quit because it was a tedious organization.[13] He had become a 'volontaire national' of the Croix de feu's youth section in November 1934. This affiliation was in keeping with the conservative but social Catholic outlook he had adopted, and was consistent with Rome's view at the time, which was hostile to Action française. The Croix de feu, with its parades, banners and uniforms, and its slogan ('Family, Work, Fatherland', later appropriated by Vichy) has become assimilated to the French extreme anti-parliamentary right. However, although it had a uniformed marching wing (as did most political parties at the time), and some of de La Rocque's supporters were involved in the riots of 1934, the Croix de feu had not fanned the flames. All the same, it was dissolved in June 1936 when the Popular Front came to power and de La Rocque recast his movement as the Parti social français (PSF). This was highly anti-communist, though not anti-Semitic, a mass conservative party that grew in popularity; it was a movement of institutional reform calling for a reinforced executive and inevitably more law and order. But it was more committed to a patriotic conservatism based on a moderate programme than it was a fascistoid sect like Jacques Doriot's Parti populaire français (PPF). The distinction is crucial, although there was movement across the boundary particularly by those conservatives angered by the Popular Front.

Mitterrand's social links had taken him into the company of Jean Delage, a 'talent spotter' for newspapers who then introduced him to journalism on L'Echo de Paris, Henri de Kérillis's PSF-leaning paper, and he wrote a column about student life from autumn 1936 to the end of 1937. This newspaper was another link with the Croix de feu/PSF, and it took the standard conservative line of the time, condemning the Popular Front, the communists and the Spanish Republican cause while supporting de La Rocque, but it was anti-Nazi and anti-Munich. Mitterrand was a weekly commentator on literature, but not on politics.

Mitterrand was drawn into the right-wing campaigns with apparent enthusiasm, as became clear on 1 February 1935 when he joined the Action française's demonstration 'France for the French' against the '*invasion des métèques*' (he referred to the Latin Quarter as a 'Tower of Babel'). This was in reality a protest against the Polish Jews who had arrived in French universities because they could not study in Poland as a result of a *numerus clausus*, and an echo of it can be found in Mitterrand's published 'regret' that the Latin Quarter had been invaded by 'outsiders'. Mitterrand denied participating despite the fact that there was a photo of him at it in *Le Figaro*[14] and that he had written to his old school chaplain about it (parts of his letter were reprinted in the school journal).[15] Mitterrand also participated in January 1936 in the extreme right demonstration against Professor Gaston Jèze, who had served as adviser to the Ethiopian government at the League of Nations when Mussolini invaded Abyssinia. The conservative and extreme right (and *L'Echo de Paris*) generally supported Mussolini. In the law faculties, the extreme right, led by Action française, mounted a virulent campaign against Jèze, which was intended to force him out of the university. This succeeded to the extent that the university had to be shut from 11 to 18 January. In response, the Minister of Education (then on the left) tried to keep Jèze's courses open, though students polarized the university. Mitterrand was hostile to Jèze at this time.[16] He is shown in a picture taken on 5 March demonstrating against Jèze and then, after the events, wrote an article in *L'Echo de Paris* implying that he had relished the clash.[17]

Mitterrand met people connected with the Action française and its splinter Comité secret d'action revolutionnaire, known as the Cagoule. The Cagoule was a secret extreme right-wing organization working to destabilize or subvert the Republic; it developed during the years 1935–40 and was implicated in sabotages and assassinations. No definitive list of members has been established, but a secret list discovered by police in a raid on the home of the Cagoulard Aristide Corre in September 1937 did not include Mitterrand's name.[18] (The list, which is in alphabetical order, runs 'Mioux, Mirabel, Mitjaville, Mohrenschildt . . .').[19] On the other hand, he would, by the nature of his milieu, have met many of its members: Jean Bouvyer, for example, who married his sister Marie-Josèphe, and Mitterrand's brother Robert married the daughter of Colonel Cahier who was brother-in-law of the Cagoule's leader Eugène Deloncle.[20] Deloncle himself was jailed in 1938 for an attempted *coup de force*, but was set free by Vichy and then started up the fascist Mouvement social révolutionnaire in 1940.

Likewise, Mitterrand was not a member of Action française according to his friend Claude Roy (who did join).[21] Action française was active in his student lodging and many friends were members, but the movement had been condemned on the Papal Index in 1926, which meant that it would not attract the faithful. Its literary and writing fraternity would nevertheless have held an attraction for Mitterrand and its animator, Charles Maurras, was an author of stature (Mitterrand regularly read the newspaper). Many of this circle, like Angèle Polimann, the deputy who lived at the Marist residence, ended up as servants of the Vichy regime, as did François Méténier and Gabriel Jeantet (at that time student leaders of Action française).[22]

Of these people, it was royalist Bouvyer who provided the first test of Mitterrand's loyalties. Mitterrand had been a frequent visitor and a friend of the family in Jarnac. Jean Bouvyer, then a naive 19-year-old, was sucked into the Cagoule's plots. In 1937, the Cagoule was asked by Mussolini's secret services to murder two Italian anti-fascists (Carlo and Nello Rosellini) and this they did with the aid of the young Bouvyer acting as a scout. His implication was suspected but not proven, and he fled to join the army in North Africa. This might have been the end of the affair for him had he not boasted of his involvement; he was then arrested and convicted. Mitterrand's part in this was to come to the aid of the family and to visit the imprisoned Jean frequently. Mitterrand's actions were those of a good friend (though beyond the call of duty), a pattern that was to recur for the rest of his life.

In 1937, Mitterrand graduated fifth from the Ecole libre des sciences politiques and received a degree in public law, but none of this was of the first interest to the young man. He had also fallen heavily for Marie-Louise Terrasse (alias Catherine Langeais) and they were engaged before the war started, though she was rather less smitten than he was.[23] It is difficult to guess at Mitterrand's state of mind on the eve of the Second World War, but he did publish his reflections in the *Revue Montalembert* in April 1938.[24] In this rambling confessional, infused with a lassitude – or fatalism – he expresses his 'shame' at the *Anschluss* (the annexation of Austria by Germany in 1938) as if he were personally 'responsible'. This came from the pen of a writer for the anti-Munich section of the conservative right and hard-line staff of *L'Echo de Paris*, but it says little else, especially on the key question of what could be done. His brother recounts Mitterrand's pervasive pessimism at this time and a jaundiced view of the Republic he was defending; attitudes that were consonant with the Vichy regime to be installed in July 1940 under Marshal Pétain.[25]

The Second World War

In September 1938, Mitterrand was called up to join the French Army. For some reason he rejected the officer training that somebody of his background might have been expected to take up and became instead an infantryman. Mitterrand did not have a military temperament and was not suited to taking orders from people he considered to be boneheaded, or to the futile tasks which are the lot of the squaddie. But he nevertheless became a sergeant in the 23e RIC (23rd Colonial Infantry Regiment), whose barracks were close enough to Paris for frequent visits. This was a new phase in Mitterrand's education, because he met people from outside his relatively limited social circle and made close friends from very different classes. He was, however, already friendly with the socialist '*pied noir*' (Algerian-born Frenchman) Georges Dayan, who was the first left-winger he really got to know.[26]

At the outbreak of war the regiment was sent to complete the Maginot line in the north of France near Luxembourg where, in different sections, the 23e RIC spent the Phoney War. But on 10 May 1940 the Blitzkrieg began and the regiment was forced to fight rearguard action, falling back on Verdun. It was in the retreat on 14 June that Sergeant Mitterrand was hit by pieces of shell, though the location of the wound varies in different accounts and Mitterrand himself was vague.[27] In Mitterrand's story (though others differ), he was put on a stretcher cart and pulled through the crowds of refugees and abandoned on the verge while enemy aircraft strafed the road. Some questions remain about this account and about whom he travelled with.

He ended up in a military hospital in Bruyères (Vosges), possibly on 18 June, but the advancing German Army had already defeated the French and were in the town, so the wounded soldier became a prisoner. In time, he was interned as a prisoner of war (POW) in Stalag IXA near Cassel and then transferred to Stalag IXC near Weimar. Mitterrand recounted the lessons of the camp in his own words:

> At midday the Germans brought basins of turnip soup or loaves of bread and left you to shift for yourself for the day. First it was the reign of the knife. . . . after all the knife is the knife, a simple principle of established

order. However, that did not last three months. . . . new delegates, designated who knows how, cut black bread in six slices to the nearest millimetre, under the penetrating stare of universal suffrage. A rare and instructive sight. *I was witness to the birth of the social contract.* [original emphasis] I will not be teaching anybody anything in noting that the natural hierarchy of courage and straightforwardness which had established itself here as more powerful than the knife had only a distant correspondence with the old hierarchy, to the old social and moral order before the universe of the camps. Mockery! The old order had not resisted the trial of turnip soup![28]

He was then still on the political right and saw the defeat, as many did, as condign punishment for the Republic's failings.

In these camps the prisoners were demoralized and felt themselves to be abandoned; usually the only contact with home was through the Vichy authorities who worked on behalf of POWs. There are hints at a sympathy for Marshal Pétain at this time – though these are no more than allusions in letters. Information about the outside world and home was difficult to come by. It is also clear that Mitterrand's distinctive personality made its mark and one prison camp drawing depicts him as an emperor, although his contribution to making life tolerable for fellow prisoners was also remarked on.[29] Those he met in camps included Jean Munier, the Legionaire Bernard Finifter, the Communist Roger Pelat and the Jesuit Alphonse Delobre. In the camps, Mitterrand was able to learn and to teach as well as to write in the prisoners' journal.[30]

As evidenced by his attempts at escape, breaking out was on Mitterrand's agenda from the early days of incarceration. Perhaps this intensified when Marie-Louise Terrasse decided to end the engagement (he had sent her 2,000 letters) and he took it badly.[31] Mitterrand's objective was to get to the southern third of France, which had not been occupied after the armistice and which was run by the Head of State Marshal Pétain from Vichy. Mitterrand was to show great physical courage and considerable determination in his escape attempts. Prisoners in IXA were relatively unguarded; walking out was less the problem than planning and preparing an escape that could succeed in crossing Germany to reach Vichy France, more than 400 miles away.

Mitterrand made two attempts to escape before finally succeeding. His wartime itinerary has been retold in a confused and contradictory manner concerning details and essentials (notably the escapes). On 5 March 1941 Mitterrand and the Abbé Xavier Leclerc escaped probably from a work group and made their way to the Swiss border. But only three miles from freedom, on 25 March, fatigued beyond endurance (in Mitterrand's account), they made the mistake of walking in daylight through a crowd emerging from Sunday mass and were seized and taken back to the prison camp. The accounts of the second break out are likewise unclear, but on 28 November he again escaped (probably from another outside work group) and this time got to Metz with false Italian worker's papers. In Metz he checked into the Cecilia hotel, only to be reported by the hotel's owner (after one or possibly two days), arrested and sent to a camp in Boulay-en-Moselle near the French border.[32] As a two-times escaper he should have been destined for a high security Stalag, but he was for some reason put to work in the relatively laxly guarded hospital part of the camp, possibly through the intervention of his cousin Yves Dautun, a leader of Doriot's PPF.

On 10 December 1941, he got away. In his own account, he slipped into a ditch and wormed his way out. He may have been on work detail in the gardens and this story may have been more than a little embellished with incident to dramatize the youthful Mitterrand's daring. He went to a café run by Maya Baron that he had heard helped escapees, and was passed through an 'underground railway' to the non-occupied zone at Chamblay in the Jura, which he reached on 16 December. He was demobilized by Vichy and lodged by cousins and friends while he recovered from the dysphonic experience of the camps. He visited Jarnac in Occupied France for New Year 1942 and also made several other dangerous, for an escapee, visits home. He had lost his fiancée, although he kept in amicable touch with her. At the Liberation he was awarded the Croix de guerre (two citations) but not the escapers' *médaille des évadés*.[33]

Vichy

Mitterrand had to look for employment, and his contacts, ambition and sympathies drew him to Vichy, where he arrived in May 1942 and where he had a flat until December 1943. Until the end of 1941, Marshal Pétain and the Vichy regime had support, and the various Resistance groups were isolated.[34] Mitterrand seems to have been an admirer of Marshal Pétain and both at home in the regime and broadly sympathetic to its 'revolution'.[35] For most French people it looked as if the war had been lost and that the best would have to be made of a bad situation. The enormous prestige of Marshal Pétain supported an authoritarian system which was an anti-Republican, anti-Semitic regime laying claim to a conservative 'national revolution'. Mitterrand, however, started as a 'pétainist' and became a Resistance leader after an intermediate period when he had a foot in both camps.

Mitterrand was only a minor official (not a civil servant) in the Vichy POW Ministry (Commissariat aux prisonniers de guerre). As such he would not have had to pledge allegiance to Marshal Pétain, but it leaves open the question of how he related to the regime. That he was unaware of the nature of the regime and its increasingly vigorous collaboration is not credible. When Mitterrand arrived in the non-occupied zone, Pétain had already introduced the first anti-Semitic laws and had published them in the Vichy *Journal officiel* on 2 June 1941. He was a politicized student of law and elsewhere stated that, alive to the new culture, he had alerted his Jewish friend Finifter to the ambient anti-Semitic prejudice. Mitterrand also said that he thought Vichy's laws concerned only foreign Jews, although these measures also removed French Jews from the public sphere and stripped Algerian Jews of their nationality.[36] Mitterrand may have continued to believe that the Vichy regime was the lesser of two evils. At any rate, his arrival in Vichy in 1942 needs no special explanation: like most people of his background – and like most French people – he was a Pétain supporter at that time even though the old Marshal's prestige was beginning to dwindle.

Vichy was a 'bear-garden' inhabited by various competing coteries, ranging from those working for the Allies and de Gaulle to the full-hearted Nazi or fascist collaborationists.[37] The orientation of the departments of government depended on the relative power of those within them. Admiral Darlan headed the government from February 1941, but Pierre Laval, who had been excluded from the government in December 1940, returned in April 1942. The fanatic Darquier de Pellepoix had been made the Vichy Commissioner for Jewish Affairs on 5 May, and in July 1942 there was the round-up of Jews in Paris (the raid of Vel d'Hiv) and from then onwards there were regular deportations to Auschwitz. On 4 September labour conscription (STO) was introduced; on 8 November the Allies landed in North Africa and on 11 November the German Army entered the non-occupied zone, although the Vichy government was allowed to continue to administer 'its' territory. Mitterrand does not seem to have changed his view of Pétain's regime as a result of these events, although the public increasingly rejected collaboration and there was a fall in support for Pétain himself.

At the end of January 1942 Colonel Cahier found Mitterrand a job administering index cards on people in the section who were helping prisoners of war in Maurice Pinot's documentation service of the veterans' organization, the Légion française des combattants. He was also, at Pinot's request, making false papers for prisoners by the summer of 1942. Vichy's Légion brought together under one umbrella the members of all the veterans' organizations. Mitterrand seems not to have shown a particular disquiet.[38] However, he resigned from the Légion in April 1942, not because he opposed Pierre Laval, but because he felt it to be a futile post.[39]

By mid-May 1942, Mitterrand had been offered an essentially propaganda place in the press office staff of the Commission for 'the Board of Rehabilitation' of prisoners, where he remained until January 1943.[40] This Commission had been created the previous October and oversaw the 200,000 or so prisoners or escapees. It was run by Commissioner Maurice Pinot, an unconventional figure at high level in Vichy, who was dismissed from the post by Laval in favour of a more amenable associate in November 1942. Pinot himself was a strong personality and, although on the right, was not a devotee of the National Revolution, but he moved towards the Resistance movement before Mitterrand did. It was Pinot who set up Vichy's Rassemblement national des prisonniers de guerre (RNPG), which became the basis during 1943 for the Pinot–Mitterrand network. Also working there was Jacques Favre de Thierrens, who was part of a Resistance network linked to the Allies and who later helped General Giraud escape. A building for ex-prisoners (Centre d'entraide) had been opened in each department within the spirit of the Vichy regime's National Revolution; the Centres were financed partly by sales of seized Jewish property.

Péan thinks that the high point of Mitterrand's Vichy fervour came around the time of Laval's return to power. Mitterrand was then lamenting the 'lack of commitment' of the supporters of the 'Revolution'; he expressed a sympathy for the Service d'ordre légionnaire, responsible for hunting down the regime's opponents, and a hope for an elite with 'heartfelt convictions'.[41] His letters show a continuing faith in Pétain in mid-1942 and 'confidence in Laval', but to whom the letters were written and what other letters show is unknown, as Péan obtained them on condition that the recipients remain anonymous.[42] However, Mitterrand was not sympathetic to collaborationism and he allegedly organized the disruption of the collaborationist Claude George's meeting in Toulouse in April 1942. This was still consistent with a commitment to the Marshal, and hostility to collaborationists was not necessarily an act of resistance.

Mitterrand also published in Gabriel Jeantet's journal dedicated to the 'Etat nouveau' – that is, to the Vichyite National Revolution rather than collaborationism. These, and other articles, are difficult to decrypt. They do, however, nod to the symbols of the Vichy extreme right. 'Pèlerinage en Thuringe' ('Pilgrimage to Thuringia'), in Jeantet's *France, revue de l'état nouveau* (reprinted in *Politique* but omitting the journal's subtitle after *France*) is a multi-layered text.[43] It appears anodyne but, for example, it uses the expression 'cent cinquante années d'erreurs' ('150 years of errors' since the Great Revolution), an Action française anti-Republican slogan from 1939, and there are criticisms of the Enlightenment, the Rights of Man and the Versailles settlement of 1919. But then Mitterrand also published a piece admiring the poetry of the Communist Louis Aragon; under the Vichy regime, where suspicion was rife and censorship heavy handed, people had to read between the lines.

At this time Mitterrand met, and may have been protected by, the Vichy official Jean-Paul Martin (a faithful companion to Mitterrand on his annual pilgrimage to the roche de Solutré), who worked as bureau chief in the Interior with Police Prefect René Bousquet who went on to become Laval's Secretary General of police. Martin was stripped of citizens' rights after the Liberation, but was then rehabilitated by Mitterrand, whose press attaché he became in 1947. He was awarded the Légion d'honneur by Mitterrand in 1983. Bousquet was the high Vichy police official who organized the round-up and incarceration of Jewish people at the Vel d'Hiv. Mitterrand met Bousquet through Martin for the first time in 1949 and he would have known about his background then.[44] René Bousquet's case became notorious and the lawyer Serge Klarsfeld accused Mitterrand in 1994 of slowing down the legal process against him.[45] (Bousquet was assassinated on 8 June 1994.)

Resistance

Slowly Mitterrand abandoned his pro-Vichy outlook and in June 1942 he attended the meeting at the Château Montmaur – but not as a Resistance member – organized by the inspirational figure of Antoine Maudit, 'the most attractive figure I ever met', remembered Mitterrand later.[46] Mitterrand claims that at a meeting on 15 August 1942 he set up a cell to find, regroup and help POW escapees and that this was an embryo Resistance movement. Although this activity was anti-German, it could have been compatible with loyalty to Pétain's Vichy regime (escaped prisoners did receive a small payment from the authorities), but when helping prisoners evolved into a full-blown Resistance movement is unclear. However, Mitterrand was in contact with Resistance figures from this time without breaking links with Vichy's anti-Nazi figures. Many people who had this divided outlook changed after the German take-over of Vichy France in November 1942: some became giraudist (especially in the army) and then took up more active Resistance activities, dropping the Vichy cover. Mitterrand's full switch took place in the summer of 1943 when a credible provisional government was installed in Algeria, but he had already met Henri Frenay, the head of the Combat network, in March. Although Pétain was still admired, there was by then a latent hostility to Vichy and the Allies were seen as liberators.

In April 1942 General Giraud escaped from a POW camp and arrived in Vichy. Giraud, a prestigious officer, was an embarrassing escapee for Vichy and he slipped out to North Africa when he was pressured to return to Germany. He was supported by the Americans in preference to de Gaulle as the head of the French Resistance, but he showed no aptitude for politics and was soon swept aside by the gaullists. However, 'giraudism' provided a bridge to the Resistance movement for many. Giraud's supporters had set up the Organisation de résistance de l'armée (ORA) in the winter of 1942–3 with the aim of working against the occupant but without a political revolution. Giraud's network was of use to Mitterrand, who in particular was able to obtain some funds from the ORA to start his own organization and, probably, to get to London.

Nevertheless Mitterrand's association with Giraud and his family (the son had a house near the Mitterrands in Jarnac) made gaullists suspicious of him and did cause difficulties. Mitterrand's problems were increased by the activities of de Gaulle's nephew, Michel Caillau, who had started a network of his own for escaped prisoners and who tried to turn his uncle against Mitterrand. By the beginning of 1943 – probably in February – the elements for the RNPG network were being put in place and Mitterrand may have decided to move from support for Pétain to a more determined resistance stance under the leadership of Maurice Pinot (no longer in Vichy's service). It might be thought that Mitterrand's prickly relationship with the gaullists stems from this rivalry and the suspicion on the gaullist side of 'giraudists' or former Vichyites. There is also the political factor that the protagonists appreciated the potential of the prisoners' associations and the weight they would have; the struggle for their control was highly political.

On 15 October 1942, Mitterrand met Pétain, but in January 1943 he resigned from the Commissariat aux prisonniers when Laval's supporter was installed at its head and he refused a post in the Commissariat aux questions juives (the Vichy Ministry for Jewish Affairs).[47] But he had not yet broken publicly with Pétain and kept an entrée to the extent that he was considered by many to be a strong supporter of this now enfeebled puppet régime. What Mitterrand's precise thoughts were in 1943 – as the war's tide clearly turned after the victory of Stalingrad, the Allied landings in North Africa and then Sicily – are impossible to establish now. Notwithstanding, he was decorated (at his request, says Arbellot) with the *francisque* medal by the Marshal's Council in May or June of 1943, when conditions for the award were stringent.[48] All nominees had to be proposed by two impeccable patrons (in Mitterrand's case, Gabriel Jeantet and Simon Arbellot de Vacqueur). Mitterrand asserted that it was awarded when he was in England in November, but he was probably decorated before that. There were only about 2,600 *francisque* medals awarded (his was number 2,202), but only – perhaps – two were given to significant figures in the Resistance ('Navarre' and Colonel Heurteaux).[49] Before it could be attributed, the nominee had to swear allegiance to the Marshal and to the ideals of Vichy, a test which meant that, for example, Raymond Marcellin of the Alliance network, although nominated, never received the medal. Mitterrand's own account of this incident was to say that it provided some cover for his Resistance work, but it was certainly the recognition of a pétainist. In the end, he was to say that it had been an error.[50]

Mitterrand, taking the *nom de guerre* of 'Morland', was in the Resistance in mid-1943, but didn't go clandestine until later, when his position became more dangerous. Early in 1943, the Occupation authorities had offered to return one POW for every three volunteer workers who opted to depart for Germany ('*la relève*' – the relief). This requirement, and Laval's determination to push it through, had been behind Pinot's resignation as Commissaire in January. On 10 July 1943 a meeting of about 3,500 people was called in Paris's Wagram Hall by the new POW Commissaire, André Masson, to promote this policy with the Vichy prisoners' organization.[51] Mitterrand claims he infiltrated the meeting, interrupted the Vichy Minister Masson in full rhetorical flood and denounced the exchange along with the Commissaire's pretence to speak for the prisoners. 'Morland' then escaped. (This account is uncorroborated.) Radio London broadcast the news of the incident six months later when Mitterrand was in London. Mitterrand, sought by the police, who seemed to have been quite well informed of his activity, lived secretly under a variety of names, was involved in Resistance activities and almost captured on at least one occasion.[52]

It became clear to Pinot that the prisoners' network had to make its presence known in London and Mitterrand was designated as the delegate to the Free French. This visit took place in the autumn of 1943, but it too is the subject of controversy. Mitterrand is supposed to have used the giraud-ist ORA to wangle a place on a flight on 16 November on a Lysander in the company of the giraudist General du Passage. But the date and conditions of departure are not plausible and his name is not on the documents.[53] He did, however, arrive in London on or around the 16 November, where he got a cool reception from the gaullists, suspicious of his connections with Giraud (and possibly also the UK's secret services). In London he met other influential politicians, including the Communist Waldeck Rochet with whom he struck up a friendship. He also managed to get from London to Algiers to meet de Gaulle on 3 December at the Villa des Glycines through the intercession of Henri Frenay.

This meeting between de Gaulle and Mitterrand has been written up in different ways at different times, but the only other witness to it was Henri Frenay (responsible for POWs) and his accounts were inconsistent. In de Gaulle's scheme of things it would have been one of many such meetings, and Mitterrand was a minor – though not negligible – quantity. However, despite Mitterrand's description (sometimes) of the meeting as a frosty one, the outcome was positive for him and his network. It was accepted as a legitimate prisoners' organization and Mitterrand achieved the acceptance by de Gaulle of his resistance credentials. Moreover, Frenay ordered the fusion of the gaullist movement with Mitterrand's. For Mitterrand, this can only be judged a considerable achievement, particularly as it was carried out to the detriment of de Gaulle's nephew Michel Caillau. Maurice Pinot was judged too compromised by his Vichy past and ordered to leave the leadership, though he remained important in the background as a supporter of Mitterrand, especially to conservatives.[54] Maudit, the other great spirit of the network, had been arrested while Mitterrand was away and died in deportation.

Mitterrand used this time in North Africa to renew acquaintances and make new ones, but some gaullists appear to have sought to delay his return to France and were accused (later) of trying to conscript him into the army in Italy. Once again he used contacts to get out of Algeria and back to London – it was General Giraud himself who made sure he was able to return.[55] In December 1943, with Giraud's help, Mitterrand reached London using a circuitous route via Marrakech (housed by the singer and actress Josephine Baker), where, through further contacts, he 'hitched' a ride in General Montgomery's air plane on 26 February. His return to France was organized and he was set down in Brittany by an MTB commanded by Lt-Commander David Birkin (father of film actress and singer Jane). Mitterrand was thus able to return claiming the support of Algiers gaullists to consolidate his position in the fused movement before the Liberation. During this period, Mitterrand also made the acquaintance of his future wife, Danielle Gouze, sister of his friend Roger Pelat's wife and part of a resistance family of the left.[56]

Once back on the ground, the creation of the united Mouvement national des prisonniers de guerre et déportés (MNPGD) went ahead, bringing together the gaullists and Mitterrand's own group but also involving the Communists, who had now entered the scene. Edgar Morin was delegated to the network by the PCF, but it was Mitterrand who brought the Communists into the movement in conformity with the policy of the new unified Resistance council (CFLN). The communist movement was non-existent, but it enabled the party to enter the CFLN and it gave Mitterrand the edge.[57] Progress, though rapid, proceeded with bad grace and the institutional tensions between gaullists and Mitterrand, and the personal rancours, were never fully dissipated. By March 1944 a small executive of two from Mitterrand's group, two gaullists and one communist was set up, headed by Mitterrand and dominated by him.[58] Michel Caillau then quit the contest. This reorganization demanded the development of one of Mitterrand's political talents: that of bringing together highly disparate, rival and suspicious groups working to a broadly common end and to control them through his own supporters. With a combination of energy, personal charm, conviction, contacts and patronage provided by influential figures, Mitterrand had risen to the top and he had unified the MNPGD under his leadership by the end of March 1944.

In general, the leaders of the new movement were well disposed towards him, but the key posts were held by his intimates – former prisoners like Pelat, Munier, Finifter, but also Beauchamp; there was a Mitterrand majority. De Gaulle's nephew was obliged to accept the fusion and more or less withdrew, leaving Mitterrand the principal figure in the MNPGD. Mitterrand's Resistance work was not easy but it was intensely political, and the network became the basis for his role in post-war politics. In 1986, just before the period of 'cohabitation', Mitterrand's Resistance group was recognized by the Minister of Defence as having been a 'fighting' movement, in defiance of the committee charged with deciding these matters, leading to the resignation of its Chair, Colonel Masset. On 11 March 1991, this recognition was annulled by the Conseil d'Etat.[59]

In the last days of the Occupation, the Milice (the Vichy secret police) and the Gestapo remained active in their surveillance and in their search for Resistance networks. There were several close escapes and living a clandestine existence was increasingly dangerous for the sought-after

'Morland'.[60] The author Marguerite Duras, a member of the Morland network, was trying to get her husband out of prison, and confirmed (through conversations with a Gestapo officer) that 'Morland' was the object of substantial Gestapo efforts and that there was a traitor in the network. Duras wrote a fictionalized account of this time (*La Douleur*), but the real state of affairs has never been fully established.

Mitterrand had not neglected to keep the Conseil national de la résistance (CNR) informed and on his side. He had friends in the CNR, notably the former Vichyite Frenay who was in a way his patron. He was nominated interim 'commissioner for prisoners' by Frenay (with de Gaulle's approval) in June 1944 – in effect, minister – until the provisional government could arrive in Paris. Allied forces had landed in Normandy in June, but before their arrival in Paris an uprising was started by the Communist leadership on 19 August. Mitterrand's group then showed its organizational and tactical abilities by taking and occupying strategic buildings. Its unit, set up by Roger-Patrice Pelat and Jean Munier, took part in the liberation of Paris in the Forces françaises de l'intérieur. Mitterrand himself occupied the Annexe of the Commissariat aux prisonniers (the HQ was in Vichy) entering Commissioner Moreau's office. A press was also occupied and the movement's paper, *L'Homme libre*, was printed and other resources were wrested from the Occupier.

The Liberation

When de Gaulle entered Paris on 25 August, Mitterrand was able to participate in the parade down the Champs-Elysées the next day. He became, at 27, the youngest 'minister' for the short time before the government arrived from Algiers on 5 September and Henri Frenay from the CNL took over. Mitterrand had already brought the Vichy Centres d'entraide for ex-prisoners under the MNPGD, and increased its reach and its budget to considerable effect.[61] Frenay offered Mitterrand the post of general secretary at the ministry, an unparalleled offer, but he refused it – probably because he had greater ambitions that would have been crabbed by this subordinate role.[62] It was while at this post that Mitterrand, trying to keep control of an increasingly radical movement, wrote opposition editorials and led a demonstration against Frenay's alleged inadequacies.[63] In the MNPGD's journal, *Libres*, Mitterrand denounced 'insulting money which disports itself amongst those for whom the wars are the best profit'.[64]

In September 1944 he found himself without a job. He was made editor of *Votre Beauté* (surely the least appropriate appointment since Rupert

Psmith took over *Cosy Moments*) through the efforts of his friend Dalle and the Schueller group. Eugène Schueller was a prominent former Cagoulard and Mouvement social révolutionnaire member, something that revived rumours about Mitterrand's attachment to the extreme right. This editorship did not last, but his affairs were such that subventions ceased to be necessary after he was elected to the Assembly. He was married on 28 October 1944 in Paris to Danielle Gouze. Tragically, a year later his first child (Patrick) died of infantile cholera at the age of only three months.

Was Mitterrand one of those who, in his own words, 'started wrongly, arrived correctly'?[65] His political evolution had not yet ended. He had started at Vichy as a *maréchaliste* but he emerged from the Resistance as a political figure of some stature with many powerful friends from both camps, as well as a circle of close associates and, of course, the leader of the prisoners' movement, which involved as many as two million people. He had shown extraordinary fortitude, endurance and persistence. His political instincts had been tested, as had his own political outlook on a number of fronts, and his views were well to the left of his opinions in the 1930s. All the same, Mitterrand's comments in the MNPGD journal *Libres* on the trial of Marshal Pétain in July 1945 cast aspersions on the pre-war politicians in particular, but do not criticize the Vichy Head of State.[66] As President, he had a bouquet of roses placed on Pétain's tomb on two occasions and then on every Armistice Day from 1987 to 1992 (when this gesture stopped after a public outcry).[67]

Over the years, Mitterrand was careful to keep alive his Resistance and POW past through such Proustian moments as the regular Easter visit to Solutré and excursions to places associated with his escape or imprisonment. But Mitterrand by obfuscation, excision and concision concealed his right-wing past from those who followed him and obscured his role in Vichy. Choices were open to people even during the war, and some people made different decisions from the young Mitterrand. But of course Mitterrand was no ordinary person trying to get by. He was a conservative student and then an ambitious employee at the heart of the regime itself, and an admirer of the figure of Marshal Pétain. But he is not unusual. The sovereign historian of the period, R. O. Paxton, remarks on the continuity of the elite from Vichy to the Liberation.[68]

Already in 1945, Mitterrand had created a network of faithful servants from very diverse milieux whom he could call on when he needed to. These people were located across the political spectrum, from the extreme right to the centre, from the left and even from the Communist Party. Most importantly, dealing with the Vichy era, is that Mitterrand never broke with the Vichyites and continued to associate with many of them into his double septennate. None of his youthful involvement in Vichy, however, prevented him from taxing opponents with Vichyism or pétainism. It can be speculated that Mitterrand's initial faith, forceful and ardent in his early life, was lost over this period. Perhaps what replaced religious faith was not another set of convictions, but a detached and instrumental attitude to political life and a weakness for the numinous. This, however, is psychological speculation.

Mitterrand was not, in writing or conversation, a political idealist, policy specialist or reformer with a briefcase of plans. His talent was for tactics and for small-scale and micro-level political action and in dealing with groups, parties, personalities and coalitions. This, as it happened, admirably suited him for the shifting, unstable alliance politics in the Assembly of the Fourth Republic.

2

The Fourth Republic

With the Fourth Republic came a new political system. The socialist Section française de l'internationale ouvrière (SFIO) remained, but the once dominant Radical Party had been humbled and many conservative formations had been compromised by their ties with Vichy. There were also new forces. In 1945 these counted notably the large Christian democratic Mouvement républicain populaire (MRP) which had emerged from the Resistance and, later, the gaullists. De Gaulle, although without organized support at first, was a huge presence. However, the major factor was the massive Communist Party which had polled 26.1 per cent of the votes in the October 1945 Constituent Assembly elections: communism was now a disciplined force in every walk of French life. Mitterrand, however, was initially going against the grain of the new Republic, which was left wing in tone.

Veterans' Minister Henri Frenay, Mitterrand's old associate, had become a *bête noire* to the Communist Party because of his determination to build up a non-communist rampart. In the press and in meetings, the prisoners' movement (MNPGD) became highly critical of the Minister for Prisoners, and this led to a massive rally on 2 June 1945 demanding his resignation. As a result, Mitterrand met with de Gaulle three days later. De Gaulle claimed to have forced Mitterrand and leaders of the prisoners' movement to back down under threat of imprisonment, an account that is unlikely, but this incident helped move Mitterrand into opposition to the General. Inside the MNPGD Mitterrand used the Communist Party to inch out the gaullists from the leadership, but in November 1946 he also removed the Communists from the leadership by easing his own supporters into the top posts, although he had to step down himself.

In this way, Mitterrand found himself going counter to the two main currents in Liberation politics, General de Gaulle on the one hand and the Communists on the other. He therefore moved into the small gathering of personalities founded in 1945 as the Union démocratique et socialiste de la Résistance (UDSR). This tiny party, a 'Mexican Army', included, it must be noted, some of the most distinguished Resistance leaders, but it was an ideologically imprecise grouping of notables federating five Resistance movements as well as gaullists, centrists, Catholics and socialists. It was, says Williams, 'too small to be feared and too essential to be ignored'.[1] Its leader, René Pleven, had gone to London in July 1940 and, as de Gaulle's finance minister in 1944, his opposition to Pierre Mendès France's measures to restore the economy caused Mendès France to resign.[2] Pleven and Mitterrand heartily disliked each other. Mendès France, although with only a brief experience of government office, was the dominant figure on the centre left with a prestige and moral authority that went beyond that of the small Radical party of which he was a member.

Finding a Constituency

After the 1946 elections, the UDSR lost many of its socialist members to the SFIO and in 1948 it lost its gaullists to the General's Rassemblement du peuple français (RPF), its parliamentary group falling from 27 to 14. In 1948–9 it was behaving as a conservative group, although later, after Mitterrand's take-over in 1953, it moved left. In the Assembly, its hinge position made it an invaluable coalition ally and its lack of an organization that might have hindered horse-trading enabled it to bargain effectively for posts. The UDSR was invariably useful for finding the extra few votes needed to support a coalition, and Mitterrand was able to hold government office for six and a half of the eleven years of the Fourth Republic. In 1951 there were nine UDSR deputies from metropolitan France and fourteen from overseas, but in the last elections of the Fourth Republic in 1956 these numbers fell to six metropolitan deputies and ten from overseas.

Mitterrand did not embody any clear political position – there were many who did – but he was competent and well placed. However, his stance did change as he found himself pushing against the main demands of his original supporters on the right and then moving leftward. Thus Mitterrand's Fourth Republic career is in two parts. In the first he is on the centre right but moves leftward under the impetus of a reforming colonial policy; this phase ended when he resigned from the conservative Laniel government in 1954.[3] The second phase started on the centre left with Mendès France's government of 1954 and continued with the Republican Front government of Guy Mollet, a trajectory that extended into the Fifth Republic.

In June 1946 there were elections for a second Constituent Assembly and Mitterrand was a UDSR candidate within Radical Edouard Daladier's Rassemblement des gauches républicaines (RGR; conservative, despite the name) in the affluent Paris suburban seat Seine 5e (Neuilly, Billancourt). For this election, Mitterrand ran a definitively right-wing anti-communist campaign stressing opposition to the governing 'Tripartite' alliance of Socialists, Communists and the MRP, and repudiating the Liberation nationalizations. Although he polled well enough to make an impression, Mitterrand's list came fifth behind the PCF, SFIO, MRP and the ultra-conservative Parti républicain de la liberté (PRL).

In reality, Mitterrand had no chance of winning in this Parisian constituency, and he acted mainly as a spoiler for the PRL's deputy Edmond Barrachin, the party's co-founder. According to Georges Riond, a PRL leader, Barrachin reportedly called Mitterrand in and asked him what his game was: 'to drop me in it or become a deputy'.[4] Barrachin, who did not want his votes siphoned off, invited Mitterrand to 'carpet bag' in the Nièvre.[5] Mitterrand had no connection with the Nièvre, deep in rural France, and was dependent on the support of Barrachin and others, particularly the Count d'Armaille, a figure who was still trying to come to terms with the universal franchise. D'Armaille's Nevers newspaper, Paris-Centre, had been seized at the Liberation for publishing under the Occupation (it became the Journal du Centre) and the Count wanted it reopened – it was later confiscated by Mitterrand when he was Secretary of State for Information (July 1948–October 1949). But the Nièvre was profoundly Catholic, and the support of Church and Chateau counted in 1946.[6] Mitterrand would later claim that his only patron was Henri Queuille, the Radical Party fixer, but he certainly had other powerful support.[7]

His vigorous anti-communist campaign and his dismissal of the 'Tripartism' of the Socialists and Christian Democrats who governed with the PCF also helped.[8] In a sense he ran as the anti-establishment candidate against the governing parties. He arrived only a fortnight before the polls opened but he did work the constituency with energy and imagination, making an impression on the local squirearchy and on the Church. Once again this was a decisively right-wing campaign emphasizing defence of Church schools, the Communist menace and the weakness of the MRP's response as well as (he Hayeked) the interventionism, bureaucracy, nationalization and regulation of the 'Tripartite' government: 'the conglomerate-state that has everywhere substituted itself for private enterprise'.[9] 'No to bankruptcy, no to high prices, no to administrative chaos, no to nationalizations, no to the installation of the Communist Party in power.'[10] He also called for an amnesty for deputies who had voted full powers to Pétain in July 1940. It was a convincing enough simulacrum of orthodox conservatism for the Centre national des indépendants paysans (CNIP) to accede to his request not to run against him in 1951. Curiously, Mitterrand's campaign manifestos from 1946 have disappeared from the archives of the Assembly, Senate, Bibliothèque nationale and departmental archives.[11]

As ever, there is doubt as to where his campaign funds came from but there was no doubt that Mitterrand's contacts in the business community helped here (as did the PRL). But it was more the support of the right-wing network than the vigour of his canvassing that won Mitterrand a victory in November 1946.[12] Nationally, the Communist Party polled 28.6 per cent of the vote and held 183 of the 617 Assembly seats. But the Socialists had lost votes and won only 105 seats and the MRP won 167 seats. But the overall shift was an anti-communist one, and fear and suspicion of the Communists was growing. In Nièvre, with 25.5 per cent of the vote, Mitterrand was ahead of the Socialists but behind the PCF's 33.3 per cent.

Mitterrand began standing for other local offices, but his roots in the constituency remained relatively shallow and he tended to concentrate on national matters in Paris. He was elected a local councillor in the departmental capital Nevers in the west in 1947 and then a departmental councillor for Montsauche in the east in 1949. He also became political director of *Le Courrier de la Nièvre* (the small departmental publication) in 1950 and wrote a regular column. In a rural department where communications with Paris were not good, *Le Courrier de la Nièvre* was the principal (and then the sole) widely read newspaper, and Mitterrand's domination of it extended over the years until it folded in 1983 (after 1958 it was run by his collaborator Georges Beauchamp). In addition, the other regional paper, the *Journal du Centre*, was favourable to Mitterrand and he cultivated the local professional and agricultural interest groups such as the Comices agricoles and the Comité d'étude et d'aménagment du Morvan to electoral effect.[13] However, his recent arrival made problems for him in 1951, although he used his access to the central government to aid the constituency (hastening post-war reconstruction, for example).

Ministerial Career

There was a further advance in Mitterrand's career when, on the recommendation of his former Resistance and UDSR associate Claudius Petit, he was made Minister for Veterans in the government of Socialist Paul Ramadier on 21 January 1947. In the musical chairs of the Fourth Republic, Mitterrand had made an early start: aged 30 and 3 months, he was the youngest minister since the Empire. The Communist Laurent Casanova had been the Veterans' Minister for more than ten months and had assisted the infiltration of the establishment so that the party almost ran it. The outgoing Socialist minister Max Lejeune had stopped this, with the result that a strike had been declared. The new minister arrived to an occupied building and he and one aide were allowed inside. In the first Cabinet meeting, the new minister announced that the building would be cleared by force if needs be, and a decree stated that the civil servants who had refused to comply were being replaced by members of his MNPGD federation. Zimmermann, the CGT civil servants' union leader, called on the young minister to lay down what would be tolerated in the building, but was met with a firm rebuttal and a refusal to deal directly with him in future.[14]

At the ministry, Mitterrand brought in his trusted associates, making it his stronghold. Robert Mitterrand ran the minister's private office, Georges Beauchamp and Resistance associate Jean Védrine were also brought in and Georges Dayan later came in from Algeria. The Communists ceded the building and leaders of the party cells were carefully weeded out by the new minister over the coming months. At the same time, Mitterrand used the ministry and its patronage to consolidate his hold on the Prisoners' Federation, in the process building a network of supporters that could be deployed either against the PCF or to support his own moves. But Mitterrand's ministry also achieved some changes in the status of ex-POWs. There were two principal measures: one was a simplification of pensions procedure and the other was an increase in their value and indexation to prevent their devaluation through inflation.

In May came the action for which Ramadier's government is chiefly remembered: the eviction of the Communists from the government. There had been no ambiguity about Mitterrand's anti-communism, and he supported the Prime Minister's firm action against the party, which looked capable of overthrowing the Republic. It was the end of collaboration with the Communists in 'Tripartism' and the beginning of the anti-communist 'Third Force' of the SFIO and MRP. 'Third Force' minorities were, however, much weaker and based on parties which found themselves back to back fighting off attacks from extremes. De Gaulle, determined to end the Fourth Republic, had started his new RPF party and it had cut hard into the MRP's electorate, while the Communists had already plucked the socialist chicken for its support. From this time onwards, faced with two major hostile forces, governments had to be constituted from the centrist and conservative parties and the SFIO and MRP were divided on major issues.

At this time in his career, Mitterrand was frequently thrown into the front line against the Communist Party and took a determined stance against it, so much so that he was the butt of their frequent attacks. In 1949, campaigning for the canton of Montsauche, he told *France-Soir*: 'I have undertaken a very difficult fight, I know that, but I have chosen it to defeat a Communist. I hope to succeed because that will mean one less.'[15] Mitterrand remained at the Veterans' Ministry for the term of the Ramadier and Robert Schuman governments from January 1947 until the end of July 1948. However, in October 1948 Henri Queuille was nominated Prime Minister and he chose Mitterrand as Secretary of State for Information, the government's cheer leader and censor, a much more exposed post.

As with other Information Ministers, Mitterrand was to seek to minimize the appearances of the Communists and gaullists on TV or radio and to tackle the chaotic position in the press resulting from the Liberation. It was as Information Minister that Mitterrand took the decision to impose an 849-line television image on France, not the USA's 605 lines or the continental 625 lines, in this way protecting the French market. He was also able to recommend his former fiancée Marie-Louise Terrasse to the television authority Jean d'Arcy, his former chief of staff. As 'Catherine Langeais', she became one of TV's best-known and most successful presenters.[16]

Africa

Another key change in Mitterrand's position came with his African involvement, after which he was no longer well viewed on the right and became assimilated to the left. After a coalition crisis in June 1950, René Pleven, the UDSR leader, was invited to form a government on 13 July. Despite their rivalry inside the UDSR, Pleven offered Mitterrand the Colonial Ministry. This ministry, though large, did not control the Empire: it had the overview of sub-Saharan French Africa, Madagascar, the Comores and Oceanic France. Pleven was perturbed at the situation in French sub-Saharan Africa, but contacts with African leaders had convinced him that the problem was potentially resolvable. Mitterrand had previously demonstrated the old colonial reflex and had shown no particular prescience in the Madagascan crisis of 1947 when he rounded on the local leaders and supported the subsequent 'pacification' of the island by the army (contrary, for example, to Defferre).[17] He had, however, visited Africa as Information Minister in 1949 and taken a long trip through the Congo, Gabon, Chad, Sudan and Egypt, developing a taste for big game hunting with an African-ist colonial friend Cornut-Gentille. He accepted the post of Colonial Minister and then kept the post under the Queuille government from February 1951 to 11 July 1951.

Within the French Empire, developments were gloomy and the evolution of the colonies was not helped by the hold that MRP politicians Paul Coste-Floret and Raymond Letourneau had maintained over the ministry since the Schuman government of November 1947. One of the many paradoxes of the Fourth Republic was that government instability was combined with ministerial stability; in the Colonial Ministry this led to immobility (*immobilisme*) and a lack of strategic planning, as the ministers involved themselves principally in a crisis management that resulted in a cracking down on dissidence. Mitterrand, no decolonizer and opposed to the nascent nationalist movements that, he feared, led to independence, wanted to put the relations of France with its colonies on a new basis.[18] This new 'autonomy' (vaguely defined) sought to make the continuation of Empire possible in a way that the incessant repression could not.

Problems were building up in the Empire: France was fighting a desperate action in Indochina and discontent was mounting in Tunisia where reforms had failed and in Morocco where the Resident General Juin was in conflict with nationalists. In sub-Saharan Africa there were civil disorders and the colonial army had been reinforced and was on alert. One of Mitterrand's first problems was the rising demand for the further repression of the Rassemblement démocratique africain (RDA) and the arrest of its leader and founder Félix Houphouët-Boigny. They were held responsible for recent demonstrations in the Ivory Coast that had left forty people dead. Houphouët-Boigny was an outstanding figure, a local chief, with a substantial land-holding but also a doctor and a deputy (with, according to de Gaulle, 'a first-class political brain').[19] In the Assembly, the RDA's six deputies were linked with the Communists, but Houphouët-Boigny was the effective nationalist leader: he had succeeded in organizing the Ivory Coast's peasant farmers into cooperatives and introduced new farming methods.

With the backing of President Auriol and Prime Minister Pleven, both colonial liberals, Mitterrand immediately sought secret talks with Houphouët-Boigny, who was guaranteed safe passage to France. Houphouët-Boigny had been contemplating a move away from the Communists, who threatened to take over his movement, but government instability had made offering concessions difficult before Mitterrand's arrival at the ministry. The talks were undertaken with a view to ending the grievances behind the demonstrations if Houphouët-Boigny would accept the legitimacy of the Empire – or 'French Union', as it was called. This ran counter to the crack-down advocated on the conservative and gaullist right and necessitated dealing with somebody sought by the police and viewed as a troublemaker by the authorities.

An agreement was reached and a paper was signed – though not made public – committing Houphouët-Boigny to keeping the colonies within the French Union. Mitterrand kept this text, possibly as a hold over the African leader.[20] As a result of the agreement, a series of changes were made in colonial governance ending requisition of labour and introducing fairer labour laws, equality in commercial dealings between French and Africans and giving the right for indigenous representatives to stand in elections. Mitterrand also acceded to Houphouët-Boigny's demand for an end to the outlawing of the RDA as well as stopping the police pursuit of its leaders. Mitterrand enforced these in the colonies through ministerial directives and by changing unsympathetic personnel, including Governor Péchoux who, on 1 May 1951, was withdrawn. A result was a relaxation of tension in this part of Africa, and it made possible the continuing close association of these colonies with France.

However, the colonialists were not pleased, and gaullists, Christian Democrats and conservatives accused the minister of dismantling the Empire.[21] In order to prevent a backlash that would come with an RDA landslide, Mitterrand limited its seats at the 1951 elections to three. In the Assembly the RDA group left the PCF and joined the UDSR, a crucial reinforcement because it was only just at the threshold of numbers entitling it to form a group, but it made Mitterrand's party an object of suspicion on the right. However, this integrated the notables of the burgeoning anti-colonial movement into the Assembly and into the French overseas system; Houphouët-Boigny became a Fifth Republic Minister for Health in 1959.

Another incident took place before Mitterrand departed from the Colonial Ministry that confirmed his place on the left and may have influenced his own personal views. A Dakar Catholic missionary publication, *L'Afrique nouvelle*, broke the law by publishing the proceedings of an action for slander brought by the Governor Paul Béchard. With the minister's approval, the two priests who edited *L'Afrique nouvelle* were then brought before the courts. They were ordered to pay a symbolic 50-franc fine and given a suspended sentence, but the use of the courts against them was a *casus belli* for the colonial right. Empire loyalists (gaullists, in competition with MRP, making the running) then portrayed this as an infamy and made Mitterrand's position in the (pro-colonial) right impossible.

The opening in February 1951 of the new port of Abidjan also marked his card: RDA deputies were among the invitees on the stand and there was a horrified outcry from colonial die-hards. It was Mitterrand's UDSR rival René Pleven who was again nominated as the next Prime Minister in August 1951, but this time he did not include Mitterrand in his cabinet. Mitterrand had overly annoyed the colonial right and his successor as Colonial Minister, the conservative Louis Jacquinot, was more amenable to the right. This choice and his omission envenomed a relationship already made tense by Mitterrand's determination to dominate the UDSR. But he had made new allies and extended his personal patronage network by using the resources of the Colonial Ministry, and had established a reputation in that area.

UDSR Politics

Mitterrand's period as Colonial Minister had marked him as a leftist and 'seller-out of the Empire'. It also made his re-election in Nièvre more difficult, although the seat was won again in June 1951. With the support of the UDSR, RGR, Radicals and PRL, Mitterrand, still in Nièvre on the right, took 17.3 per cent to the gaullists' 22.9 per cent, the SFIO's 16.6 per cent and the Communists' 29.9 per cent. Nationally, by changing the electoral law and by using the advantages of the incumbency, the gaullist and Communist challenges were beaten off. In 1951 the MRP's vote fell by 2,700,000, the Socialists lost 668,000, and the PCF 450,000 votes, but the RPF won four million votes. In the 1951 Assembly of 627 the RPF held 120 seats, the SFIO 107, the Communists 101, the Radicals 76, MRP 96, the Conservatives 98 and there were 24 overseas independents.[22]

Nine UDSR deputies were joined by fourteen from Africa. With this new infusion into the UDSR, Mitterrand's own hand was strengthened against Pleven. Mitterrand had called to his aid the former prisoners from his movement who joined the party and gave him a majority – probably overwhelming – although in 1951 Pleven was unanimously re-elected as leader.[23] Mitterrand emerged within the UDSR as a champion of the leftward move of the party and took up a position that was critical of the subvention by the state of (private) Church schools under the Barangé law. At the party's Nantes Congress in November 1953 Mitterrand became president of the UDSR – nobody voted against him – and he had 51 supporters to Pleven's 19 on its Directing Committee.

On 20 January 1952, the Radical Edgar Faure formed a short-lived government and made Mitterrand a Minister of State with a brief to handle Tunisia. Tunisia had expected to be moved on the track to independence, but had been plunged into crisis when, the month before, this had been abruptly revoked. Mitterrand's solution, consistent with his démarche in West Africa, was to devolve powers to local politicians (self-government based on a representative Assembly) but to retain French authority through a continuing association within the French Union. In effect, this was a prolongation of the protectorate status that Tunisia had with France, and whether it would have been a success in the long term is a moot point. But the Faure government was turned out of office on 29 February and replaced with the very conservative Pinay government. Mitterrand promoted his ideas and reputation in a book published in 1953, *Aux frontières de l'union française*, his new political position marked by an introduction by Mendès France. In this work he defended what were the reformist positions of the time against the hard line of previous governments.

However, the government's policy change to a clamp-down in the colonies did not prevent Mitterrand from joining Joseph Laniel's Cabinet, the most conservative government of the Fourth Republic, in June 1953. There had been a long crisis, and Laniel's major claim to head the government was that he was unknown. Lacking leadership, the government was both conservative and shiftless, taking '*immobilisme*' to a new low and evading problems where they could not be swept under the carpet. Largely because it did little and therefore made few enemies, what was expected to be a temporary government to overcome a ministerial crisis wound on until its final reckoning in June 1954. What was Mitterrand's motive in taking a post in this government other than wanting to stay inside the ring where decisions were made? Or was it in the expectation of changing the inflection of the government, a move too clever by only an eighth?

Europe

Mitterrand was made Minister for Relations with the Council of Europe, a post created because of the salience of the European issue. This was not, however, a title that meant much. Europe is often believed to have been the guiding theme of Mitterrand's political career, but his *Drang nach Westen* did not start at this point.[24] Although he was present at the first meeting of European federalists after the war at The Hague in 1948 and he was never anti-European, his stance was more nuanced and less determined than that. Mitterrand supported European integration (most politicians did at the time, even de Gaulle) but 'federalism' has a different meaning in European discussions and was seen as consistent with patriotism, especially when it was assumed, as it usually was, that France would be the motive force in this new Europe. Mitterrand was not, unlike Giscard d'Estaing and Gaston Defferre in 1955, a member of Jean Monnet's Action Committee.

Thus in the Fourth Republic Mitterrand supported European integration, but he had other priorities and those had to be reduced or eliminated before his European commitment rose to the top. For him then, Europe was secondary to other issues – notably the French Empire. With a disregard for novelty, he ranked French interests in the western Mediterranean and Africa above Europe, although Europe was more important than Indochina. What emerges from Mitterrand's politics in the Fourth Republic is an outlook of enlightened colonialism. Often accused of inconsistency, he pursued this policy with a single-mindedness that ignored its increasing unreality.[25]

Mitterrand's views on the developments in the colonies were incompatible with Laniel's. Morocco and Tunisia were the first problems. In Morocco, a round-up removing opposition leaders was followed by the deposition of the Sultan on 24 August and that provoked a general strike. This action by the colonial authorities was not authorized by Paris but, in a pattern that was to become familiar in Algeria, was endorsed by Paris as a fait accompli. In the Cabinet, Mitterrand and Faure protested, but in September the way the government was going became clear when Pierre Voizard, a hard-line colonial official of the same unyielding stamp, was nominated as Resident General of Tunisia. With that appointment, recognizing that the direction of the government was contrary to his, Mitterrand resigned and associated himself with the left – notably with Mendès France, for whom he had come to be regarded as a second in command.

Mitterrand's view remained that the war in Indochina detracted from the effort needed in Africa.[26] Joseph Laniel's government fell a year after its nomination after the psychologically devastating defeat of the French Army by the Vietminh insurgents at Dien Bien Phu in June 1954. After that military disaster for the French Army there was no possibility of retaining Indochina as a French colony, and the government, which had not known what to do, resigned to make way for Mendès France, who did.

Mitterrand and Mendès France

Mendès France's government was decisive, authoritative and reforming, and Mitterrand owed his place not to his progressive stance on colonial reform (which would have angered the die-hards) but to the complicity between the two men which, at this time, was great. Mitterrand, who knew his way round the fauna of the Assembly as Mendès France did not, had a considerable influence on the formation of the government. But Mitterrand was not one of the many disciples, and the new Premier did not see the young minister as an equal, merely as one of the brilliant newcomers he promoted. On 19 June 1954, Mitterrand became Minister of the Interior (despite representing only the small UDSR) in the Mendès France government, where he had responsibility for Algeria, governed not as a colony but as part of the Republic.

Mendès France embarked on a negotiated peace for Indochina that was concluded at Geneva on 22 July, but for Mitterrand there was the first major obstacle of the 'leaks scandal'. Like most scandals, this was a convoluted affair with many loose ends and unsolved problems, but the essentials were simple: it was aimed at discrediting Mitterrand.[27] One of Mitterrand's first decisions as Interior Minister had been to sack the Paris police prefect Jean Baylet, a right-wing plotter who then intrigued against the new minister. Just prior to Mendès France being nominated Prime Minister, accounts of Defence Committee meetings and secret briefings were appearing in left-wing publications as well as in the Communist daily *Libération*, and some were also finding their way to the Vietminh fighting the French Army in Indochina. It was clear that somebody had leaked these documents and these leaks had continued since Laniel's departure. One purpose of revealing the leaks under the new government was to compromise Mendès France's attempts to decolonize Indochina and destroy the Interior Minister, as had happened to Roger Salengro in the 1930s.

One of Baylet's men, commissioner Dides, who had been dismissed from the Prefecture of Police, went to the gaullist Minister of the Colonies, Christian Fouchet, asserting that the leaks came from Mitterrand. Mendès France was informed and assumed Mitterrand's innocence, although he ordered a secret inquiry. But, about to depart for Geneva for negotiations to end the Indochina war, he omitted to inform Mitterrand. That omission became the cause of much bad blood between these two politicians, even though the Prime Minister vigorously defended his Interior Minister in parliament six months later.[28] Mitterrand was informed of the inquiry on 8 September, and the leaks were followed up by the secret services; these investigations led to uncovering an extreme right network in the administration and police. For Mitterrand, the 'leaks affair' was an appalling and trying time and one when Mendès France had failed, in his view, to support him as he should have done. The slanders made a mark and they continued during the trials of the miscreants: 'slander, slander, something will always remain'.

Algeria

The other test case for Mitterrand was Algeria. French governments came and went, paying little attention to Algeria, and were reassured by the local authorities that things were 'calm', with their only need being for further investment and support from Paris. Algeria was regarded as part of France and few even on the far left disputed this assumption, but the situation was one of a colonial apartheid even if the numbers of settlers was relatively high (10 per cent).[29] Mitterrand had some connections with Algeria, notably through his close friend Dayan who lived there and whom he visited, and through his brother and his brother-in-law. The problem in Algeria was that the nine million or so Muslims were treated as second-class citizens, while the privileged settler minority of one million ruled. As Interior Minister, Mitterrand was receiving alarm signals from Algeria, from the Governor and the police, about the possibility of an insurrection, but he did not pass these on to the Prime Minister.[30] On 1 November 1954 there were seventy attacks in the streets and a guerrilla war started in the mountainous Aurès region in the east; the 'Algerian war' had been launched by the FLN. Eight people were killed and forty were injured. Talks with the rebels could not be resumed and the government adopted an uncompromising stance, declaring that 'Algeria is France'.

Mitterrand had responsibility for the three departments constituting Algeria, but his main response to renewed nationalist attacks on settlers (and rival nationalists) was to treat them as matters of internal order.[31] Thus, like most mainstream politicians, he approved of the use of troops and the 'restoration of order' and dismissed any idea of leaving the territory to the insurgents. Algeria would remain French as far as public opinion – and certainly Mitterrand – was concerned. Once again, Mitterrand does not seem to have departed substantially from the orthodoxy of the time, except that he did plead the need for reforms like the promotion of Muslims in the civil service, even though he was very prudent in urging change on the settlers.

Various reform measures had been proposed, but the settler minority sabotaged even those that were applied, so that little real progress had been made. The SFIO's Edouard Depreux had placed quite extensive reforms on the statute book in 1947, which had proposed an Assembly in which the representatives of the settler minority would be equivalent to the Muslim majority, but these proposals had been emptied of content by the settler administration. Mitterrand realized this inequity and addressed it verbally with a determination to provide equal opportunities for all those born in Algeria.[32] But the Muslim majority had fallen so far behind the minority that in retrospect it is difficult to imagine that these outdated reforms, belatedly applied, could have retained Algeria as part of France. Moreover, Paris would not have accepted the genuine incorporation into the Republic of such a large number of Muslims. In Algeria, the settlers were not willing to dismantle their privileged position; the suspicion that Mitterrand would impose 'one man one vote' was behind much of the right's hostility towards him.

Mitterrand, clearly worried about Algeria on the basis of his West African experience, wanted to push the reforms ameliorating the situation of the majority. Again, this was an enlightened view at the time when few thought of independence and it was assumed that equity and better living standards would tie Algeria to France. Thus, to cite one example (among many), Mitterrand wrote in *L'Express*: 'Our presence in North Africa, from Bizerta to Casablanca, is the number one priority of French policy. Nothing is more important', and again: 'without North Africa there is no historic prospect for France'.[33] In February 1958, he was to assert that the 'abandonment of Algeria would be a crime'.[34] Mitterrand was an 'advanced' but not an adventurous thinker on this matter and at first he repudiated, amongst other ideas, the federal solutions.

Settler opinion was on the alert because Mendès France had decolonized Indochina. Many in the colonies – who took any reform to be the first step to independence and in effect decolonization – saw him as an enemy, although his intention was to enforce French authority. But such reform impetus as there was reckoned without the blocking powers of the settlers in the colony and in Paris and the deterioration of the situation in Algeria. Forced onto the back foot by this refusal to contemplate change, Mitterrand remarked that: 'Algeria is France'.[35] This affirmation, unexceptional at the time,[36] was enough to keep the vital margin of settler votes behind the government in the Assembly for a while. In this struggle, Mitterrand's position on Algeria was hard line (more so than on Africa) and not in harmony with Mendès France's own attempts at negotiation with the insurgents to the extent that he perhaps risked dismissal from the Cabinet.[37]

In February 1955, the gaullist Jacques Soustelle, who had a reputation as a liberal on colonial matters, replaced Roger Léonard as governor-general in Algeria and in January the Algerian police forces were integrated into the metropolitan service. The police had been responsible for torture and for zealously imposing the local settler supremacy and it was hoped, by this manoeuvre, to transfer the more ardent spirits out of the country and instill some discipline into the corps. Soustelle was expected to confront the local potentates and impose the 1947 Depreux statute on the departments, but he, like many others sent to Algeria, 'went native'. At the same time, the search for those responsible for the attacks went ahead, while Mitterrand responded with hard-line measures. He dissolved the one serious competitor with the FLN – and an object of its violence – Messali Hadj's independence party, Mouvement pour le triomphe des libertés démocratiques (though it was not involved in attacks), while moderate Muslims were being forced out of institutions.

If Mitterrand's strategy of reform was intended to create a middle ground on which the French authorities could negotiate, then in fact he was undermining the moderate and Francophile leaders. Mitterrand declared that the action of the insurgents 'make unthinkable, in any way whatsoever, a negotiation', and that was interpreted by others as a hard-line refusal to compromise on 'order'.[38] The re-establishment of order by the army was, however, meant to be a prelude to reforms. These reforms, although they were subverted, were too much for the settlers, and their opposition to the government in turn became implacable. As a result, the Mendès France government fell on 6 February, voted down by 319 to 273, animated in part by their Algerian policy, but like all such votes in the Fourth Republic there were other contributory factors. Mitterrand came out of this Algerian imbroglio with the reputation on the right of a dangerous radical.

Mendès France's government had also faced the other big question of Fourth Republic politics: Europe. It was René Pleven who had first suggested the creation of an integrated European army including German units under a supranational authority. German rearmament had become pressing with the Korean War, and the European Defence Community (EDC) would have rearmed Germany within a context reassuring to its neighbours. However, the EDC was bitterly attacked by its opponents, many of whom saw it as entailing the disappearance of the French Army. Most Fourth Republic governments were not willing to put the issue to the Assembly for fear of being overthrown until Mendès France decided to settle the issue one way or another. With a divided majority and dubious himself, Mendès France was unwilling to stake the fate of his government on the EDC: its ratification was not made a question of confidence and the Treaty was roundly defeated by 319 votes to 264, with both the Communists and the gaullists voting against it. But the issue that Mendès France had hoped to side-step had weakened the government through resignations by provoking the hostility of the MRP – another factor in Mendès France's eventual fall. Mitterrand's lack of enthusiasm for the EDC was held against him by the MRP. Pleven blamed him for the fall of the EDC, as did some other Europeanists, and this may have contributed to keeping him off the list of prime ministers. He was evicted from the European Movement by vengeful Christian Democrats.

Mitterrand and the Left

Algeria remained, however, the principal problem for governments after the departure of Mendès France. Edgar Faure's government, which followed Mendès France, did not include Mitterrand. Faure undercut Mendès France's attempts to reorganize the Radical Party by asking the President to dissolve the parliament, and snap elections were held on 2 January 1956. A Republican Front was hastily put together by Mendès France's Radical Party supporters, the SFIO and other leftward leaning groups in which Mitterrand emerged as a leader along with some more progressive gaullists.[39] There was no coordination, but the 'mendésiste' label was distributed by the journal L'Express to candidates in lieu of any formal party or coalition arrangement. A substantial wrangling over candidacies was involved, a great deal of bitterness was generated and there was considerable confusion, with the result that candidates ran against each other (the UDSR was a big loser from this).

However, there was a new force rising on the extreme right: the Poujadists. Pierre Poujade's anti-tax 'jacquerie' directed its barbs at the political class as a whole: it was a nationalist and vigorously 'French Algeria' movement, which momentarily captured many shared discontents. Poujadists regarded Mitterrand as a prime example of a Fourth Republic oligarch and set out to defeat him in the Nièvre. Although both the mendésistes and Faure's coalition endorsed Mitterrand himself, the violent Poujadist onslaught made the election far from certain: local Socialists still opposed a politician they regarded as on the right, as did the Communists. But, polling better than he had in 1951, Mitterrand was elected in the multi member constituency with 18.2 per cent of the votes. The Communists polled 29.9 per cent, the Socialists 18.3 per cent and the gaullist remnant Républicains sociaux polled 10.3 per cent (each had one deputy) – but Mitterrand's electorate was moving leftward.

Nationally, too, it was a vigorously fought election and there was a high turn-out, but it returned a fragmented Assembly with a swing to the left that produced about 150 Republican Front deputies, more of them SFIO than Radical. There were 150 Communist deputies, 200 Conservatives and 52 Poujadists, but the survival of Edgar Faure's conservatives meant that the Republican Front needed allies and could not govern alone. As a result of this failure, the mendésiste modernization impetus ran into the sands, Mendès France did not lead the next government and of the twelve outgoing members of UDSR, only four were returned. Of the nineteen UDSR deputies, ten were metropolitan and the rest were RDA members. But the key to the future was the Socialist Party, and Mitterrand would have to demonstrate that he could work with the SFIO.

Guy Mollet, the leader of the SFIO and some 100 deputies, became Prime Minister. In this government of the left, Mitterrand was made Minister of Justice, Alain Savary became Minister for Morocco and Tunisia, Mendès France became Minister without Portfolio and Gaston Defferre became Minister for Overseas France. General Catroux, who had introduced reforms in Morocco, was named Governor-General of Algeria. A reform policy for Algeria appeared to be back on course, but the Prime Minister back-tracked, Robert Lacoste replaced Catroux and the French forces in Algeria were increased to half a million in a policy that had now become 'first win the war'. In March, and with Mitterrand's support, a near state of emergency was introduced in Algeria along with a virtual military justice. On 17 March 1956, Mitterrand signed over the administration of justice in Algeria to the army, enabling it to apply the emergency laws and to use such means as it thought appropriate to deal with the insurrection. On 23 May 1956, Mendès France, dismayed at the abandonment of reform and the intensification of repression, resigned from the government.

Although it was not the issue over which Mendès France resigned, the question of the use of torture and Mitterrand's attitude to it cannot be evaded, particularly as his participation in government despite these usages is still held against him by many. Unrestrained warfare led to the use of torture in Algeria on an extensive scale and the behaviour of the French authorities, with the use of round-ups and disappearances, recalled that of the Nazi Occupation. As Mendès France's Minister of the Interior, Mitterrand had tried to bring the police in Algeria under control with a view to eliminating these methods and removing unreliable people, and he was able to use his weight in the Mollet government to reduce the numbers of executions and inhuman imprisonment. As Minister of Justice, he refused to grant political status to FLN prisoners or to waive the death penalty. The number of executions during Mitterrand's tenure as Minister of Justice was, at 44, at its highest. Intended to reassure the settlers, the executions only redoubled the ferocity of the insurgents. In April 1957, he condemned the use of arbitrary arrest in Algeria, but he had defended the Suez expedition and the kidnapping of the Algerian leader Ben Bella with vigour.[40] In keeping with Cabinet responsibility, he retained solid support for the government, a stance which, whatever his reservations or those of his associates, meant that he remained a member of the Fourth Republic political class.

Despite this change of policy, resignations and egregious mistakes, the Mollet government was the longest lasting of the Fourth Republic and, armed with 'special powers', it launched an all-out war on the FLN. In fact, France was at war with the insurgents during the Mollet government and with it came the use of torture by the army, whose practices had come to public notice.[41] Also there began the seizure of journals that printed articles believed to be unhelpful to the prosecution of the war and searches of those journalists who wrote these disobliging pieces. During this time, Mitterrand remained in government as Minister of Justice in the Cabinet while being well aware of developments in his domain, even though he had signed away the power to the military in Algeria. But Mitterrand limited himself to the occasional protest about particular actions, unlike Alain Savary, for example, who had resigned after the kidnapping of Ben Bella.

All the same, incursions increased and, with them, the disaffection of the Algerian Muslims. An integrationist stance was difficult to maintain as the re-establishment of 'order' necessarily involved counter-insurgency operations that violated human rights, and yet no other course was proposed by Mitterrand. In fact, there were few who were prescient at this time, but Mitterrand's views were mainstream: he neither foresaw decolonization nor fought against the policies of the Mollet government from inside, as did Gaston Defferre. As things in Algeria got steadily worse, Mitterrand's standing with the left, both Marxist and Catholic, diminished. However, although nominally third in rank in the Republican Front government, he was increasingly marginalized and as Algeria became the Prime Minister's consuming problem, he was inevitably sidelined by the ministers directly involved in the war.

After the fall of the Mollet government in May 1957, there was a rightward shift that included Mollet, but under the right-wing Radical Bourgès-Maunoury as Prime Minister. Although he was invited to stay at the Ministry of Justice, Mitterrand declined a further spell in office to use the time to rethink his policies: one result was the book *Présence française et abandon* (1957). In this book he drew the lesson from Indochina that change was necessary within the Empire. Mitterrand argued that the experience in West Africa showed that consolidating reforms were possible. Thus in Algeria, the die-hards who rejected change should be repudiated or that country and the Empire would be lost. It was far from evident that such a solution was possible for Algeria, and that case was not made in Mitterrand's book. However, his public pronouncements were restrained and supportive of the government. By 1957, Mitterrand seems to have been prepared to envisage the federal solution he had previously repeatedly rejected and the UDSR launched a campaign for a new Franco-African community.[42]

But this plan lagged behind developments in Algeria and the state of opinion there even while Mitterrand told the Assembly that 'the Mediterranean and no longer the Rhine is the very axis of our security, thus of our foreign policy'.[43] But even the small steps Mitterrand was now prepared to envisage for the French Union and Algeria would have been too much for the National Assembly to bear. In September, the Bourgès-Maunoury government fell trying to promote a timid change in the governance of Algeria and was replaced. It is possible that Mitterrand may have thought his appointment as Premier was nigh, but he had no support on the right at a time when the Assembly – and the settlers and their supporters – were highly sensitive to a move to the left. In other words, the basis on which to build a more authoritative policy was not there for Mitterrand to use. Gaillard's government watered down the already weak proposal for Algeria and had it passed in the Assembly, with Mitterrand one of those voting against it. On 15 April 1958, Félix Gaillard's government was overthrown and allegations about torture became more insistent when a report by the former colonial governor Delavignette made them impossible to ignore. In May 1958, the Fourth Republic entered its last agonies.

3

De Gaulle's Republic

With the return of de Gaulle to power in 1958 the whole axis of French politics shifted: it became a duality, for or against de Gaulle. Mitterrand himself, in early 1958, had anticipated de Gaulle's return to power.[1] In the Fifth Republic there would be bipolarization, a left/right cleavage and a need to choose camps. There was no immediate prospect for Mitterrand; in the medium term, an anti-gaullist coalition had to be built but there was the prospect of power in the longer term. Between Mitterrand and de Gaulle there was a gap of mutual disdain which it would be difficult to bridge and de Gaulle's return to power meant a complete change of ruling class in which Mitterrand would have no place.

Mitterrand's strategic insight gave him the edge over de Gaulle's other opponents. As Martinet has remarked, Mitterrand was the most strategically far-sighted leader the French socialist left had ever had, far superior to both Mendès France and Léon Blum.[2] By seeing that the route to government lay in an alliance with the Communist Party and in pursuing that goal in a clear-headed and unsentimental way without the distractions of the socialist tradition, Mitterrand was more than just another *arriviste*. While denouncing the presidential system, he realized the importance of the new institution and of how direct election could be used to reshape the political landscape. He also realized the necessity of rebuilding the non-Communist left and the implications of this action before others had done so, and this insight kept him ahead of any rivals.

He set this out in 1969:

> Democratic socialism, to be able to exercise its leadership inside the new majority, must enlarge its audience on the left (through the precision of its economic programme) and on its right (through its political liberalism). Hence the importance I attach to the formation of a political movement able first to balance and then to dominate the Communist Party and finally to hold by itself, and in itself, a majority vocation.[3]

But this was a strategic outline and not a political programme. Mitterrand was, in 1958, a centre left figure – a 'Republican' – and that suited the early

1960s. Later in the 1960s Mitterrand was to realize the need to reconcile the pragmatic and programmatic at a rhetorical level. In other words, by espousing a 'socialism' that was neither social democratic nor communist he was able to bring together very dispersed groups and place himself more firmly on the left. Once again, at a rhetorical level, Mitterrand proved to be adept at 'speaking socialist' (to use Mollet's phrase), although he was uninterested in the interminable marxiological debates then current on the French left. But, to use the old adage, Mitterrand might well have said: 'I know that you believe you understand what you think I said, but I am not sure that you realize that what you heard is not what I meant.' Mitterrand's move left also began the long soap opera of antipathies and conspiracies on the left.

De Gaulle's Republic

When de Gaulle's hour came, it was on the back of a military uprising in Algeria. There were demonstrations on 13 May 1958 in Algiers that rapidly turned into an insurrection when a Committee of Public Safety was formed, headed by General Massu. De Gaulle, however, did not want to come to power through a military coup and sought the backing of the Assembly. On 29 May President Coty called on him to form a government. Mitterrand's attitude to this was to demand that de Gaulle disavow the generals in Algeria. De Gaulle, however, was determined to avoid this, but at a meeting of parliamentarians Mitterrand confronted him, demanding that he repudiate the putsch. An account is given in Mitterrand's *Mémoires* which has de Gaulle asking whether ' "you [Mitterrand] want my death, is that it? I am ready!" and stomping out'.[4] For Mitterrand, de Gaulle's 'I prefer to re-establish order than to disown disorder' was the original sin of the Fifth Republic.[5] When Mitterrand spoke in the Assembly he asked de Gaulle rhetorically: 'Why seek investiture here when you have it already from the generals in Algeria?'[6]

On 1 June, de Gaulle was invested by 329 deputies to 224 against. Those who voted against him included Mitterrand and Mendès France and forty Socialists, and the UDSR was split. Mitterrand's response was that 'de Gaulle once had two companions, honour and the country. Today these two companions are brute force and sedition.'[7] On 7 July, Mitterrand, with Mendès France and other figures of the left, joined the Union des forces démocratiques, a group of those opposed to de Gaulle's return to power. In September, the Fifth Republic's Constitution was approved by 79.25 per cent in a referendum and in the Nièvre itself the 'Oui' won a total of 94,808 votes (74.8 per cent) to the 'Non' vote of 31,997 (25.2 per cent). France went to the polls on 23 and 30 November to elect a new Assembly under the old Third Republic two-ballot plurality electoral system. The anti-gaullists suffered a crushing defeat: Mendès France was ousted, as was Mitterrand; the Poujadists and the Communists were the other big losers, the PCF being reduced to 18 per cent of the vote and ten seats. In part, this defeat was due somewhat to the new electoral system, but mostly it reflected the popularity of de Gaulle. The UDSR was one of the victims, pulled by centrifugal forces either to the gaullists or against them. Of the UDSR's fourteen metropolitan deputies, ten joined de Gaulle.

Mitterrand had decided to base himself in the eastern part of the department, where he was a general councillor and where there was some industry and, in consequence, a Communist presence of some size, but his opposition to de Gaulle was costly. In Nièvre's 3e constituency he came third on the first ballot behind the little-known gaullist Jehan Faulquier and the SFIO's local notable Dr Daniel Benoist. Mitterrand used his national opposition to de Gaulle (voting against the investiture and 'no' in the referendum) to get Communist support for the second ballot, but he declined to withdraw and created a three-way run-off with the gaullists and the SFIO. But although the Communist Party's candidate withdrew in his favour (a local a precursor of the alliance of the left), the gaullist Jehan Faulquier was elected with 15,318 votes to Mitterrand's 12,219 and the SFIO's Dr Daniel Benoist who polled 10,489 votes.

Defeat forced Mitterrand to return to the constituency and build up a more extensive following in the Nièvre, though this time in the left-leaning Morvan. In 1959 he abandoned the western Nevers council (where he had been elected from 1947 to 1959) to became mayor of Château-Chinon on a joint list with the Communists that defeated the Socialist list. He was re-elected as a councillor for the canton of Montsauche in 1961, 1967 and 1973. In March 1959, he defeated his SFIO rival Dr Benoist by 330 votes to 256 and in April was returned to the Senate for Nièvre (as 'Gauche démocratique') with other defeated personalities of the Fourth Republic. In 1964, he became president of the departmental council. During these years, working like a reverse Rastignac coming from Paris to make his fortune in the provinces, Mitterrand extended the local roots that sustained him as a deputy for the Nièvre in the elections of 1962, 1967, 1968, 1973 and 1978.

The Observatoire Affair

Mitterrand was not yet the leader of the left nor the principal personality in the opposition to de Gaulle. However, he was making his name as a fierce critic of the regime when there occurred one of the most peculiar of France's post-war scandals – the 'Observatoire Affair' of 15–16 October 1959. This affair can be described but not explained. Mitterrand claimed that his car had been followed and then shot at, turning it into a colander. He claimed that he had escaped this attempt on his life by getting out and leaping over the gates of the Paris Observatoire and hiding in the bushes. Those responsible, Mitterrand then announced, with a strict economy of sincerity, at a press conference called especially to denounce the perpetrators, must have been Algerian extreme right-wingers out to decapitate the progressive left. This attack turned Mitterrand briefly into a hero of the anti-war left.

However, eight days later Robert Pesquet, a louche former Poujadist deputy with links to the far right and the gaullists, claimed that the attack was a fake organized by Mitterrand himself.[8] Pesquet produced letters postmarked before the events describing the affair in detail and had them opened by a bailiff in front of a judge. Mitterrand had concealed from the examining magistrate both that he knew Pesquet and that an attack was imminent and was consequently accused of contempt of court. Mitterrand, as Pepys remarked of Major General Harrison who was about to be hanged, 'looked as cheerful as any man could in his circumstances'. His standing fell to nothing and he was ostracized by the political class and by many friends but not, significantly, by *L'Humanité* (the Communist Party's daily newspaper). Public incredulity increased as his story was examined more closely;[9] not since the death of Little Nell had there been so much hilarity. Mitterrand's parliamentary immunity was revoked by a vote of 175 to 27 by the Senate: supporting Mitterrand were 11 of the 14 Communists. Some people never forgot this affair, and Viansson-Ponté, head of *Le Monde*'s political desk, held it against him for years after. As was reported in *Le Monde*: 'a former Minister of the Interior, for whatever reasons, contributed to the misleading of the police and the investigating judicial authorities.'[10]

There are too many loose ends to this affair for definitive conclusions to be reached. Was the government involved, as Mitterrand claimed? Was Mitterrand that credulous? Did he believe Pesquet, and why did he not tell the police or at least close associates? Mitterrand met Pesquet three days after the 'attempt' in the Cristal Bistro on the Avenue de la Grande Armée. What did they discuss? On the Holmesian basis that, once you have removed the barking, whatever remains must be true, a real attempt on his life is unlikely, and the idea of a plot arranged by Mitterrand himself is implausible, but that he knew of it in advance seems certain. There are published testimonies from Pesquet, Dumas (Mitterrand's lawyer) and of course Mitterrand himself, but these have inconsistencies and are not compatible at crucial points.[11] Mitterrand may have been a victim of his overconfidence that he could exploit the affair against his enemies and of his penchant for secrecy. He was given amnesty in 1966 and Pesquet's case was dropped the same year, on the grounds that there was no basis for prosecution. Mitterrand, for his part, never committed the sin of admission.

Churchill remarked that politics is worse than war because in politics you can die many times. Mitterrand's climb back from the abyss began immediately, but in a low-key manner and, although he appeared at many meetings, he stayed in the background. In the first place, the organization of a party network to replace the defunct UDSR went ahead, supported by close allies. These initiatives found a response amongst the various clubs then in vogue on the left (like the Club des Jacobins and the Club Jean Moulin), intended as think-tanks to pilot the way ahead under gaullism.[12] These clubs worked assiduously over the period but they were intellectual forums and not quasi-parties.[13] It was from this small world of intellectual and political clubs that Hernu's and Mitterrand's Ligue pour le combat républicain developed, designed to propel his presidential candidature, although that was not stated as an objective at that time. This Ligue joined with other clubs and became Mitterrand's Convention des institutions républicaines (CIR) in June 1964, of which Louis Mermaz became secretary general.[14] In fact, the CIR was the Archemedean lever with which Mitterrand was going to move the world of the left and it was ideologically and programmatically light.

But Mitterrand's standing had first to be rebuilt, and this started with a visit to China, with his new associate François de Grossouvre, and a long talk with Mao. Mitterrand's visit resulted in the partly admiring, partly critical but also imperceptive book *La Chine au défi*, in which he introduced the country and presented the Great Wall as if he had just himself knitted it. Mitterrand went out of his way to offer a toast to French Algeria in front of his Chinese hosts.[15] But his book made its mark and the visits were followed up by others to Sékou Touré's Guinea (ostracized by de Gaulle), Asia, the United States and elsewhere. Mitterrand was the only major figure on the non-Communist left to attend the funeral of those killed in February 1962 at the anti-Algerian war demonstration at the Charonne underground station (seven out of the eight dead were Communists). He remained attentive to the Communists and often voted for their amendments in the Senate. He also attended the many small meetings of the left and alternative left which were trying to work out the future direction of socialism in the new Republic. However, it was not until a year or so after the 'Observatoire affair' that he began to re-emerge as an effective critic of the Fifth Republic. Gaullist criticism provoked a bespoke attack on de Gaulle and gaullism in what he called his 'best book', *Le Coup d'état permanent*, but it was strident and excessive in tone and argument. It was a success perhaps because it flung intemperate accusations at de Gaulle without restraint, calling him a 'dictator' and comparing his regime to Vichy.[16]

Moving Left

Mitterrand's views on Algeria and on the colonies had slowly changed since de Gaulle came to power and, though not moving beyond the consensus, he came to accept the independence of Algeria and the West African states (not without regret for what might have been). In April 1962, de Gaulle concluded peace with the FLN and France abruptly withdrew from Algeria, abandoning its struggle for a special settlers' statute or for rights in the Sahara. As a result, Algeria slipped off the political agenda for metropolitan France. De Gaulle then turned the corner that Mendès France had been unable to take in 1955, to move from an opposition to the war to a durable coalition supporting the government. He achieved this by dissolving the Assembly.

Mitterrand denounced both the direct election of the presidency and the method (the referendum of 28 September 1962) used to amend the Constitution. But strategically the key point was that he knew that direct election of the President was now permanent. While others on the left thought of replacing or humbling it by getting a symbolic figure elected, for Mitterrand it was a fixture and an opportunity because it would be a competition between individual politicians, not parties. Although French voters overwhelmingly supported the gaullists, Mitterrand won a famous victory, going against the national trend, and was returned to the Assembly in the general elections of November 1962 from the Château-Chinon constituency in Nièvre by 21,705 votes against the gaullists' 10,510. Once again the Communist candidates stood down in his favour on the run-off, a decision that must have been made by PCF leaders in Paris, but so too did his old rival of the SFIO Dr Benoist. Mitterrand, a newcomer in 1946, had become, as election results were to show for the next three decades, a 'favourite son'.

Mitterrand's next years consisted of working through a strategy of realignment that was to continue persistently throughout the next thirty years. This was the alliance, in different forms, of the non-Communist left with the Communist Party. Given the domination of the gaullists over the conservative right, success looked a distant prospect and, given the size and nature of the Communist Party, it appeared impossible. But without the Communist Party's support, the left could not prevail against the gaullists, so some method had to be developed to deal with this difficulty. There were broadly two. One was that of Marseilles' mayor Gaston Defferre to consolidate the non-Communist left and then to seek alliance with the Communists but from a position of force. If the non-Communist left were sufficiently broad and included Socialists, the Christian Democrats and the Radicals, it would balance any fear of a Communist-dominated alliance. But, the other method, Mitterrand's, was to treat the Communists as legitimate partners in the coalition.

But Mitterrand's démarche raised doubts. On the left, the Communist Party was regarded with suspicion and awe. It was the best organized political force in France, with a huge membership and with front organizations, a press and publishing empire of some size and the control of France's main union federation, the CGT. On the other hand, it was an arm of Soviet foreign policy and had clashed violently with the governing parties, including the SFIO, only ten years previously. Most politicians on the left felt that it could only be managed as a small part of a large coalition and that the public would need guarantees that it was the junior partner.

Journalists on *L'Express* magazine led by Jean-Jacques Servan-Schreiber started an artful publicity campaign describing the sort of person, unsullied by the Fourth Republic, who would be needed to stand against de Gaulle in the presidential elections in 1965. This was the 'Mr X' teaser in which the journal described the politician bit by bit each week and the features of Gaston Defferre slowly emerged. Defferre's strategy was to consolidate a *grande fédération* with the MRP and the Radicals, but he would not cooperate with the PCF until conditions could be imposed from strength.[17] Defferre's bid, after an optimistic start, failed in June 1965.

This left little time, but the way was now open to Mitterrand – *faute de mieux*. Few people thought that de Gaulle could be defeated or even forced onto the second ballot. Mitterrand was an isolated figure with no party backing to speak of and had never been a Socialist. However, he turned these to his advantage. In October, he was credited with only 15 per cent of the vote and expectations were so low that 25 per cent would have been considered a 'good' poll against the General.[18] Isolated and without a major party, Mitterrand appeared to pose no threat to the established parties, and if the campaign, as expected, went badly he could be easily disowned. Mitterrand moved into the gap but, unlike others, he consolidated his position with the PCF carefully. In this he was helped, because the Communists were willing at this stage to pay a relatively high price and Mitterrand, who had been prepared to treat with the party since 1958, was ready to deal with them. Mitterrand was their way into the opposition coalition and they were prepared to support an independent who would bring them in from the cold.[19]

But the trick in this, which Mitterrand managed in the run-up to the campaign, was to engineer Communist support without appearing to be their mouthpiece. In fact, Mitterrand could hardly have conceded less. There were go-betweens who dealt with the PCF and sounded out the intentions of its leader, but Mitterrand himself avoided public meetings with the PCF hierarchy. Communist leader Thorez had raised the issue of a 'Common Programme' (a joint manifesto) at the party's 17th Congress in May 1964, and had even threatened to run a Communist candidate if this were not granted, but this was not asked of Mitterrand in 1965.[20] Waldeck Rochet demanded a public commitment to an alliance 'with nobody excluded', and Mitterrand made this commitment at a press conference on 21 September.

An embarrassing meeting with the PCF immediately afterwards was avoided by Mitterrand, who invented an appointment in Brussels, sending Dumas as an emissary in his place. Dumas arrived, by chance, at a meeting of the PCF's Central Committee and was solemnly interviewed as a plenipotentiary.[21] The day before, the Central Committee's agenda had been changed to include the presidential elections and Waldeck Rochet spoke on the item, putting his authority as party leader behind the choice of Mitterrand as candidate.[22] On 23 September, the PCF publicly called on its supporters to work for Mitterrand, thereby provoking a schism by the Sorbonne student section.[23] It must have looked, to the party, a familiar step to take (in 1936 they had preferred the Radical Daladier to the SFIO's Blum) and the Communist Party might expect to maintain pressure on the Socialists to push them into a more formal alliance.

Presidential Elections in 1965

This bald survey does not do justice to the patient work undertaken by Mitterrand and his allies to prepare the ground for his bid, nor to the finesse with which the various components were put together, nor to the timing. Three preconditions were set for Mitterrand's candidature, and by the summer of 1965 these were achieved: he had the support of Mendès France (in *France observateur*),[24] of the SFIO's Mollet and of the PCF leader

Waldeck Rochet.[25] Mitterrand's tactics looked improvised and hasty but they were very carefully worked out 'to the nearest millimetre' leaving as little as possible to chance.[26] Mitterrand had to support the major personalities like Defferre, Daniel Mayer (of the Ligue des droits de l'homme) and Mendès France and then let them declare themselves non-combatants before he himself entered the ring with their blessing. Finally, the Communist Party's support had to be obtained without negotiation and by side-stepping its demand for the joint manifesto that it had been making for over a year.

But the party was willing, aided by Mitterrand's openness to the PCF since 1958 and (possibly) by its new Secretary-General Waldeck Rochet who had visited Moscow on 21 August 1965. At that meeting the elections must have been discussed and he was presumably given the go-ahead, but the PCF's desperation to enter the party mainstream meant that it would accept a fairly general joint platform. De Gaulle's disruptive and anti-American foreign policy found favour in Moscow and hence with the PCF, which referred to the 'positive aspects' of de Gaulle's foreign policy in *France nouvelle*.[27] But for the period of the elections the reference to these 'positive aspects' was dropped by the Communist Party. One thing for which the Communists might have hoped was that the election would put an end to the accusation that they were *gaullistes de fait*. Mitterrand's candidature was announced after de Gaulle's press conference on 9 September at which the General declined to say whether he would stand. (On the alternative left, the tiny PSU supported Mitterrand but declined to participate in the campaign and *Combat* reminded its readers that Mitterrand was pro-Algérie française, pro-Atlantic and defended the USA in Vietnam.)[28] Mitterrand's declaration of candidacy after de Gaulle's press conference made very difficult the search for alternative personalities who might represent the left.

At the beginning, Mitterrand's 'democratic union' campaign was run by a small group of mainly long-time associates, but they were joined by newcomers.[29] Behind this group, of course, lay the network of the prisoners' movement bolstered by other volunteers and ready to be mobilized for Mitterrand's campaigns. Local campaigns were organized under the aegis of these committed supporters. Mitterrand's declaration was centrist in tenor and lacked the aggressive polemics of the past. His 'democratic union' campaign was an anti-gaullist 'republican' one, stressing the nature of the regime, repeating many of the criticisms of the Fifth Republic but without the strident socialist note that would appear later. Mitterrand's main line of attack concerned the disrespect shown by the gaullists for the law and the independence of the judiciary.[30] Most of the options he set out

at first were insubstantial to the point of invisibility, although the emphasis on 'women's rights' was a novelty in French elections. But this impre-
cision was a necessity given the heterogeneity of the coalition supporting
him and was possible because his lack of party ties gave him a free hand.
(A party might have determined the manifesto.) Later, on 25 November,
they were supplemented by 'twenty-eight proposals', which were a careful
admixture of suggestions designed to appeal to both the Communists and
the Socialists but, although they did suggest a French investment bank, they
did not propose nationalizations.

In the campaign Mitterrand called for a re-establishment of parliamentary responsibility and the removal of the elite that, he said, had usurped
the public's decision-making powers. This was linked with the theme of
democracy, manhandled by the gaullists; he then turned to progress
and growth, which he said should be determined on principles of social
justice and as part of the European community. Individual freedom,
freedom of information and of trade unions and local autonomy were to
be prioritized. Among the few definite promises were abolition of the
nuclear force and the repeal of Articles 16 (emergency powers) and 11
(referendum) of the Constitution. These 'proposals' were supplemented
by a manifesto that included a strong defence of Europe and the Atlantic
Alliance. On the institution of the presidency itself, Mitterrand emphasized
the need for it to respect republican traditions and in particular stated
that the Assembly, not the President, would be the authority if he were
elected.

But Mitterrand's campaign was given further impetus by de Gaulle's disdainful refusal to campaign and his uninspiring election broadcasts on TV.
De Gaulle did not descend to the arena on the first ballot, but the gaullists
attacked the heterogeneous coalition backing Mitterrand, underlining the
President's imperious 'moi ou le chaos'. Gaullists were told not to attack
the Communist Party, nor did they bring up the subject of Pétain's very
own OM, the francisque awarded to Mitterrand by the Vichy regime.[31]
Apart from Mitterrand and de Gaulle, the candidates were the Christian
Democrat Jean Lecanuet, the independent Senator Pierre Marcilhacy,
the marginal syndicalist Marcel Barbu and the extreme right's J.-L. Tixier
Vignancour. MRP's Jean Lecanuet, with new techniques and great élan,
began to revive the old Christian Democratic centre.

Although, in what was the first televised election, Mitterrand proved a
mediocre television performer, this was managed by arranging interviews
rather than straight talks. However, he excelled at the massive rallies that
were arranged across France and came to the fore in a whirlwind cam-

paign, sometimes holding four meetings a day. It was an energy that few of his associates could match. On 5 December 1965, de Gaulle was forced into a run-off: he polled 44.6 per cent, Mitterrand polled 34.7 per cent and Lecanuet took 15.5 per cent. It was Lecanuet who, with a lively campaign, had taken votes from de Gaulle and ensured that there would be a second ballot, but the rules allowed only the top two to go through into the run-off.

There was a feeling that the left was reviving and that the General had been rebuffed (though the brute figures hardly suggest that). Mitterrand ran as a candidate of the left, regrouping the parties of the left in a 'democratic union' in the first round and of the centre as well in a broad front of those who rejected the General in the second. However, this support in the second ballot when he ran as a candidate of 'all the republicans' included some of the extreme right, who regarded de Gaulle as Pétain's opponent and as the most infamous of decolonizers. Mitterrand had supported Tixier Vignancour in the trial of the rebel General Salan, but the extreme right's support lost him the active presence of Mendès France at his side (who wanted Mitterrand to disown the Tixierists).[32] It was a campaign that snowballed as the bipolar presidential competition had its effect and drew the opponents of de Gaulle to Mitterrand's side.

Mitterrand's electorate was the traditional electorate of the left, and he came ahead in twenty departments, six in the centre and fourteen in the south-west and Midi. For the second round the campaign had a new élan and, garnering 45 per cent (the General polled 55 per cent), the outcome was seen as a victory. Mitterrand announced that it was 'not a victory for François Mitterrand but for the entire left'.[33] However, he had not garnered the whole of the Fourth Republic left's potential vote. Although he had a majority amongst the workers, his support was concentrated in the less prosperous and less dynamic areas.[34] Fauvet estimated that Mitterrand was lacking about three million votes from the traditional left and those were in working-class areas such as the Paris region (where they were 40 per cent lower) and in the Nord, Pas-de-Calais.[35]

De Gaulle's set-back served only to bring him back into the ring with greater determination and the second ballot saw a vigorous gaullist campaign – and the President returned to the TV screens. Gaullists started by denouncing Mitterrand as a prisoner of the Communists, but that was dropped in favour of more diverse attacks. It was a well-financed onslaught and one with which Mitterrand could not compete, but he made the best of TV and radio appearances and numerous large rallies. Jean Lecanuet proposed a pact with Mitterrand for the second ballot but that would have alienated the PCF and was refused; the bulk of his support would probably not have transferred to Mitterrand in any case. Both Lecanuet and Tixier Vignancour (through anti-gaullism) declared their support for Mitterrand on the second ballot (as did Barbu and Marcilhacy in a back-handed way), but there was no possibility of de Gaulle being defeated. Mitterrand styled himself as the candidate of 'all the democrats' and welcomed support from other candidates.[36] On 19 December, the second round results gave de Gaulle a large margin in the highest ever French election turn out (85 per cent). Mitterrand's vote increased by three million (many from the centre and extreme right), but de Gaulle was re-elected with 55.2 per cent (13.1 million) of the vote to Mitterrand's 44.8 per cent (10.6 million).

Leader of the Left

In many ways, however, Mitterrand had won. By taking the lead in the 1965 presidential campaign against de Gaulle, Mitterrand, though he never came near to being elected, had become the major personality on the left. There was some cheer for the PCF which had, because it was the only organized mass force on the left, gained members (as did Mitterrand's CIR) and it had begun to make progress towards a left-wing alliance around a joint manifesto. However, it began once again to demand a 'common programme' as the price of future progress.[37] On 10 September 1967, in time for the elections, a federation of the non-Communist left had been hastily bolted together: this was the Fédération de la gauche démocrate et socialiste (FGDS). The FGDS brought together the Radical Party, the CIR, the UDSR (still a name but with no members), the SFIO and some small clubs. Its moderate programme emphasized economic expansion and made some relatively modest proposals for nationalization (of arms, space and some banks) along with the increase in local powers and union rights.[38] It was started as no more than an electoral cartel to prevent destructive run-offs in the upcoming 1967 general elections, but Mitterrand had other plans for it in his long-term aim of uniting the non-Communist left and then agreeing a programme with the PCF. Power, however, still lay with the parties and these, strong in their own traditions, did not intend to cede anything to another party or institution.

But with the prestige gained from the elections and legitimacy as the unifier of the left, the presidency of the FGDS became a more important post than was originally planned. By threatening resignation and by out-facing the old leaders, a degree of progress was made. These leaders resented the newcomer and were not necessarily going to be helpful to him or his small party. This loose federation became the vehicle for the next stage of Mitterrand's regrouping of the opposition and a fusion of parties was envisaged but, unlike the parties, he saw its vocation as 'catch-all' and not as a socialist rally. For the operation to succeed the two-way stretch was necessary, reaching out to the PCF (with its demand for a 'common programme') and to the centre (Atlanticist and European). Mitterrand's determination to tread this sinuous route resulted in many curious turns, but he was well placed to take it.

A 'shadow cabinet' was created in the Assembly as a way of countering the gaullist assertion that between them and the Communists there was nothing. However, as with all actions in the FGDS, the 'shadow cabinet' showed only too clearly the effects of negotiations between the partners, even though some promotions of 'Mitterrandists' were made. This 'front bench' was not a success: its composition was derided and its functioning was poor. In this enterprise, as in the rest of the FGDS, the old parties would not let themselves be dominated by an outsider and tensions mounted inside the federation.

Meanwhile, on the alternative left the PSU was organizing intellectual energies and mounted its Grenoble conference in April 1966, intended to modernize the Socialist left and update its programme. These intellectuals put the renovation of policy and programme before the conclusion of electoral and institutional agreements, in contrast to Mitterrand. Mitterrand was not present and the conference was dominated by people from the PSA and PSU, some of whom had refused to accept his application to join their party (and were well-disposed to Mendès France but often quite hostile to Mitterrand). This small splinter of the left, although it joined the electoral agreement, was wary of the Communist Party and difficult to bring into the fold. It was to be the root of several later difficulties.

By 14 July 1966, a joint FGDS manifesto had finally been negotiated and published, a necessity before a platform could be negotiated with the PCF. It was left-leaning in domestic policy but it was circumspect in foreign policy. There were long-standing disagreements between the Socialists and the Communists on foreign policy, and on these Mitterrand was firmly on the Socialist side. Nuclear weapons, which were condemned by both sides, were not at issue, but Europe and the Atlantic Alliance, which the Socialists had always supported and the Communists opposed, were. These differences remained a problem throughout the alliance and they were one reason why Moscow was inclined to the gaullist right rather than to the union of the left. De Gaulle, with his criticism of the USA in Vietnam and his withdrawal of France from the Nato military command, had given the

USSR diplomatic gains in the West that would not be repeated if the left won.

All the same, the conclusion of an agreement between the FGDS and the Communists went ahead. In the elaborate minuet leading up to the negotiation of a common platform, Mitterrand suggested, first, that there had to be agreement on single FGDS candidates in each constituency before a platform could be concluded and then that the 'seven options' of his 1965 campaign should be the platform. In December 1966 an agreement was concluded bringing together the PCF and the SFIO for the first time since 1947. There was agreement on an economic plan and the nationalization of banks, arms industries and on the 'democratic' management of nationalized industries. However, once again the disagreements on foreign policy surfaced and these were simply noted as a fact of life. This was a small step towards the common programme of government so ardently desired by the PCF, a demand made by Waldeck Rochet at its 18th Congress in 1967.[39] The deal opened the way for an agreement on standing down to be made with the PCF in December.

Pompidou's change in the threshold of votes candidates had to pass in order to qualify to run on to the second ballot, from 5 per cent to 10 per cent of the registered voters, made the FGDS agreements imperative and it was intended to force the centre to choose between the left and the gaullists. Georges Pompidou was for a long time de Gaulle's close political associate and a driving force in the building of the gaullist movement. Although not a Resistance figure, he ran de Gaulle's private office and was then Prime Minister from 1962 to 1968. He had not initially intended to undertake a political career, but he developed a taste and a talent for political action to become a formidable politician. By January 1967 single FGDS candidacies in 413 of the 487 constituencies had been agreed, of which 216 were SFIO, 97 were Radicals, 97 were CIR and 21 were independent leftists. It was arranged that the two partners would stand down for the 'best-placed' candidate – that is, the one who could defeat the gaullist – and that allowed the PCF to give several 'presents' to the FGDS. It also enabled the FGDS to support candidates who were hostile to 'personal power' but not necessarily on the left at all (for example Frédéric-Dupont, in Paris). Despite Lecanuet's attempts to revive the centre with a new Centre Democratic Party, the bipolarization trend continued. Mitterrand was not quite the 'leader of the opposition' (Mendès France had the moral stature of the leader), but he was the principal politician on the non-Communist left. In Nevers on 22 February, a three-hour debate between Prime Minister Pompidou (leading the government's campaign) and Mitterrand ended in a draw. However, it enabled Mitterrand to re-emphasize his criticism of 'personal power' and to reinforce his position at the head of the left.

The 1967 National Assembly elections were very closely fought. On the first ballot the government majority polled 8.5 million votes (37.3 per cent), but the FGDS took 4.2 million votes (19 per cent) which was below the combined 1962 vote of the SFIO and Radicals (20.1 per cent). But the Communist Party's support increased by one million votes to five million (22.5 per cent), seeming to confirm its dominant place but still below its Fourth Republic totals. Lecanuet's 390 candidates polled three million votes (13.4 per cent), below his presidential result, but far from a humiliation, although they were the victims of bipolarization. Mitterrand himself was elected on the first ballot in Nièvre with 56 per cent to the gaullists' 33 per cent and the Communists' 10.6 per cent. It was the second ballot that would distribute seats and decide the Assembly's composition, and that was a victory both for Mitterrand's strategy and for his group.

'Republican' discipline, or the transfer of votes to the 'best-placed' candidate, worked: it gave the FGDS 118 seats and the PCF 73 (an increase of 32). CIR candidates did well out of the agreements on seats: 17 were elected, many of them Mitterrand's close associates, including Georges Dayan (Nîmes), Roland Dumas (defeating Jean Charbonnel in Brive), Claude Estier (defeating Alexandre Sanguinetti in Paris), André Rousselet (Toulouse), Louis Mermaz (Vienne) and Georges Fillioud (Romans). De Gaulle's supporters, with 245 seats, had won a narrow majority. On 20 May the government won a vote of confidence by a mere eight votes, an illustration of the narrowness of the gaullists' victory. However, Lecanuet's 41 centrist deputies constituted a potential 'reserve' for the government.

Mitterrand began to make declarations as the opposition leader, for example, replying to de Gaulle's press conference on Israel in August. In late 1967 he visited the Czechoslovak Communist leader Novotny, thought to be one of the new generation of liberal communists.[40] This was badly judged: Novotny was deposed in January 1968 at the beginning of the 'Prague Spring'. These events made headlines and were fully reported, while the party leaders, such as Mollet, had difficulty getting attention. But the FGDS was a ramshackle structure and no further progress could be made within its confines, so it was proposed in January 1968 to fuse the component parts of the federation. Before that could be got under way, a joint programme with the PCF had to be negotiated and this was concluded on 24 February 1968. There were divergences over the EEC and UK entry, European integration, the Atlantic Alliance and Israel.

1968

Mitterrand was largely absent from the events of May 1968, though he was one of their principal victims. Nobody had seen it coming and few people, if any, understood the student uprising as it was happening. Mitterrand had devoted his energies to the building of an alliance on the left between party leaders, and the student 'psychodrama' was an unwelcome intrusion into that. As a summary of the situation, his comment in *Ma part de vérité* that 'I missed the revolution, but there had not been a revolution' was accurate enough, but the virtuosi of class war were on song.[41] Perhaps, though, many could have been excused for feeling that the Fifth Republic's original sin of *coup de force* was now being paid back. Unlike Mendès France, Mitterrand had no empathy with the students or they with him, and they saw him as a figure of unsavoury electoral negotiations and backroom deals. Cohn-Bendit, the nearest to leader the students had, declared that Mitterrand was not an ally but he 'might be of some use to us'.[42] All the same, many of the ideas of May '68 and some of its student leaders were later to resurface in the Parti socialiste of the 1970s and 1980s.

As he lived in the left bank of Paris on the fringes of the university area, Mitterrand would have seen the skirmishes and the barricades and could have met students without undue difficulty. On 13 May 1968 the CIR had organized a meeting in Paris to deplore ten years of gaullist usurpation, but it was entirely overtaken by the mammoth demonstration the unions had organized to coincide with their call for a general strike. The demonstration had started in the working-class districts and extended through the Latin Quarter, but the politicians were largely unnoticed in the middle of the crowd. By the end of that week strikers had paralysed the country and more buildings had been occupied. Mitterrand's interventions in the Assembly were designed to make the government as uncomfortable as possible and played on the paradox that it was an uprising that had brought de Gaulle to power ten years before. On 14 May, he demanded an amnesty for students, denounced police brutality and called for the government to resign. A censure motion failed by a predictable margin in the Assembly on 22 May; but it was not in the Assembly that the events were being played out and he was absent from the main arena. (Though he was, as *Paris-Match* illustrated, dining at the Lipp restaurant when the students went past.)[43]

There were two further things that emerged from May '68 for Mitterrand. One was the rift with Mendès France and the other was the shattering of the FGDS and the left-wing alliance. Mendès France was the man of the hour and was widely talked of as the likely saviour of the situation, for he was popular with the students – unlike Mitterrand. After meeting together on the 23 May, the two men decided not to mix with the student crowds to avoid what they feared might result in an incident. But the next day, when the students invaded the stock exchange and violent actions took place, Mendès France decided to intervene to calm things down. This he did, but Mitterrand, hearing of Mendès France's appearance amongst the students and of his enthusiastic reception, felt that he had been side-lined. Mendès France's remark that Mitterrand's intervention would have been unhelpful or even counterproductive was apposite. Along with Michel Rocard, Mendès France attended the meeting at the Charléty stadium on the 27 May.

The next incident was more serious and was of Mitterrand's own making. De Gaulle's broadcast of 24 May proposing a referendum had gone badly and had in fact made things worse for a country still paralysed by strikers, its streets filled with students. A conventional press conference was arranged at the Hôtel Continental on 28 May. Here, Mitterrand made the observation that, were de Gaulle to resign following a 'no' in the proposed referendum, he as leader of the opposition would stand for the presidency in the ensuing elections. Before these elections, an interim government, as in 1944, 'open to all' (i.e. including Communists) led by Pierre Mendès France, should be installed. None of this was exceptional, possibly even banal, but although the effect was at first thought highly positive it quickly turned to disaster.[44] Pompidou, who as Prime Minister controlled the television services, had the press conference edited to show a dictatorial Mitterrand mounting a virtual coup d'état. This montage ruined Mitterrand's stock and he once again suffered ostracism and derision.

Neither Mendès France nor the Communists had been consulted about this press conference and were taken aback, and the PCF was not ready to have its conduct decided by the non-Communist left. The Communists organized their own demonstration on 29 May and used it to call for a 'popular government' with Communist participation.[45] De Gaulle's government may have been temporarily feeble in early May, but it was not good politics to treat them as such. Mendès France had been slipped into Mitterrand's scenario to play the secondary role to the President. But the Communists would not accept Mendès France as Premier and they wanted guarantees of ministerial portfolios. Next day, General de Gaulle dramatically disappeared and then returned to make a magisterial speech and dissolve the Assembly. May '68 came, fizzled out and the scene was set for a gaullist landslide.

De Gaulle had turned round the situation from one of rejection of the gaullists to an embrace of law and order and there was little or nothing that the FGDS could do to prevent the gaullists from reaping the harvest of anxious voters rejecting the student *'chienlit'*. Although the Communists, as in 1967, rejected single left candidatures, the pact was maintained and a mutual standing down on the second ballot was agreed. For the first time in the history of the Republic a single party won a majority in the Assembly. With 296 seats (8.2 million votes: 37 per cent) the gaullists had no need of their Independent Republican allies who had 67 seats (1.7 million votes: 7.7 per cent) and were hardly threatened by the FGDS's 57 seats (3.7 million votes: 16.5 per cent) or the Communists' 34 seats (4.4 million votes: 20 per cent). All Mitterrand's associates in the CIR were defeated and he survived a bitter campaign in the Nièvre only on the second ballot. (The centre, the PDM, with 2.3 million votes, 10.3 per cent, took 33 seats.)

A scapegoat was needed for this débâcle.[46] In August, the Warsaw Pact forces invaded Czechoslovakia and ended the 'Prague Spring' tentative experiment in freedom that the Communist Party had begun. True to form, although after hesitating, the French Communist Party, never an enthusiast for the Czechoslovak experiment, fell in behind Moscow; Prague's problems thus became anathema to those on the socialist left as well as to the centre and right.[47] Although Mitterrand did not close the door to the PCF, it seemed to others to confirm the 'bolshevik' nature of the Communist Party and its submission to Moscow and to make an alliance impossible.[48] An FGDS Bureau meeting was unable to come to a decision because it was torn between those (SFIO and CIR) who wanted to continue to seek an alliance and those who wanted a break with the Communists.[49] But the FGDS was already dead and had no further power over events. Most of the activity now moved to the creation of a new unified socialist party, and the components of the FGDS took up their positions on that issue: the CIR and SFIO were in favour and the Radicals were against. On 7 November 1968, his position untenable and his person and policy discredited, Mitterrand stood down as President of the FGDS.

4

The Common Programme

One of the essentials of leadership, as Galbraith remarks, is the ability to convey conviction to others in a world in flux where consequences are uncertain.[1] Power in these cases goes to those who show self-belief, a capacity Mitterrand did not lack, even if it was not accompanied by an equivalent ideological or programmatic commitment. Yet, after ten years in opposition, Mitterrand was back at almost the point of departure by the end of 1968. On the positive side, he was still one of the politicians who incarnated the determination to unite the left and he might still get the backing of the Communist Party.

But there were many negatives. Mitterrand had been sidelined once again and was not trusted by many of the political elite, as mid-1968 showed, much less so than Mendès France (in polls only 9 per cent preferred Mitterrand as the replacement for de Gaulle[2]), who stood aside from Mitterrand's unifying work. Mitterrand was alone in the Assembly, sitting as a non-party member. Many criticized him for seeking to corral Mendès France as his junior and for blocking the possibility of a call for a Mendès France presidential candidature.[3] Within the non-Communist left, the parties had demonstrated their resilience by undermining the FGDS experiment and the Radical Party had departed leaving the left crucially short of centrist votes. Mitterrand was not from the socialist family and would somehow have to make his peace with the barons of the SFIO if he were to progress within a new coalition structure. Finally, the invasion of Czechoslovakia made the PCF an object of suspicion to everybody.

Joining the Left

Mitterrand started once again to construct the pyramid out of billiard balls. But as 1969 unfolded, things did not get any better for him or for the left. Building an alliance of the left while at the same time consolidating the centre and centre left had been a long-term affair starting in 1958, and there had been few tangible signs of success. This process had to be restarted, but before anything could be done the left had to meet the challenge of de Gaulle's 1969 referendum on the reform of the Senate and regions, followed by the General's resignation and new presidential elections.

Mitterrand, while campaigning against de Gaulle, was kept at arm's length by the left. Meanwhile, he put together a half-autobiographical and half-philosophical book (in interview format) setting out his credentials to lead the left: *Ma part de vérité* (published later in the year). Once again there was a back-up in his memory's septic system when it came to wartime politics. This process continued with the issue of *Un socialisme du possible* in 1970, another extended interview, in which he declared his belief in 'reformism' and in the necessity for socialism as a way of eliminating exploitation.[4] As set out in these works, Mitterrand's stance emphasized old socialism of the French left while ignoring the 'social democracy' of the northern European countries. 'Social democracy' was to become a hissing and a byword on the left in the 1970s.

There was only a small chance that Mitterrand would be the left's candidate for the 1969 presidential elections. He himself summed up the difficulties faced by the fragmented left and declared that he was 'not a candidate for anything'.[5] In fact, the left splintered into several candidatures: Gaston Defferre came from the ranks of the old SFIO, Michel Rocard from the new PSU and the avuncular Bolshevik Jacques Duclos was run by the Communist Party. Guy Mollet, conscious of Mitterrand's poor standing in the polls and still the SFIO's leader, proposed non-political candidates, as he had done in 1965. There were many on the left who supported the centrist Senate Speaker Alain Poher who, had he won, would have reduced the presidency to its modest Fourth Republic dimensions.

In the first round, on 1 June, the front runners were the gaullist Georges Pompidou and Alain Poher. However, Pompidou polled only 9.8 million votes (44 per cent) and Poher, who had at one time led in the polls, took a mere 5.2 million votes (23 per cent), coming only just ahead of the Communist Duclos who polled 4.8 million votes (21.5 per cent). Duclos's vote was in fact a ceiling for the PCF, which had faced no real competition on the left and which ran a well-organized campaign stressing the need – in the future – for a united left. Defferre, on the other hand, even running in tandem with Mendès France, received a humiliating 1.1 million votes (5.1 per cent). Thus, removed as a serious presidential contender, Defferre's centrist strategy was definitively discredited, and he also ended Mendès France's position as alternative leader of the left. By contrast, with 3.7 per cent of the vote and a shoestring budget, the PSU's Michel Rocard made his appearance on the political stage in what was judged to be a successful campaign. On the second ballot Pompidou won easily with 10.7 million votes (57.6 per cent), though on a reduced turnout of 59.1 per cent, the Communists having called for abstention in the absence of a candidate of the left.

De Gaulle's unforeseen defeat had also interrupted the process of remaking the SFIO into the new Parti socialiste. At Alfortville in May 1969, the old SFIO held its conference before disbanding and decided the route to the creation of the new Parti socialiste. In the intricate quadrille between the old guard of the SFIO and the supporters of Mitterrand, the CIR had been effectively excluded by being offered conditions that would have made it a subordinate partner. Mitterrand had lost a skirmish in which he and Mollet had tried to force constraints on the other.

The New Parti socialiste

At the next congress in Issy-les-Moulineaux in July 1969, the Parti socialiste (PS) was officially created and Alain Savary became its First Secretary.[6] Savary was a former Socialist, a Resistance leader, well liked and upright, and he decided on a very different course from Mitterrand's. Savary and Mitterrand also had very different styles and a personal antipathy to each other.[7] Savary tried to modernize the left, to strip it of its revolutionary rhetoric by reducing expectations to modest dimensions. His perception of the need for doctrinal modernization was one reason for his undertaking a frustrating philosophical discussion with the PCF. The old leadership around Mollet hindered Savary from modernizing the party, although, in his stolid style, he did start the rebuilding and renovation of the party and attracted new members to it even if he failed to rouse the enthusiasms of those involved.

Savary's was a 'mendésiste' line, eschewing nationalizations and critical of Soviets, which had been confirmed at a special conference and which he had set out in his book.[8] A 'Common Programme of Government', the Communists' minimum demand, was not yet being negotiated (without that there would be no alliance) and this was postponed until after the PS 1971 congress. A good part of the problem was that the Socialist Party was still dependent on anti-Communist alliances at municipal level and these, still the party's main resource, inhibited any leftward move to accommodate the PCF. But by the time of the next Socialist Congress, in June 1971, the municipal elections would be over and the problem could be shelved for a few more years.

In 1970 the spectacular (if brief) revival of the Radical Party under the leadership of Jean-Jacques Servan-Schreiber in a by-election victory at Nancy showed what might be done. Savary proposed to bring in any socialists still left outside the 'big tent' of the new PS and on 8 November 1970 the CIR proposed the unification of their party with the PS. Unlike Savary, Mitterrand intended an immediate political change and expected that that would pay dividends, but he regarded ideology and the building of the new party as secondary. It was the end of Mitterrand's attempt (which he now saw as hopeless) to manage the left through a tiny splinter group.[9] In the negotiations, the CIR's membership was very generously reckoned at 10,000 and the PS's at 70,000.[10] This prepared the way for the PS congress of Epinay-sur-Seine of 11–13 June 1971. In some versions of this congress, Mitterrand is cast as Bottom to the Socialist Party's Titania, but there were good reasons for the alliance. A plot was hatched to bring Mitterrand to the leadership of the party between the dude proletarians of CERES and the machine politicians Defferre and Mauroy; and developed (astonishingly) in complete secrecy and with not a little James Bondery. While Mitterrand kept out of the foreground, CIR members acted as if nothing was afoot and even managed to misdirect the leadership's attention elsewhere onto secondary questions.

Savary himself was not a schemer and could not see a potential danger, but in truth it would have required a paranoid mind to have realized what the opposition coalition was. Even had he recognized the threat, Savary was no match for the plotters and would have been like an operatic tenor called on to fight a real duel. For most people the main question was the alliance with the Communist Party and how that would operate, although, of course, the problem of leadership lay only partially occluded behind that. Each of the components of the Mitterrand coalition had tabled their own motion. On the 'right', Mauroy and Defferre wanted a series of guarantees in any negotiations with the PCF, while on the left Mermaz and Robert Pontillon proposed immediate discussion of a 'Common Programme of Government'.

Chevènement's CERES tabled a disquisition on the need to destroy bourgeois society and to break with capitalism and, as their flagship issue also, demanded an immediate 'common programme of government' with the Communists. It was not certain that Mitterrand's supporters had a majority, so a trial run was made. This test of strength was provided by the resolution that the party's Directing Committee (its 'parliament') be elected by proportional representation. Hence, unlike the old SFIO, the different factions would all be represented on the Directing Committee but the key point was that no threshold would be needed. This stipulation would allow CERES, which perhaps would struggle to make 8 per cent, to enter the Directing Committee and play a part, perhaps the determining one. Moreover, allowing smaller factions like CERES to play a balancing role would produce a majority for Mitterrand on the Directing Committee. This motion succeeded and a general tumult followed when it was realized that the leadership had been defeated by a combination of the party's right and its *gauchisante* left. Savary and his supporters had 38 members elected, to 23 Mauroy-Defferre supporters (Nord, Bouches-du-Rhône) and 13 CIR; the 7 CERES members would make the difference by rallying to Mitterrand.

Next day, on Sunday 13 June, the new majority motion was ratified by 43,926 votes to 41,757 (a majority of 2,169 that was probably bigger than the membership of the CIR). Mitterrand, making his first speech to the Congress, exceeded himself in rhetorical flight and, using language from the haute sixties cracker box, managed to condemn 'capitalism' and 'money' and to declare that their purpose was revolution, to the delight of the activists.[11] To some, however, this 'socialist' talk had the effect of a cat sliding down a blackboard.[12] Three days later, Mitterrand was leader of the party. Most observers reacted with surprise and some reflected on the 'unnatural alliance' of the new majority and doubted its solidity. There were those in the party, and not just Mollet, who thought that they had been swindled out of 'their' heritage by an adventurer.[13] More to the point, the victory of the left around Mitterrand destroyed Savary's slow modernization of the Socialist Party and put the old anti-capitalist project at the heart of the new party. This was announced by Mitterrand himself in his speech to the congress denouncing 'the system' and, obviously finding the French language inadequate, asserting that whoever did not accept the 'rupture with capitalism' was no socialist.[14]

The Common Programme

Most disturbing of the reactions to the coup, in view of the need for an alliance of the left, was the sceptical response of the Communist Party which was apparently more impressed by the presence in the new majority of the party's anti-Communist municipal bosses than by CERES and Mitterrand's CIR. *L'Humanité* reacted with contempt to the take-over of the party and then denounced the demands for 'guarantees' to be given before any alliance was forged. It did, however, repeat in forceful terms its demand for a joint manifesto – a 'Common Programme of Government'.[15]

Mitterrand's declaration that the non-Communist left had to be reinforced to 'rebalance' the left had been noted and deplored by the Communist Party.[16] In the meantime, partly as a basis for the negotiation of a 'Common Programme' and partly to occupy the PS and its turbulent left wing, the PS began to put together its own manifesto. If this rebalancing could be achieved, Mitterrand would become, for the second time, the artisan of the alliance of the left and would be the principal beneficiary of that dynamic. In a short time the 'rose in the fist', the new symbol of the Epinay Party, did become familiar.

The Parti socialiste's manifesto, *Changer la vie*, was under the charge of the ardent mimeographers of Jean-Pierre Chevènement's CERES, who called on a range of experts to contribute. This lyrical programme, prefaced by Mitterrand, envisaged far-reaching changes in society that would make their undoing impossible and at the heart were nationalizations. Three headings were crucial, nationalizations, Europe and international politics, and the emergence of a left wing became significant particularly as these were themes the Communists also promoted. It was not that CERES were fellow travellers in the old sense, but they used the Communist Party's massive presence in the alliance to lever themselves into key positions. Much as Mitterrand might have liked to repudiate these 'young Turks', this was difficult to do without at the same time dismissing the PCF's arguments. At the same time, of course, the recently ousted old guard was looking to break up the coalition around Mitterrand, but for the main part it held.

It was this manifesto as much as anything else that brought to the fore the term *autogestion* (self-management) and made it the banner of the new Socialist Party. 'Self-management' had no dictionary definition but it was new as it derived from the movements of 1968. It served to mark out territory for the Socialist Party and differentiated its members from those of the Communist Party to whom the word was anathema. 'Self-management' held out the promise of a greater control by workers over their own working lives and at the same time had the whiff of radicalism that enthused the activists and made bridges to other campaigns. Nationalization was seen on the French left as the test of 'socialist' commitment, a point made by Mitterrand in the manifesto's introduction; 'self-management' thus went alongside a bizarre commitment to a long list of nationalizations. To it was added, by the combination of CERES and the Mollet supporters, the right of workers to demand the nationalization of their own company. This stipulation became a source of difficulties later on. Subsequently, the Communist Party in its own programme produced a much longer shopping list of nationalizations in a Dutch auction at the expense of the Finance Ministry. *Changer la vie* had to conciliate pro- and anti-Europeans and pro- and anti-Americans as well as nuclear weapons supporters and disarmers and for that reason 'left the darkness unobscured' on many points. The manifesto was adopted by the party on 12 March at a congress in Suresnes. As far as Mitterrand was concerned, the manifesto was a form of phatic communion with the PCF: necessary but not binding.

But *Changer la vie* was only the prelude to the negotiation of the 'Common programme' manifesto with the Communist Party. There were four working groups. The Socialists' representatives were 'institutions' led by Joxe and Bulloche, 'economics' led by Chevènement and Piette, 'social problems' led by Bérégovoy and Mauroy, and 'international politics' led by Jacquet and Enock. All these areas had their difficulties, as the PCF wanted the dissolution of the Assembly if the coalition disagreed, an anti-European slant and more nationalization than Mitterrand was willing to consider. Before this manifesto could be concluded, President Pompidou held a referendum on the enlargement of the EEC to take in the UK, Denmark, Eire and Norway, a subject calculated to split the left along the Communist/Socialist fissure. Their manoeuvre proved misplaced, for the signature of the agreement was barely halted. While reaffirming the PS's commitment to Europe, Mitterrand side-stepped the elephant trap by calling for abstention in a campaign that was not seen as relevant by the public. Disagreement over Europe did not last as an obstacle to agreement, as the Communists, once enlargement had been ratified by referendum, were content to drop the issue.

A final meeting of the two parties was held on 28 June. Communist negotiators abandoned the demand for a dissolution if there were a disagreement, and Socialist negotiators accepted the Communist formula of the 'simultaneous dissolution of the two blocs' (a Soviet demand, and which would have left Western Europe open to the USSR) as well as France's nuclear strike force. After long discussions, the list of nationalized industries was reduced from the PCF's 25 to 9, although the steel and petrol sectors were to come under a state majority holding. Mitterrand had persistently intervened in these difficult negotiations and organized tête à tête meetings with the Communist leader Marchais when things looked particularly difficult. It continued the line Mitterrand had laid down at Epinay in promising to 'break the domination of big capital' and to 'transform society opening the way to socialism'.

Even after the signature there remained outstanding issues. These included *autogestion*, international politics – Mitterrand supported the

Atlantic alliance and Israel – Europe and presidential powers, which the PCF wanted to see restricted, while other issues were left hanging. There was a big difference over conditions in Czechoslovakia even though the issue of its invasion by the USSR had diminished in importance during the 1970s. And the question of whether Communists would relinquish power ('alternance') or accept an alternative majority during the parliament (as happened in the Fourth Republic) also remained unresolved. But the most important thing – beyond the details – was the symbolism of the gesture, and it was largely agreed (the left wing of the Radical Party signed on 12 July). A Radical Party split was consummated in the autumn of 1972 when the main part of the old party, following Servan-Schreiber, dissociated itself from the minority who had signed the Common Programme. They refused to subscribe to a programme that they regarded as extreme and unrealistic, a view which was, perhaps, not far from Mitterrand's own. Whatever the case, this was a competitive alliance from the outset.

The 1974 Presidential Elections

A new dynamic was now under way in which the 'unity of the left' (in alliance) was a source of strength to the respective parties; by the same token, whoever was perceived to have destroyed the alliance would suffer in the eyes of the voters. A curious looking-glass war thus began in which disagreements were either kept under wraps or used to throw the responsibility on to the other partner, while at the same time each tried to maximize their position in the alliance. Mitterrand was no slouch at this game, but it was the Socialists who made the immediate progress within the alliance without, however, initially displacing the PCF as the bigger partner. Mitterrand was careful not to pose as the leader of the opposition, which would have been grounds for offence, but at the Communist Central Committee immediately after the signing of the Common Programme the PCF's leadership reiterated its distrust of the Socialist Party.[17] All the same, the PCF flung its organization into the printing and diffusion of the Common Programme of Government (with Marchais's introduction) on a scale that the Socialists could not match. Mitterrand, aware that they would lose on this terrain where large numbers of activists could be deployed, ensured that there would be no joint undertakings. Crucial here was the point Mitterrand made himself that the Socialists had to be the senior partner if the alliance were to win.[18]

To that end François Mitterrand began to build himself an international reputation and a profile in France as a statesman of distinction. At the

Socialist International meeting in Vienna shortly after agreeing the Common Programme with the PCF, Mitterrand explained to a sceptical audience that he intended to take three of its five million voters from the Communist Party, a comment that, as Jules Moch noted, lacked something in elegance.[19] Access to the major figures of the European (and world) socialist left did not confer power, but it did give prestige, conferred stature by association as well as enabling him to explain his party's strategy to a wary but influential audience. One of his first visits was to Salvador Allende, and he also went to Cuba to meet Castro, a pilgrimage that, at the time, was essential for those on the left of the left. Mitterrand's first tentative steps to raise the problem of repression in Czechoslovakia, though not the Soviet role, were met with hostility from the French Communists. To reinforce this message a threat to withdraw the scheduled October 1972 meeting with Brezhnev and the USSR's leaders was made and Mitterrand went quiet.

At the same time, things on the right were not going well for the gaullists and elections would be due in March 1973. President Pompidou's government was becoming scandal-prone and the Prime Minister Chaban Delmas had clashed seriously with the President over the direction of policy. In July 1972 Chaban Delmas was dismissed and replaced by the more conservative but committed gaullist Pierre Messmer, whom nobody could accuse of either scandal or deviousness. Pompidou's revival of the gaullist right revolved around attacking the Socialist-Communists' Common Programme, which provided a choice target for conservative politicians and the possibility of an institutional conflict ('cohabitation', as it was not yet called). In truth, the programme presented a barn door target with its ambiguities and its state-dominated view of the economy, but subjecting it to such violent attacks, elevated its importance to symbolize the principal line of cleavage in French politics.

General and Presidential Elections

The revival of the right, concessions to the centre, the radical Common Programme and the residual lack of trust in the left meant that the conservatives were able to rouse their supporters and win a narrow victory. Moreover, on the first ballot many more lead candidates were Socialists than Communists (220 UGSD to 180 PCF, unlike 1967 when it had been 205 FGDS to 267 PCF), with the result that the Socialists had 104 seats to the PCF's 73 in the new Assembly. Running as the UGSD together with the Left Radicals, the Socialists' audience was growing and beginning to rival the Communists. In the general elections, although the combined right and centre won with 11.2 million votes, the Socialist alliance polled 4.9 million votes (20.8 per cent) to the PCF's 5 million (21.4 per cent). The Socialists had started to do well in the Catholic regions of France, where socialism was traditionally distrusted (Normandy, Brittany, Alsace-Lorraine).

A new generation of Socialists entered the Assembly. It was a conservative victory: with 8.5 million votes (36 per cent) the gaullist coalition of centrists, giscardians and the UDR took 268 seats, and they had a reserve of 33 centrists who would support the President if it came to it. All the same it was possible that one more heave would see the left back in government. And there were problems. Inflation and unemployment began to climb and in October 1973 the OPEC oil cartel put prices up, to which the President responded with a crash programme of nuclear power. Mitterrand's strategy had been vindicated in one respect and the party's progress was largely imputable to him, but it was not just his internal party supporters who reaped the benefits.

Inside the new Parti socialiste it was the CERES that was growing rather than the mainstream of the party, and at the Grenoble Congress of June 1973 they had 20 per cent of the mandates. In October, a new war in the Middle East polarized the left beween the pro-Palestinian Communists and the pro-Israeli Socialists and the socialist Bagnolet Conference developed a European policy that was more integrationist than before even if expressed in 'anti-imperialist' terms. This caused problems for the leadership, but the Epinay coalition around Mitterrand remained welded together even if the signs of stress were beginning to show. For the time the PCF decided to continue the alliance and supported a single candidate of the left for the presidential elections due in 1976.

Mitterrand was a practitioner of the slow approach and the strategic build-up, but time was foreshortened by President Pompidou's unexpected death on 2 April 1974. Although unanticipated, the 1974 election would prove to be the high point in the harmony of the alliance of the left. Mitterrand cannot have nourished illusions about the competitive nature of the alliance. In the circumstances, with a new Communist leader (Georges Marchais) only just in post and the Common Programme newly signed and having supported Mitterrand in 1965, a single candidate of the left was agreed. An early campaign had been anticipated so that the presidential team could be quickly assembled and a platform published, but the mature preparation, which would have come to fruition in 1976, was curtailed. Chaban Delmas was the first to declare his candidacy, followed by Edgar

Faure two days later and then Giscard d'Estaing and Mitterrand, four days after that.

Delay was seemly in the circumstances and it also enabled Mitterrand to get support without appearing to negotiate: on 3 April the Communist Party's representatives called for him to volunteer as the left's single Common Programme candidate – in a futile attempt to tie him to it.[20] Although the Communists were annoyed to be given a response by the 'interim' First Secretary of the PS Pierre Mauroy, and not by Mitterrand himself, and by his repudiation of the title as the Common Programme candidate, they went along with his initiative. They had little alternative, for Mitterrand had made himself the natural candidate of the whole left.[21] Although the Communist Party flung its organization into the campaign for Mitterrand, they were not part of the campaign team, and, although they had representatives at the campaign headquarters, the party's bêtes noires Rocard and Mendès France were also both there. This was irritating but went unremarked by the party during the election itself, in which it played an exemplary role as an undemanding ally, for Mitterrand stated that he would nominate Communist minsters 'as de Gaulle had done', and declared that his platform was to be drawn (in some unspecified way) from the Common Programme – though he issued his own manifesto.[22] He was supported unconditionally by the PCF, PS, MRG and PSU.

Mitterrand's campaign was run from the modern Tour Montparnasse, by a team brought together by Mitterrand around his programme, not by the parties which were not involved as such. It was a very personal campaign, which Mitterrand ran in his own style, calling on different groups from different milieux and coordinating them himself. His slogan was: 'The right has only one idea: to keep power; my first project is to give it to you;' he promoted himself as a president for all French people under a series of five broad headings in the manifesto. On economic policy, he stressed the importance of sound money and the fight against inflation (to this extent it did anticipate the problems of the later 1970s) as well as a redistribution to the less well-off, reduction of the working week (a Popular Front measure) and a lowering of the pensionable age to 60. While the economic part of the platform was devoid of the lyricism that characterized the Common Programme, it did caparison its prescriptions in anti-capitalist language and envisage, amongst other things, an end to 'production oriented to profit'.[23] For the rest, this manifesto was European, Atlanticist and stressed women's rights, liberty, decentralization (both to the regions and in businesses), fraternity and the environment. As the PCF was to point out later, this all added up to an original programme, well short of the state-centred radicalism of the Common Programme (there was no reference to nationalization).

A quasi 'primary' election was being conducted on the conservative right which turned in favour of Finance Minster Giscard d'Estaing. Giscard's campaign offered a change with continuity and its face was both youthful and modern, but fatally, it later transpired, it did not have the unreserved support of the gaullist party which rallied to him only to keep out the 'marxist left'. Other 'minor' candidates fell by the wayside as the right/left polarization crystallized by Giscard and Mitterrand had its effect: these 'victims' included the first ecologist René Dumont.

On the first ballot on 5 May, Mitterrand won 11,044,373 votes (43.24 per cent) to the centrist Giscard d'Estaing's 32.6 per cent, the gaullist Chaban Delmas' 15.1 per cent, and Jean Royer's (an independent conservative) 3.2 per cent, Trotskyite Arlette Laguiller's 2.3 per cent and René Dumont's 1.3 per cent, the six other runners taking 2.19 per cent, between them. Mitterrand's percentage was, in the campaign arithmetic (adding his together with Dumont and Laguiller – the left's putative vote), within striking range, although it did not reach 50 per cent. He began the second round determined to make a fight of it. With gaullist votes to be picked up, Communists extended a hand to them in between ballots.[24]

Interest in the election was immense and the mobilization of the electorate was, at 90 per cent on the second ballot, at an all-time high. Ideologically and in practical terms much seemed to be at stake both in the 'choice of society' and in the perceived need for social reform in conservative France. This 'choice of society' notwithstanding, Giscard was treated to the visit of the Soviet Ambassador Stefan Chervonenko on 7 May in between ballots, ostensibly to discuss trade issues. This was in truth an indication of who the Russians supported and their appreciation of de Gaulle's foreign policy, which they hoped to see Giscard continue. The visit embarrassed the PCF, which condemned the visit and continued to play its supportive role.[25] But it also indicated an unresolved tension in the alliance of the left which was to influence future events.

Communist voters expected only minor portfolios, but the PCF called for 'six or seven'.[26] The instincts and interests of Giscard's supporters led to a vigorously anti-communist campaign on the right. Those who watched the television debate – and Giscard's victory was by the slimmest of margins (400,000 votes out of 26 million; 50.7 per cent to 49.3 per cent) – thought that the Minister of Finance, with his command of complex economic figures, had won it, but also that his riposte to Mitterrand (*'Vous n'avez pas le monopole du coeur'* – 'you don't have a monopoly on compassion') was effective. Mitterrand's electorate was similar to that of 1965, but he progressed in the industrial areas at the expense of the gaullists and in some traditionally conservative areas at the expense of the Catholic centre. Coming so close, the let-down was the greater for his supporters, but Giscard's narrow victory meant that next time it could be Mitterrand's.

Setbacks

Mitterrand, as a *hombre de espera*,[27] continued his *festina lente*, an outlook oracularly expressed by Mitterrand as: *'il faut qu'on laisse le temps au temps'* ('make haste slowly').[28] A further attempt was made to bring together the last fragments of the left with an 'Assises du socialisme' to enlarge the Parti socialiste to include the remaining 'self-management' left, of which the main component was the small, intellectual PSU. PSU politicians had played an important part in Mitterrand's campaign. From the point of view of Michel Rocard and his supporters, there were clear advantages: they were in difficulties in a leftward-leaning party and the process of rebuilding the Parti socialiste had been almost completed without them. It was their last chance to join the new expanding PS before they were completely sidelined. In this ambition they were aided by PS sympathizers, but these 'social democrats' were admirers of Mendès France's austere moral approach to politics and his modern technocratic outlook and they were hostile to the Communist Party and not Mitterrand's natural allies. This Assises meeting, bringing in anti-Communist PSU members and former gaullists (like Edgard Pisani), centrists and union leaders (like Edmond Maire of the CFDT), did not pass unnoticed by the PCF, which was also suspicious.

Mitterrand's success in 1965 had brought recruits into the Communist Party and had been a crucial first step in bringing the party out of its isolation, but the dynamics of 1974 were different. This time Mitterrand had his own party, which was the beneficiary of the momentum of the campaign while the Communist Party had more difficulty in discerning benefits. To these reservations should be added the important (but unquantifiable) weight of the USSR, which clearly distrusted the strategy of alliance with the Parti socialiste and preferred the gaullist right to the Atlanticist and pro-European Mitterrand. This had also been true in 1965 when Tass (the official Soviet news agency) had made the remarks of the same general tenor, but it was not regarded likely at that time that Mitterrand would win. After 1974 a victory by the left dominated by

Mitterrand in the near future was probable. Mitterrand, mindful of his presidential strategy, was not a participant in turning the public mood against Soviet regimes that was taking place at that time, assisted, notably, by the publication of Solzhenitsyn's work.[29]

If Soviet preferences remained consistent, the balance of forces between the PCF and PS and the economic situation had changed completely: the optimistic assumptions of post-war growth were no longer plausible. Instead, the left might find itself elected not to distribute the fruits of growth, but (in the jargon of the time) to 'administer the capitalist crisis'. Mitterrand's presidential platform, put together on the economic side with PSU help, did not eliminate the possibility that a dose of deflation might be the appropriate if bitter medicine. There was a divergence of appreciation of economics here that put the two parties at opposite ends of the spectrum but which had been papered over by the Common Programme. On the one side, the Communists regarded the problem as another 'capitalist crisis' that could be resolved by 'socialist measures'; on the other, the Socialists had diagnosed a problem of inflation and slow growth ('stagflation', as was said) that would require a difficult cure. None of the Socialist Party's economists thought that the crisis could be overcome by the Common Programme measures or by further nationalizations.

Six by-elections in October 1974 made the position plain: the Socialist Party was advancing and the Communist Party was not. Over these six constituencies the PCF lost 1.3 per cent and one seat (to a gaullist), but the Socialists and their Radical allies won 8.23 per cent more and five seats. Yves Péron, the Communist who lost in the Dordogne, failed to garner the full complement of the left's votes, whereas the transfer from Communists to Socialists was highly effective. Communist voters were willing to vote for the Socialists but the Socialist voters, and especially Radicals, remained reluctant to some extent to vote for the Communists. This reluctance was seen by the Communist leadership as unjust and disloyal, although what the PS could do about it was uncertain.

The Communists then started – on 13 October – a 'polemic' with the Parti socialiste that continued with fluctuations from 'hot war' to 'cold war' (usually before elections) until 1994. On 24 October the XXIe Communist Party Congress in Vitry criticized the PS for its alliances with the centre in some town halls (like Marseilles), of the 'disloyal' transfer of votes, the newcomers from the PSU and the leadership, which was accused of taking a right turn. Mitterrand's response to these serial attacks was to reaffirm his commitment to the alliance of the left and the Common Programme, but not to concede points to the PCF. A constant barrage of criticism from the PCF, some of it personal (Mitterrand was described as 'dominating and sure of himself'), was met by a stolid persistence and a refusal to review the strategy.[30] Despite changes of line by the leadership, the Communist voters were still willing to vote for the Socialists while the Socialists were picking up floating voters as well. In the mid-1970s, with the PS only recently formed and newly established in French society, it was easy to assume that the losers would have to be the Socialists. By 1974 Mitterrand's strategy of alliance with the Communist Party around a Common Programme had lasted two years, although a purely electoral deal continued, bringing the non-Communist left the anticipated benefits of votes, activists and elected members, but not rewarding the PCF.

Opening out an argument with the Socialist Party was not, for the Communists, an immediate success. In France the climate had changed since the 1950s and the nature of the Soviet system itself was under attack. Students in May 1968 had contested the Communist Party, and more open and libertarian forms of marxism that it found difficult to counter had undermined its creaking bolshevism. A major problem was the impact of Solzhenitsyn's *Gulag Archipelago*. French intellectuals took up the cause with vigour and promoted a bleak view of the USSR. The Communists, especially *L'Humanité*, endorsed the Soviet side and with tired old arguments. Events in Portugal, where the 'Carnation Revolution' of April 1974 had removed the Salazarist regime but where the Communists seemed unwilling to allow its replacement to be decided by free elections, also became part of the 'polemic'. Subsequently, Portuguese Communists had been involved in 1975 in an attempted coup d'état and in the suppression of the Socialist paper *Republica*, and these actions were condemned by Mitterrand. These rebukes to the Portuguese Communists, restrained though they were, enabled the PCF to make accusations of not helping the 'fight against fascism'.[31] Mitterrand went to the USSR in April 1975 with a Socialist delegation, where he met the regime's ideologue Mikhail Suslov and President Leonid Brezhnev on the assumption that that was where the real authority lay.[32]

Communist attacks on the Socialist Party had their internal effects in the PS and this was seen at the February 1975 Pau Party Congress, where the Epinay coalition that had brought Mitterrand to the leadership was split. The problem was the left-wing CERES, which was growing too fast for Mitterrand's liking with 25 per cent of the mandates at Pau, and which was also making relations with the Communist Party more difficult than they had to be by echoing the Communist line. CERES was ejected from the leadership and the supporters of Michel Rocard, more likely to hold firm against the Communists' attacks, were brought in to make up the new majority. CERES was also under attack at the Suresnes conference on 'self-management' in June 1975, when its positions were pushed aside in favour of those of the ex-PSU newcomers. This was the point at which 'self-management' fever began to subside in the PS. CERES, however, now in opposition to the leadership, proved no easier a faction to control. Mitterrand ended the Congress by berating the government for its 'submission' to international capital and underscoring his determination to break with the old 'capitalist society'.

The PCF continued with a twin-track strategy: it attacked the Socialists while attempting a renovation of its own façade in the hope of enticing floating voters into its camp. This involved the then fashionable (but previously rejected) term 'Eurocommunism', which the Spanish and Italian Communists had taken up and which proved a marketing success even if its content remained unspecific. It was in this context that the party's XXIIe Congress opened in February 1976 under the banner of 'Socialism in French Colours'; at the same time the party announced that 'l'union est un combat' and a certain coolness entered relations between them and Moscow. One innovation was the willingness of the PCF to admit that there had been 'crimes' committed by Stalin and that, from time to time, things did go wrong even in the contemporary USSR. This admission was, of course, well behind what outsiders of every political stamp knew and it was not entirely new for the PCF, which had 'firmly condemned' Stalin's excesses in the 1960s. But the reservation remained that the USSR was a 'socialist system' (in that lexicon it was on the way to perfection) and that just because there were spots on the sun it did not mean that there was no sun.

There was a limited distancing of the PCF from the CPSU, but that was probably more over the USSR's view that the conservative right in France was more useful in foreign policy than the left could be – a point the PCF would not at that time accept. All the same, the package of criticisms of the USSR, the dropping of the notion of 'dictatorship of the proletariat' (unanimously), a social policy of personal freedom and a stress on freedom of expression looked like fundamental change. These changes were made with the intention of disputing the terrain of the left and centre with the Socialist Party, but they came too late and their only effect was that they made the PCF more attractive, they made voting Socialist easier and did not swell the Communist Party's ranks. Doctrinal changes of this nature could, given the disciplined democratic centralism of the party, be reversed very easily, as they were just over eighteen months later.

There was, however, no let up in the polemic with the Socialists and in June 1975 the party published a book of texts from 1972 (*L'Union est un combat*, edited by the hard-liner Etienne Fajon) critical of the PS and of the alliance. But none of this stopped the left from profiting from the mistakes and divisions of the Giscardian presidency. In September 1976, the left had a majority in the local cantonal elections, but here again the principal victor was the PS, which won an extra 195 seats, giving it 529 to the PCF's 249. Municipal elections were due in 1977 and these, providing the PS switched alliances from the centre to the left, would provide substantial gains for the Communist Party and lock the Socialists into the national alliance. Negotiations were taken in hand by the redoubtable Maxime Gremetz who faced a divided Socialist team, the Communists wrung several concessions from the PS (notably Reims and Saint-Etienne) – to Mitterrand's disquiet – and joint lists were established in 202 of the 221 big cities. There was a great victory for the left in March in which, with 52 per cent of the vote, they won two-thirds of the cities and placed the right in a minority in France as a whole. This victory, which enabled the PCF to win 72 big cities (as against 50) and the PS to win 81 (as against 41), was a major and tangible gain for the Communists, in part at the expense of the Socialists, but it tied them into the alliance with the Socialist Party as much as vice versa; if they broke that, they would lose their very important place in local government.

Developing the Parti socialiste

In the mid-1970s, aided by the gains of the Parti socialiste and his own authority in the party, Mitterrand began to advance younger politicians, promoting a generation that owed him its victories but did not rival him. A group of young, mainly technocratic, cadres was quickly promoted. These included the rising stars of Lionel Jospin and Laurent Fabius and other 'sabras', but also seasoned CIR figures such as Edith Cresson. Because of the importance of a local base to French politicians, the big victories in municipal elections were a key component in this renewal of political personnel. It was also a generation attuned to May '68 and to the marxist dialogue being conducted by the PCF but, unlike the old guard, without attachment to the old SFIO or an inferiority complex when confronted with the PCF. Renewal of the party's cadres was not without its problems: few were blindly inclined to follow the leader, but it brought a new vigour to the party and was artfully managed by Mitterrand.

No sooner were the local elections over than the polemic on the left restarted with vigour. At stake here was the 'updating' of the Common Programme to provide a platform for the general elections of 1978. Proposed by Marchais at the end of March, a meeting was arranged for 17 May. But before that, on 10 May, the PCF published a recalculated costing for the Common Programme far more lavish than anything previously imagined.[33] These figures were a real slap in the face to Mitterrand, coming as they did two days before he was due to debate on TV with the Prime Minister Raymond Barre. The manoeuvre increased the party's radical pretensions and its timing placed the Socialists in a difficult position, forcing them to reject proposals and take on the onus of undermining the alliance. Communist defence specialists also proposed the retention of the French nuclear strike force, confronting the Socialist Party with an accomplished fact. (In the Common Programme the USA's foreign policies were condemned but not the USSR's.)

At the party's Congress in Nantes in 1977, Mitterrand's coalition was reelected. Mitterrand had remarked that if CERES took a third of the mandates he would depart,[34] but his determination to grind down CERES was beginning to pay off. The Mitterrand leadership took 75 per cent and although CERES still polled strongly with 24 per cent, it was kept in opposition (there was no composite motion). It was a congress at which Mitterrand's status was confirmed but factionalism was under control in the party – and not just CERES. Rocard made a speech, noted at the time, that was a veritable hymn to the market economy and counterpoised it with a criticism of the state-interventionist left. Lines, in other words, were set out for a future challenge to Mitterrand, who, however, reaffirmed his vocation at the Congress to break with capitalism. But there was an unmistakable air of fête about the Nantes Congress, and the party confidently looked forward to the 1978 elections that would, they felt, see the victory of the left and the emergence of the PS as the biggest party in France.

Nothing, it seemed, could stop Mitterrand becoming Prime Minister after the general elections of 1978. President Giscard, fearing that the left would win, gave a speech at Verdun-sur-le-Doubs, half anticipation and half admonishment, that envisaged a 'cohabitation' with a Common Programme government of the left. Giscard told the public that no president could prevent its application, although its application would, of course, the President warned, be disastrous. Although divided between Giscardians and neo-gaullists, the conservative right had certainly not given up. The centre parties were regrouped under an umbrella as the UDF, and Chirac's gaullists flung themselves into the fight against the 'marxist left'. The right was, however, reckoning without the self-destructive impulses of the left.

5

Alliance Problems: 1978–1981

Mitterrand reportedly noted of the alliance with the PCF that 'if the left wins it will be because the Socialist Party has won 30 to 35, perhaps 38 per cent of the votes'.[1] This was not a prospect the Communists viewed with equanimity and if their strategy of alliance around a joint platform risked leading to that result they would end it. It was clearly in trouble when the Communists demanded an updating of the Common Programme and the party took a radical turn over the summer of 1977, including Marchais's theatrical return from vacation ('Liliane, pack the bags'). Communist leaders were evidently prepared to envisage defeat for the alliance in the 1978 general election if that was the price of the party retaining its position at the head of the left. But in Mitterrand's strategy, the PCF had to relinquish its leading position if the left were to win.

In all probability the decision to break up the alliance had already been taken by the Communists before the long tripartite (Socialist/Communist/Radical) negotiations began in the summer of 1977, and in all probability Mitterrand had assumed that the Communist Party wanted them to fail.[2] From Mitterrand's point of view, if the agreement was doomed it was important not to be seen to be the cause of the break-up but to make it clear that it was the PCF that had decided to end the alliance. Unfortunately, the break, when it came on 14 September, was nothing like as clear; it was largely because the small Left Radical Party, irritated at the evident ill will and lack of progress, decided to announce the obvious that the negotiations had failed. Ostensibly the problem was the extent of the nationalizations, but the causes were to be found in the attitude of the USSR to Mitterrand and in the PCF's subordinate position.

1978

In 1977, opinion polls remained optimistic for both Mitterrand and the Parti socialiste (credited with 30 per cent or over) and a victory still seemed plausible because the left ostensibly had a majority. Communist attacks, many of which, like the demand for Communist ministers (which was emphasized for the first time by Marchais on 13 January) became a refrain over the following weeks, while slogans like 'make the rich pay' were designed to both turn away the floating voter and consolidate traditional Communist support.[3] Mitterrand again had to steer a difficult course between not ceding to Communist demands on the one hand and avoiding the blame for intransigence and destroying chances of reconciliation on the other. On the issue of Communist ministers, he neither denied the possibility, which would have given the party a pretext for a break, nor confirmed that there would be any, which would have frightened off floating voters. Meanwhile, the Communists hammered home the message that Mitterrand had sold out and that the Parti socialiste had veered to the right.

There was a high turnout (bigger even than 1973) for the 1978 general elections, which, despite the lack of a joint platform, seemed to be the alliance of the left's best chance – only 16.6 per cent abstained. But the continual battering from the conservative right, with Mitterrand as the principal target, and from the Communists had their effect and the Common Programme left polled only 45 per cent to the right's 46.5 per cent. When the first ballot results were counted the PS was the biggest party on the left, ahead of the Communists for the first time since 1936, with just under seven million votes (23 per cent without the Radicals) to the Communists' 20.7 per cent, but the results were far short of the 30 per cent or so that had been anticipated. Inside the party it was the more depressing because the conservative right was on the way to a comfortable victory.

President Giscard's divided conservative coalition had pulled themselves together on the run-off just enough to win a comfortable majority against a badly divided left. In the Assembly, the right won 290 seats to the left's 202 (114 PS and 86 PCF) divided between Jacques Chirac's 150 gaullists and 138 UDF centrists (and two independents) – a conflict that would become important later. The Communist Party won almost as large a share of the vote as in 1973, avoided its nightmare of falling below 20 per cent and picked up thirteen extra seats; the Socialist landslide predicted by the polls in the mid-1970s had not materialized. On the second ballot, the transfer of votes between candidates was not good despite a hastily put-together agreement of the left between ballots that was presented as an updating of the Common Programme (possible because the Communists abandoned all of their demands). Months of continuous argument on the left had taken their toll and the heralded victory did not materialize.

After the general elections the settling of accounts began in earnest. For the Communist Party there was the surprise that their reputedly monolithic organization was riven with dissent and onlookers were treated to a public dispute. This dissent was articulated principally by intellectuals, but by no means confined to the voluble, who opened a second front against the leadership in the 'bourgeois press'.[4] This internal war hindered the party's leadership in its objective of placing the blame for the election defeat on the Socialists and forcing Mitterrand to declare that the Common Programme was a dead letter. With its union of the left strategy in tatters, the PCF decided to turn its back on the alliance, to harden its position as part of the world Bolshevik movement and perhaps to let the Parti socialiste destroy itself and, they may have assumed, reject Mitterrand.

The Communists' attitude was possible because there were also problems inside the Socialist Party, though this time not from the CERES left but from the so-called 'second left' newcomers of the PSU and the left-wing Catholics who had joined the party since 1969. A long factional war was begun on 19 March, the evening of the election defeat, by Michel Rocard, who used the opportunity of a television broadcast to launch an oblique but unmistakable attack on François Mitterrand as a strategist and policy-maker. Jacques Juillard summed it up when he said that the left had a programme incontestably less popular than the left itself. Rocard, speaking to a demoralized party audience, remarked that 'the left had just missed another rendez-vous with history but that the setback was not fatal'. Reading from a carefully prepared set of notes, Rocard criticized the strategy of the left and launched an alternative. This was a notification that he was available as nominee for the candidacy in 1981 and this was a more serious factional challenge than that of the left-wing CERES, none of whose members was of 'presidential timber'. But the left had been out of power for twenty years and, as was said, 'Mitterrand is Poulidor' (for many years inevitably second, and never first, in the Tour de France).[5] A lesser man would have given up.

Rocard's Challenge

Michel Rocard was born in 1930 and after a Blue Riband career in the IEP and then ENA he had become a civil servant in the Inspection des Finances. Like many of that generation, he regarded Mendès France as his guide and had a technical background, giving him an advantage over the more lyrical of the left. He had emerged as a critic of the state interventionist social-

ism of the mainstream left, sceptical of the Common Programme and its
unrealistic promises, but he was not in Mitterrand's circle. Rocard could
not displace Mitterrand within the party where the First Secretary controlled the main levers, and his strategy was to work on public opinion to
force the Parti socialiste to accept that he was the only credible candidate
for 1981. This was a very difficult undertaking, as Rocard's stock would
have to rise very high and the First Secretary's to fall very low before
Mitterrand's party would move to defenestrate its creator and install the
regicide. Under Mitterrand, the party had steadily risen in vote, in deputies,
in councillors and mayors, and had improved its position in 1978. But in
the meantime Rocard's criticisms of Mitterrand as 'archaic' – and of the
Socialists' platform as well as of the strategy alliance with the Communists – were telling.

Mitterrand could not continue the Epinay alliance because the Communists had rejected him. What he did was to respond to the PCF's attacks,
but without repudiating the alliance and keeping the door open to its maintenance. His strategy depended on retaining the confidence of Communist voters that he was not going to sell out to the right (the PCF's constant
refrain) and Rocard's campaign may even have helped somewhat on that
score. Rocard forced Mitterrand to maintain the 'socialist' or left-wing
credentials of the party against internal attack and provided an implicit
rebuttal of Communist charges that the PS was looking rightward. By
the same token, however, Mitterrand's room for manoeuvre in the centre
was reduced. The split in the Parti socialiste was time- and resource-
consuming and focused attention on personnel and policy rather than
conveying the positive message.

Mitterrand organized to defeat Rocard, starting by trying to ensure that
his old allies of the Epinay congress (Mauroy and Defferre) remained solid.
In addition, he brought in others who had not always been on his side, like
Poperen and Bérégovoy. Mitterrand deployed emissaries to travel the
federations across France to ensure that he was not losing votes in the
provinces, and petitions of backing were organized, in order to be published to demonstrate and consolidate support. The lists of names rallying
to Mitterrand's side were impressive. Jacques Delors, for example, whose
policy and outlook were similar to Rocard's, signed the 'contribution of
30' repudiating the 'so-called modernism' of Rocard and reaffirming the
importance of the alliance of the left. Crucially, leaving nothing to chance,
a new young (former Shell executive) Paul Quilès was asked to prepare
the 1979 Metz Party Congress and a small team was set up to organize
Mitterrand's support at it.[6]

In the vote on the resolutions for the 1979 Metz Congress, Mitterrand's authority was firmly established but not by enough for him to dispense with allies. Mitterrand's motion (signed by 39 deputies and 13 senators) took 40 per cent, Rocard's 21 per cent (signed by 39 deputies and 10 senators), Chevènement's 15 per cent (signed by 6 deputies and 3 senators), Mauroy's 17 per cent and Gaston Defferre's 6 per cent. The main substance of dispute was Mitterrand's strategy, although his monarchical style also came in for criticism. His proposal to the Congress once again spoke of ending capitalism rather than transforming it and breaking with the all-powerful logic of the market: 'our objective is not to modernize capitalism or to ameliorate it, but to replace it with socialism'. CERES had lost some key support (Wolf, Pierret and others), but persisted in seeing itself as the true socialist defender of the alliance, the principal opponent of the so-called 'American left' of Rocard and Mauroy.[7] Chevènement's view at this time was that 'without the Socialists the Communist Party is powerless, but without the Communist Party the Socialists are exposed to the temptation to default'.[8]

Mitterrand's viewpoint, relayed by lieutenants during the Congress, was that the strategy of alliance with the Communist Party ('union of the left') had to be continued. Principal amongst them was the rising star Laurent Fabius, who in a rabble-rousing intervention declared that Rocard was wrong in his contention that between the Plan and the market there was nothing: there was socialism. Once again, at the Congress, as at Epinay, Mitterrand had reconfirmed the revolutionary line, including some quite startling propositions (for example that the 'laws of economics' were capitalist inventions). On Mitterrand's behalf, Fabius rejected the 'modernistic' socialism proposed by Rocard and repeated the need for an alliance with the PCF that would come about, he claimed, if they persisted in offering a Common Programme (the Communist demand from 1962 to 1978). Rocard had, in any case, insufficient support within the party to deprive Mitterrand of the nomination, and that was clear at the Metz Congress.

Rocard and Mauroy were pitched into the opposition while Mitterrand concluded an alliance with CERES. While rejecting some of Chevènement's more outrageous proposals, Mitterrand made a virtue of necessity, devolving to CERES the task of writing a 'project' for the party and encouraging it to attack Rocard with its customary vigour. Mitterrand held the cards once again: he was not much constrained by CERES's participation in the party executive and he could decide to run when it suited him. Rocard, on the other hand, was in a small minority and at the mercy of Mitterrand's timing and strategy. For Mitterrand the position vis-à-vis the

Communists had to be maintained: 'the programme, the whole programme and nothing but the programme'.[9] In strategic terms, that was
what brought victory, but the price was the promotion of a Common Programme and a resolution to break with capitalism and transform the class
character of the state.

Communist attacks on the Socialists continued, but their effect was not
always evident. At the cantonal election of March 1979 the conservative
parties lost 107 seats while the PCF won 32; the Socialists meanwhile won
158. But the cantonal elections were not crucial and were an uncertain indi-
cator of the 1981 elections. On the other hand, Mitterrand's strategy
seemed to be a losing one when it became necessary to campaign for the
first European parliamentary elections in 1979. At these elections the
problem of 'southern enlargement' to Spain and Portugal was particularly
acute because it affected socialist agricultural areas and the Communist
Party was hostile to it. There was division on the right but the conservatives won the biggest vote, with Giscard's UDF taking 27.6 per cent and
the PS garnering a poor 23.53 per cent. These European elections may have
given President Giscard the impression that the left was too divided to win.

Chevènement hoped that by being given charge of the party's programme, the *Projet socialiste*, he might anchor the party to the left. The
Projet was based on the replies to a questionnaire to activists, approved by
the party membership after having been discussed at a convention at
Alfortville in January 1980 – it was not the presidential candidate's platform. Mitterrand's introduction to the *Projet* once again stated the revolutionary sources of the socialist idea and his determination to cleave to the
Epinay line. Its 380 pages were a long prosecution case against 'capitalism'
and depicted the contemporary 'crisis' in apocalyptic terms whilst averring
that the Parti socialiste was the dynamic part of the left. Although
approved by 85 per cent of the members, the status of the *Projet* 'wish list'
was uncertain; it could certainly not have been retained by any presidential candidate. This ambiguity allowed Rocard and Mauroy to accept it, and
Mitterrand, during the presidential campaign, to ignore and then disown
it. But it served the purpose of demonstrating the balance of power in the
party, of appealing to the Communist electorate and giving little purchase
to criticism from the PCF's leadership.

The Run-up to Elections in 1981

The years 1978–80 had not been a good period for Mitterrand. Georges
Marchais, who was only officially designated the Communist Party's can-

didate on 12 October 1980, had in fact been campaigning over this time and Communist organization was as efficient as usual. There were revelations in *L'Express* about Marchais's far from heroic war record (he passed the time as a skilled worker in Germany rather than in the Resistance), although the Socialist leader was publicly silent on the matter.[10] Communist leaders continued to take Mitterrand to be the principal figure on the left (not Rocard), but claimed that he wanted to salvage Giscard's policies and had taken flight to the right.[11] But the Communist Party had its own problems, expelling their dissident members attached to the union of the left. In January 1980 Marchais had supported the USSR's invasion of Afghanistan while retreating into an extreme anti-Socialist mode. This fed the sense that the PCF's change in line was a response to Soviet pressures rather than to Socialist misdeeds. *Pravda*, on behalf of the Soviet leadership, made it clear that it supported Giscard d'Estaing.[12]

As the election approached, the Communists' tone became more aggressive. This strategy of 'plucking the socialist chicken' by pulling away sections of Socialist support was an old one (baptized 'unity at the base') but confirmed at the party's 23rd Congress in May 1979. Mitterrand, replying in kind, stated that the Socialists had to be dominant on the left if the left were to win.[13] 'Union at the base' was inimical to a Common Programme strategy, but the unanswered question was whether the PCF's voters would follow its lead. Reputable studies made Rocard the best candidate for the left, although Mitterrand's private pollster was at this time reassuring him that he could defeat Giscard.[14] On 19 October 1980, Rocard announced his candidature from his town hall of Conflans-Sainte-Honorine. Rocard's declaration had been impetuous (Mitterrand waited) and badly bungled in presentation. Mitterrand's supporters were relieved by this blunder but effected to see in it an appalling act of *lèse-majesté*.[15] Although he had been 30 per cent ahead of Mitterrand in the polls at the beginning of 1980, Rocard had, in truth, lost the battle for the party nomination at the Metz congress.[16]

Mitterrand appeared unperturbed by Rocard's announcement, continuing to make observations on the domestic and international scene or lay down philosophical principles of a general nature.[17] But, even though he worked with a furious energy, he refused, as he had done for over a year, to talk about a 'candidature' even while he had continued his non-campaign and wanted to appear to have been drafted by the party.[18] To this end he engaged in a hesitation waltz of key interventions, meetings with potential supporters (film-makers or scientists, for example) and visits to party federations. These visits were undertaken with the rhetorical question 'should I be candidate or not?', to which the liturgical response was 'yes'. In Marseilles on 26 October, Mitterrand declared to a meeting orchestrated by its Mayor Gaston Defferre for the undeclared candidate that he 'would be a candidate should the members of the party demand it'. At the beginning of November his book *Ici et maintenant*, which was more or less a presidential manifesto, was published.

On 8 November, Mitterrand wrote a letter to the party's Comité Directeur which announced that he would be putting forward his candidature 'in response to the demand from the party's membership'. Rocard then withdrew. But Mitterrand, candidate for the candidacy, continued to 'non-campaign', visiting the USA, Israel and attending the Socialist International meeting in Madrid. This was an intentional absence from the domestic scene accenting the non-partisan nature of the candidate and had been carefully planned. It would be difficult to say what effect this 'non-campaign' had, but it placed Mitterrand apart from the minor candidates as an inclusive presidential figure above the fray. Mitterrand looked down on the country's problems. Like Yeats's 'long-legged fly upon the stream', he seemed to float above the petty squabbles of minor politicians. This was the position Giscard should have been in and the President did not declare his candidacy until 2 March.

The Presidential Elections

By then Mitterrand was close to being off-hand even if his period of inactivity was superseded by a very well-planned short campaign of one hundred days or so, starting on 7 March at Beauvais and ending on 24 April at Toulouse. Mitterrand's comportment was captured by Séguéla's campaign slogan of *'la force tranquille'* (Blum's phrase used when presenting the Popular Front government to President Lebrun).[19] In accordance with the timetable set out the previous year, the congress to nominate the Socialists' candidate was held on 24 January 1981. At this Congress, Mitterrand was designated candidate by 83 per cent of the votes, with 96 per cent of the delegates' vote from Corsica and the Pas-de-Calais, but the 'Rocardian' federations like Morbihan, Maine-et-Loire and Manche (only 60 per cent) were notably less enthusiastic.

Mitterrand's platform of '110 propositions' was far-reaching and it advanced a number of necessary reforms, but it was not a revolutionary one nor did it talk about 'transition to socialism' and 'rupture'. Mitterrand's thought was, however, impregnated with the voluntaristic and state-centred socialism that Rocard had repudiated and the manifesto included the list of industries to be nationalized (from the Common Programme). The more modest '110 propositions' were organized under four headings: peace, employment, liberty and France, although the first proposition was a demand for a Soviet withdrawal from Afghanistan. But the more restrained nature of this platform, relative to both the *Projet* and the rhetoric of the 1970s, raises the question of whether a clearly reformist approach would have won and avoided later problems. Lionel Jospin was made interim First Secretary of the party and the campaign team involved all the factions in the party, including the renegades of Metz: Mauroy, who was made porte-parole, and Rocard, who was also active. Jacques Séguéla was made campaign publicity counsellor with his own team and considerable autonomy (not to everybody's liking). Mitterrand then disappeared on a visit to China.

In the 1981 presidential campaign there were nine candidates. In addition to the representatives of the 'gang of four' (the PS's Mitterrand, the RPR's Chirac, the UDF's Giscard and the PCF's Marchais), there were also the dissident gaullists Michel Debré and Marie-France Garaud, the PSU left-winger Huguette Bouchardeau, the Left Radical's Michel Crépeau and the ecologist Brice Lalonde. Michel Debré and Marie-France Garaud ran resolute campaigns against Giscard. Garaud campaigned on the President's 'weak' foreign policy and promoted the view that the only threat to France came from the USSR. Giscard's meeting in Warsaw with Brezhnev and his failure to condemn Soviet expansion in Angola and elsewhere was a mistake that alienated many on the right. Crépeau and Bouchardeau, on the other hand, would support Mitterrand on the second round.

Mitterrand entered his third election campaign in conditions that differed from the other two. In the first place he was the leader of the now biggest party of the left, while still incarnating the mobilizing ideal of unity. Although it had been contested by the PCF, his position as the unifying force had been reinforced through his fight with Rocard. On the other hand, Giscard d'Estaing, the outgoing President, was less popular than in 1974. He had initially advertised his presidency as that of the 'ordinary man', but he became increasingly monarchical: in a lofty way he had been unwilling to explain a gift of diamonds from the Central African Republic dictator Jean Bédel Bokassa. Giscard ran a bad campaign which could not hope to recover the ground lost by an austere government over the previous three years and he was portrayed as a man of the past, something that prevented an attack on Mitterrand's age and his presentation for the third time.

Giscard was still the predicted winner in the opinion polls, even into 1981, partially, no doubt, because of the divisions in the PS, but for the Barre government the years of deflation had taken their toll and in by-elections the PS was moving ahead strongly. In mid-January, by which time Mitterrand was unambiguously the Socialist candidate, the polls made him a possible winner. Unemployment obstinately continued to rise, growth was sluggish and for some key groups, like the marginal farmers, living standards fell in 1980–1. Giscard had not, in a word, done enough to ensure his re-election and the novelty of 1974 was now old. In addition, he faced the hostility of the biggest party of the conservative right, the neo-gaullist RPR, which nominated Chirac and then conducted a campaign against the government. Chirac's RPR lacked a strong incentive to see the conservative right re-elected and his campaign was vigorously anti-Giscard, a big factor in the President's defeat. Many of Chirac's remarks were used by the Socialist Party against Giscard. Although the left was divided, the right was even more fractured and this could not be hidden for the entire election campaign. Hence, although Mitterrand did not make a direct appeal to the disillusioned gaullists, the attacks by the mayor of Paris took their toll and were often repeated by the left.

The Campaign

Mitterrand's third campaign was much better organized than the previous two and compared with his best.[20] It also worked on television and other mass media with efficiency and sophistication in a way they had not. There were 28 mass meetings, but the media were given greater priority and, of course, more funding. By the standards of previous campaigns, funds were lavish, but the exact amounts are unknown and their provenance is still unclear. Lieutenants were deployed to promote a reassuring message stating that there would be 'no change of society'. Thus, on 27 January 1981 on television Jospin said that there was no question of a 'bouleversement', while Mitterrand, for his part, stripped all eschatology from his programme. His campaign concentrated on attacking the record of the outgoing president, particularly on rising unemployment ('employment is our principal obligation' was his slogan) and the inequalities of contemporary France, which was then suffering from the inability to push economic growth back to its 1960s' levels.[21] During the campaign the need to restimulate growth through the domestic market and create jobs through a reduced working week, public works and nationalizations were emphasized. But there were also attacks on the President's foreign policy – some of them bitter – and on Giscard's indulgence – as they saw it – to the Soviet Union. Jospin said that the Communist Party would have to change, but mentioned only its attitude on Afghanistan, Poland and immigration, demanding, in effect, very little as a price for cooperation.[22]

Marchais, as presidential candidate, proved to be severely hampered by the revelations about his wartime past in *L'Express* and by the desperation of the Communist campaign (including the blockading of an immigrant hostel). There can be no doubt that the Communists were intent on driving voters away from Mitterrand. Yet, during the campaign Mitterrand continued to stand firm under the PCF's attacks, neither over-reacting nor allowing them to go unanswered. Once again the party tried to drive moderates away from Mitterrand with demands for Communist ministers and other radical measures.[23] Marchais commented about the 'honeymoon' for a new government that he had lived through in 1936, when 'honeymoon' meant the fight against the bosses.[24] At the same time he reiterated the accusation that the Parti socialiste was moving to the right. These two attacks were counterproductive because the move to the right reassured moderate voters and the contention that there would be Communist ministers reassured the PCF's voters.

Worst of all, Marchais could not convince Communist voters that it was Mitterrand who had broken the alliance, while the floating voters were convinced wrongly that indeed the Socialists had refused in 1977 to follow the PCF onto even more extreme ground. Some moderate voters may also have been convinced by the Communists' attacks that the break with Mitterrand was definitive and that they could vote for him with impunity. Mitterrand's attitude of indifference to or contempt for the Communist Party's attacks paid off in these elections. It was also possible to throw back some of their own charges at them and demand a change in the party's line if there were to be Communist ministers. Mitterrand had stated that he would dissolve the Assembly and that an interim government would be nominated, but he committed himself to very little, stating simply that it depended on the new majority returned to the parliament and that he would 'respect the choice of the French people'.[25] Communist leaders might have liked to call for abstention on the second ballot, but the pressure from their voters, on which Mitterrand had counted, would not make this possible. Whether this pressure would have worked similarly for another candidate of the left (Rocard) is one of the imponderables, though the strategy adopted by Mitterrand minimized this risk.

Opinion polls were not published in the final two weeks of the campaign and the results on the first ballot were therefore a surprise (though the candidates themselves had access to private polls). Although Giscard led on 26 April with 28 per cent he was only 715,000 votes ahead of Mitterrand's 25.8 per cent, and Jacques Chirac polled 18 per cent. Mitterrand's vote was considerably above the predicted 23–24 per cent and contributed to the momentum that was, by then, expected to bring victory. He was supported by 33 per cent of the workers (as against 30 per cent for Marchais) and 29 per cent of employees (as against 18 per cent for Marchais and Chirac). However, only 14 per cent of small business (9 per cent for Marchais and 35 per cent for Giscard) and 23 per cent of farmers voted for him (as against 33 per cent for Giscard and 36 per cent for Chirac). Mitterrand's support amongst practising Catholics was, at 12 per cent, dwarfed by Giscard's 50 per cent and Chirac's 26 per cent.[26]

In simple arithmetic, Giscard's votes plus those for the gaullists and the minor candidates of the conservative right and some ecologists might have seemed to indicate that the President's victory could still be secured. However, the dispersal of the right's vote and the hostility to Giscard from the mainstream and minor candidates meant that many conservatives would not vote for the President on the second ballot – while something like 10 per cent would eventually vote for Mitterrand. On the next day, and at a time when Giscard needed every vote, Chirac was content to give a lukewarm endorsement to the President and effectively stood down the gaullist party machine.

Most commentators saw the fall of the Communist vote as the key to the second ballot. Georges Marchais's vote fell to 15.3 per cent, at that time a historic low point; there could no longer be any credibility to the accusation that the Communist Party would dominate Mitterrand. Indeed, many Communists had supported Mitterrand on the first ballot and the party was forced to accept the consequences and to call on its voters to support Mitterrand, which a great many would have done regardless of the party's advice. Thus Mitterrand, through the collapse of the Communist vote and the divisions of the right, would start the second ballot campaign from strength, but this did not prevent the President from suggesting that the left was in thrall to the PCF and raising the question of Communist ministers. Mitterrand easily brushed this aside, but the Communists, not universally keen on a Socialist victory, raised the question again in between ballots.

A late surprise came from the *Canard enchaîné* which published revelations that one of Giscard's ministers, Maurice Papon, had been a Vichy official in charge of the deportation of Jewish people.[27] Between ballots, the main event was the debate between the two candidates that had been demanded by Giscard (it was accepted under stringent conditions). In 1981, with his campaign flagging, he needed to win the debate to turn the polls in his direction. This did not happen and, if there was a victor, the effect of the debate was minimal, although it was seen or heard by two-thirds of the voters. In the event, Mitterrand was well prepared on the economic ground that the President was supposed to master, and pulled off a notable coup with what boxers would call a 'sucker punch', feigning a reluctance to answer a point on the rate of the Deutschmark. Overall, Giscard appeared less presidential and Mitterrand more so than in 1974. But Mitterrand only needed to retain his advantage in the polls, whereas Giscard had needed the debate to destroy his opponent.

There were then some guerrilla actions by Giscard as the campaign was closing. Mitterrand's war record was raised by the head of the Légion d'honneur and two days after the campaign debate some of the *Projet social- iste's* rather more peculiar sections were read out by Giscard in an attempt to discredit Mitterrand's platform. Socialists intervened and demanded a right to reply, which was delegated to Rocard, who pointed out that these planks were not incorporated into Mitterrand's platform. But Giscard's failing support was too friable to be shored up in the last days of the campaign and Mitterrand's position was too strong to be destroyed in such a short time. Perhaps as many as one million of the six million conservative voters who did not vote for Giscard on the first ballot chose Mitterrand on the second, and another million abstained.[28]

Sunday 10 May saw a high turn-out of 85.86 per cent for the second ballot, although it was below the level of 1974, possibly as a result of some RPR non-voters. With 15.7 million votes – over a million more than for Giscard – and 51.8 per cent, Mitterrand was elected President on 10 May and Giscard left office on 20 May. Although practising Catholics voted pre-ponderantly for Giscard (80 per cent), compared to 1974, Mitterrand's vote had increased everywhere since then except in Provence, and he made notable gains in what were the traditionally conservative Catholic regions. His vote was particularly high amongst men (56 per cent), those aged 18–34 (63 per cent), employees (62 per cent), workers (72 per cent) and public service workers (73 per cent), but it was low amongst the farmers and small business milieux, where Giscard obtained 68 per cent and 64 per cent respectively.[29] Despite the failure of the conservative right to rally to Giscard, the number of abstentions and spoilt ballots fell on the second ballot. Communist voters had moved massively to Mitterrand, as had the votes of the minor candidates and the ecologists.[30] It was a historic victory, the first time in the Fifth Republic that the left had won the presidency, and it was also the first 'alternance' in the Republic.

Mitterrand's Victory

L'Humanité's headline on 11 May was 'Victoire de l'espoir' ('Victory of hope'). The stock exchanges celebrated Mitterrand's victory with a spectacular run on the franc and there were many who thought that there should have been an immediate devaluation. (This was rejected by Mitterrand himself.) Raymond Barre's government published an 'audit' of the nation's (principally financial) affairs, with the conclusion that the Socialists were inheriting an economy in sound condition. There was a ceremony in the Elysée to transfer powers a day later than originally envisaged and a short meeting with the outgoing President. Accounts of this meeting differ, but four 'secrets' were supposedly imparted, although none of them in any account was fundamental, apart, perhaps, from the collaboration with the USA on nuclear technology.[31] Giscard, unfortunately, had to make his way out of the Elysée through a crowd that had come to welcome the new president and he was treated to some unpleasant shouting. Mitterrand had already turned to the composition of the new government, but provided for his own portentous celebration at the Pantheon, organized by Jack Lang, which took place on 21 May.

Pierre Mauroy was, to no surprise, nominated as Prime Minister and a first government was put together by Mitterrand of Socialists, three Left Radicals and the independent Michel Jobert (once Pompidou's Foreign Minister) with some contributions from the Premier. It was a government that had to combine a hint of radicalism with reassurance to the floating voters who had given Mitterrand the presidency – a difficult balance. Mitterrand also had to pay off old debts to people who had helped and to reward allies or close companions. It was an artful series of nominations, leaving several discontented hopefuls, but it was Mitterrand's own: the prince is known through the quality of his collaborators. Globally, the ministers were drawn preponderantly from amongst Mitterrand's supporters, who were very well represented, and the victims were Rocard's supporters who paid for their 'treachery' at Metz.

Number two in the government was Gaston Defferre, who would have been Premier in 1974. Ageing but combative and determined, he asked to be made Minister of the Interior, in charge of decentralization – one of the main measures of the presidency. The other principal policy (nationalization) came under the Minister for Industry, Dreyfus. Chevènement, for his part, was rewarded with the Ministry for Research, but CERES as a whole was not generously rewarded. Michel Jobert, who was made Trade Minister, had left the gaullist party and carved out a career for himself as a critic of the Giscardian right and was known for his pugnacious defence of French interests. Claude Cheysson, with whom the President would have to collaborate most closely, was made Foreign Minister and Charles Hernu (a Mitterrand follower since 1956) was made Defence Minister – an equally presidentially sensitive post. Jacques Delors, whose financial ortho-doxy and expertise would be invaluable, was made Finance Minister and Mitterrand's protégé, Laurent Fabius, was Budget Minister to shadow Delors. In a controversial appointment in a turbulent and hostile sector, Edith Cresson was made Agriculture Minister. Party faction leaders were all given the prestigious title of Minister of State, including Jean-Pierre Chevènement and Michel Rocard, who was in internal exile at the Plan-ning Commission. Nicole Questiaux, Solidarity Minister, became the first woman to be made a Minister of State.

A series of measures were announced to reassure various of Mitterrand's constituencies. For the ecologists, the building of the nuclear power station at Plogoff was stopped and the Larzac army camp was vacated. At the same time, the human rights campaigners were satisfied with the ending of the state security project and the freeing of 31 people detained for threatening state security, while those condemned to death were reprieved when France became the last European state to abolish the death penalty. Popular and low income demands were met with an increase of the minimum wage, an increased old-age pension, higher family allowances and housing allowances (some employers' contributions were also reduced). In the public sector 54,290 posts were created to help ease unemployment, and exchange controls were reinforced. These measures were also a sign that the new President was determined to be seen to fulfil his promises. It was the beginning of the voluntarist economic policy that hoped to stimulate the economy through increased internal demand, but its impact was principally, because of a deterioration in the balance of pay-ments, an adverse one.

Mitterrand was in the position that the Socialists had always aspired to of domination over the Communists, and he could dictate conditions. A formal negotiation had to take place and this was conducted before the general elections at which it transpired that the Communists were pre-pared to accept the Socialist demands. When the agreement was signed, on 22 June, it stated that the two parties should defend Mitterrand's 'new politics', that there should be 'unfailing solidarity', that there would be nationalizations and faster economic growth but that the French economy would be open and would be balanced. More surprisingly, it also called on the USSR to withdraw from Afghanistan and it underlined support for Europe. Georges Marchais denied that there had been a capitulation, but the Communists had signed an electoral agreement in the expectation of participating in government. It was followed up after the general elections by a general governmental agreement between the two parties. Mitterrand had said in 1978 that he never discussed the composition of a government in advance and would not do so until after the second round and he once again held to that position.[32] In this government there were no Communists, but Georges Marchais went to the Elysée on 25 May and felt able to declare that the party was ready to 'take on the responsibilites of government'. Mitterrand simply said that the Communists' place in government depended on their electoral comportment.

Mitterrand's team at the Elysée also had to be chosen. Pierre Bérégovoy, one of the few in the Socialist élite with a genuine working-class background, a former mendésiste and Savaryist, was put in charge of Mitterrand's transition team. Bérégovoy, who would have liked a ministry (he left for one in 1982), was somewhat disappointed to be Secretary-General of the Elysée heading the presidential staff. André Rousselet, Mitterrand's long-time collaborator and finance raiser, became head of the President's private office. Jean-Claude Colliard, the political scientist, who came under Rousselet, was given the task of determining the organization of the Elysée. Jean Glavany was given control of the diary, travel in France and meeting the party officials and deputies, but was independent of Rousselet. Michel Charasse from the Conseil d'Etat was in charge of constitutional questions, Hubert Védrine followed the diplomatic and strategic policies, Michel Vauzelle became porte-parole and Nathalie Duhamel ran the press office. Jacques Attali, who was hoping to be secretary-general, was made special councillor and given a separate status. Other staffers included Régis Debray, François de Grossouvre and Charles Salzmann.[33]

In principle the Elysée is organized with civil service precision and each staff member has an appointed and well-defined role. In reality the structure is not so simple. Mitterrand liked one-to-one contacts and preferred to control information without having to be dependent on any one person. Contacts were diversified and tasks overlapped, staff often did not know exactly where they stood in the president's estimation and it was a difficult place to work. Often a collaborator would be given a task only to find out later that somebody else had been given the same directive; as a result, rivalries were promoted that could be demoralizing. Mitterrand's staff and collaborators were less managerially and more politically organized than administration theory allows. But Mitterrand had a Byzantine system of courtiers and councillors beholden only to him and in which people manoeuvred to get his ear. This was true not just of the Elysée staff but of the Cabinet as well, and Mitterrand took virtually no notice of it when it met.

General Elections

The Assembly elected in 1978 was a conservative one and would not have supported a government of the left; in keeping with the statements made during the campaign, on 22 May Mitterrand ordered a dissolution. Georges Dupeux showed that the Popular Front elections were the result of a small change in votes and a redistribution internal to the left.[34] Much the same happened in 1981. Compared to 1978, the 1981 general elections did not see a big rise in the vote for the left, despite the increase in the number of voters by 1,350,000. There was a slump in the vote for the conservative right and an increase in abstentions, but inside the left there was a shift from the Communist Party to the Socialist Party. Against demoralized conservatives and with the enthusiasm of the left behind him, the general elections of 14 and 21 June provided Mitterrand's Socialist Party with an overall majority, only the second in the history of the Republic to that date.

On the first ballot the Socialists and their Radical allies took 37.8 per cent and the Communists, who played on their local strengths, recovered slightly to 16.1 per cent. Such was the surge in the Socialist vote in all regions and all social categories that the Communists came second in many of their former strongholds and in 42 of their 68 seats they had to stand down for the PS. A rapid negotiation between the conservatives managed to impose single candidates in 385 of the 474 metropolitan constituencies. But the demoralization of the right led to a poor turn-out in their traditional bastions, despite the repeated raising of the Communist threat.[35] Compared with 1978, there were 5,416,246 more abstentions and a very large number were voters of the right. On the second ballot the Socialist swing was amplified and they won 265 seats, which, along with 20 of their allies, gave an overall majority of 78, and there was no need for Communist support. But if this contingent was combined with the Communists' 44 deputies and the 4 other left-wingers, it gave a government total of 333 to the opposition's 159. Importantly for Mitterrand, the new Socialist deputies were overwhelmingly Mitterrandist: there were only 47 Rocardians, 47 Mauroy supporters and 36 CERES.

After the election, a second Mauroy government was formed and the principal issue here was the extent and nature of Communist representation. They were offered posts in keeping with Mitterrand's strategy of alliance of the left to bind the Communist Party to the government, but the ministries would not be sensitive ones. American leaders, surprised by Giscard's defeat, were apparently reassured (notably US Vice-President Bush, who visited shortly after the victory) by Mitterrand's attitude to the Communists and his conviction that they would lose further votes as the left continued in power.[36]

Conditions were propitious for Communists to participate in the government and they were anxious to be a part of the majority, even if they were latecomers, and for Mitterrand this would have the advantage of associating them with government policies. Communist participation in government would not guarantee a social peace, and weaknesses would be exploited if they could be found. Unlike the Popular Front of 1936 (when the party stayed out of government to put pressure on the Socialists), the PCF this time had decided to enter. They demanded five portfolios but were offered four, in proportion to the party's parliamentary representation. Of those ministries they requested, they only got Transport and Health. They had to accept a small representation in the second Mauroy government, with four ministerial portfolios for Communists who were neither union leaders nor defeated in elections. Mitterrand, of course, would not accept anybody who had copiously insulted him in the elections (including Marchais). Charles Fiterman, Marchais's secretary, had the highest rank as Minister of State for Transport, Marcel Rigout became Minister for Professional Training, Anicet Le Pors became Minister for Public Administration and Jack Ralite became Health Minister. In July, *L'Humanité* made clear its first low-key disagreement with Mitterrand by commenting that the President's demanded preconditions for negotiating with the Soviets on the withdrawal of their SS20 missiles 'went even further than Nato'.[37] Roland Leroy commented in September that the 'PCF was in government but not of government', warning, if such were needed, that the 'union was still a combat'.

Other posts were reshuffled and the main portfolios went to Mitterrand's supporters, whereas the other factions in the party were not so well treated. Rocard's was frozen out, given only two ministries: Jean-Pierre Cot (Africa) and Louis Le Pensec (Marine). Chevènement was moved to the Ministry of Industry and his faction, with Questiaux at

Solidarity and Edwidge Avice at Youth and Sports, held some important posts. Michel Crépeau, leader of the left-wing Radicals, became Environment Minister. Charged with managing the party, Jospin was Mitterrand's representative and derived his authority from that perception, though he declined to organize his own faction. He was deprived of the 'ministrables' and the advisers who had departed into government, but Mitterrand's majority was reinforced on the PS secretariat and at the grass roots.

At the end of 1981, Mitterrand had everything he needed for his own politics. Authority and initiatives flowed from the summit and the jacquerie or Bolshevik system of Soviets that the right feared never materialized. In the Assembly, the Socialist group was at the forefront and dominated by his own supporters. The PS was content to be in power again and supported the President's initiatives and there was no obstruction from the Communist Party or the unions. On the right, the conservatives had been winded by the defeat and left leaderless and divided. Opinion polls and by-elections showed the continuation of the presidential 'honeymoon' and the continued popularity of the Socialist Party. In these conditions, Mitterrand held more power than previous presidents and certainly more than de Gaulle, whose 'coup d'état' he had criticized, or Giscard, whose monarchical pretensions he had guyed. But the next five years were to teach Mitterrand what the Greeks had known: that the worst punishment can be having one's wishes fulfilled too completely.

6

The First Socialist Governments: 1981–1985

Mitterrand's victory first in the presidential elections and then in the general elections was a famous one, but its importance should be kept in proportion. There had been, in the past, many victories by the left. In the early Third Republic Gambetta's defining clash with President Mac-Mahon determined that France would be a parliamentary Republic and not an authoritarian system. Many left-wing governments took office in these years, including those of the anti-clerical Emile Combes (June 1902), Georges Clemenceau (1906) and the Socialist René Viviani (June 1913). In the 1920s and 1930s there were the Cartel des gauches of 1924 (led by Edouard Herriot), Herriot's government of 1932 and the Popular Front of 1936 led by Léon Blum. However, if the left was successful in the early Third Republic, it was disastrous in the later years, and in the Fourth Republic the only remembered success was that of Mendès France in 1954, though Ramadier's government of 1947 must be counted as one of the more vigorous. There were, however, many left-wing governments, and there were the 'Tripartite' and Liberation governments, so much so that the conservative right believed, until Antoine Pinay's nomination in 1952, that they were excluded. Pinay was preceded by the governments of Léon Blum and Paul Ramadier and succeeded by Mendès France and Guy Mollet (though not immediately).

The left's problem in the 1920s, 1930s and 1950s was not so much winning power as keeping it. Had it overcome this fragility then the history of these Republics might have been very different, giving the left seven years of government rather than the meagre four it actually had. But it was internal politics rather than the 'mur de l'argent' ('wall of money') or the manipulations of outsiders that let the conservative right claw its way back in most cases. In other words, the left would come to office in previous Republics, make mistakes, divide over policy and lose power virtually within the year. An unedifying story of political incompetence, perhaps, but not a conspiracy to keep the left out of power.

Nor was the left excluded from power in the Fifth Republic: rather, it was the inability of the Socialist Party, burdened with its unelectable Communist ally, to convince electors in the Fifth Republic at regular consultations of its capacity to govern successfully. Its previous failures lay in its inability to maintain a hold on authority or to become a 'natural party of government'.[1] And indeed there were those in the Mitterrand circle who did not see the left's task in these terms, but rather as the need to make a few principled reforms and then retreat back into the wilderness. However, Mitterrand's large majority and the solidity of the parliamentary party enabled a longer-term view to be taken. Duration, rather than a sprint, was what the victory of 1981 offered. Victory did inaugurate a radical government (comparable with the great reforming governments of the past), but the ability of Mitterrand's left to govern was also its historic test – duration, if circumstances allowed, was paramount because Mitterrand was informed by his two doctors in November 1981 that he had a fatal prostate cancer. This was kept secret. The regular medical bulletins on his health published by the Elysée were falsified, but, almost unprecedentedly, the cancer went into remission for ten years.[2]

But Mitterrand's euphoric return to power presaged the same problems as the Cartel, the Popular Front and the Liberation, with their high hopes and poor preparation for the exercise of power. In any case, the *Projet socialiste* and the 110 propositions as well as the revolutionary language still employed were intended to dispose of Rocard and the challenge from the mendésist left on the one hand and the PCF on the other. Mitterrand's quasi manifesto *Ici et maintenant* stated that the new world would soon arrive and that 'to leave the nodal points of our society in the hands of big capital would be totally absurd'.[3] The key thing was that property had to change hands.[4] Other examples could be multiplied endlessly, starting with Mitterrand's speech to the Epinay Party Congress and continuing through the years into the Common Programme, the *Projet* and the 110 propositions of 1981. The claim was, of course, rhetorical, but at the opposite end of the spectrum from Mendès France. In the event, the 110 proposals were invoked when Mitterrand felt the need, or forgotten if they were a nuisance. Either way, Mitterrand arrived in power having raised unrealistic expectations, in an overly optimistic perspective and with a programme that could not be applied. As it was, learning had to be undertaken in government and an attempt was made to carry out the candidate's commitments – starting with the 'dash for growth'.

Government Policy

In practical terms, May 1981 revolved around a 'dash for growth' in unpropitious circumstances that did not work with a subsequent retrenchment conducted so as to limit political damage. This 'dash for growth' was not hopeless and was not without foundation – many expected a world upturn at the end of 1981 – and was similar to what had been tried by the conservative right in 1975–6. It was a standard Keynesian reflation based on public works, housing, job creation and other measures intended to promote the less well-off and reduce imports. It was imprudent, but might have been attempted by other politicians and it was not contested when it was first imposed. In Rocard's Interim Plan of October 1981, growth of 3 per cent was envisaged, as was the creation of 400,000 jobs per year and the reconquest of the internal market.[5]

Mitterrand, to the extent that he commented about economics, intended to stimulate growth and hence reduce or eliminate unemployment, through increased internal demand in the economy. Contrary to Marx, history can repeat itself several times and by no means necessarily in farcical form on the second or third occasion. Thus came the controversial question of devaluation. There had, of course, been a run on the franc in 1981 of dramatic proportions. That year, it had been overvalued against the Deutschmark. What happened was that devaluation was, as in 1936, postponed and substantial reserves were dissipated in a vain defence of the overvalued franc. But Mitterrand had himself on 21 May refused to 'welcome the victory of the left with a devaluation' and preferred a Wilsonian fight – raising interest rates to 21 per cent – against the markets in a vain attempt to prove that he was not the President to devalue.[6] It is true that there were general elections that had to be held in June, but the 'honeymoon' was unlikely to be ended by a devaluation that could be blamed on the outgoing administration. In putting off the devaluation, the President repeated Blum's mistake of 1936: deferring the inevitable and stimulating demand too quickly for industry to meet it, in that way drawing in imports.[7] In the early months the spectre of an IMF intervention was already being invoked.[8]

Other measures that could have been taken to offset the overvalued franc do not seem to have been contemplated in the Elysée, although Mauroy and Delors developed a deflation strategy.[9] A fight against devaluation was not, however, in the original plans and no policy evolved until the summer of 1982. Protection, mooted as a possibility by Michel Jobert, the Trade Minister, amongst others, was, as imports flooded in, in the background.[10] In addition, the effect of then trying to stimulate the economy at a time when French industry was ill-prepared and suffering a balance of payments crisis in the face of world recession made the situation untenable and forced a U-turn. This, however, Mitterrand accepted, rather in the spirit of the lady who informed Carlyle that she accepted the universe. There were ultimately three devaluations of the franc, accompanied by revaluations of the Deutschmark: the first on 4 October 1981, the second on 12 June 1982 and the third in March 1983.

Mitterrand's first year was marked by an expansionary budget presented by Fabius in September 1981, which had been put together by the Budget Minister and the Elysée. This process left out the Finance Minister and other recalcitrants and had the intention of stimulating economic growth and in that way reducing unemployment. Mitterrand's imprudent campaign estimate of 5.2 per cent growth in 1982 was not retained, but a rate of 3.3 per cent was optimistically anticipated; the talk was of employment, purchasing power and quality of life. In the same spirit, the government committed itself to investment which, it was assumed, the private sector was unwilling to do. This had to be paid for, and taxes went up despite the broadcast view that there was no need to increase direct taxes. This hit hard when the economic growth that would have taken the edge off the tax increases failed to materialize and it also bore down on the newly won-over middle classes.

The nationalizations of 1981 were part of the strategy for obtaining power. They were assumed to be the price for the adhesion of the Communist Party's electorate (or perhaps the PCF itself) and a way of showing fidelity to the traditions of the left. They did indeed lift the state's participation in the productive economy to the highest in the Western world: 30 per cent of sales, 90 per cent of deposits and 85 per cent of credits. They dominated the beginning of the government and kept other issues off the foreground even when Delors demanded 'a pause' in the reforms at the end of November 1981. Inside the President's circle the partisans of an alternative course – Delors, Rocard, Badinter and Jobert – were in a minority, but one that, if it had been more adroit, might have won concessions. At that time the nationalizations were seen as the key to the socialist economy and Mitterrand had made them a priority for his septennate.[11] Nine industries were taken into public ownership, as were the large banks. This programme also reinvigorated the right and a protracted and venomous debate took place.

But no prior consideration had been given to how these nationalized industries would be run, what they would entail or even what they would contribute to the economy. By insisting on the complete nationalizations (100 per cent – a point of debate between ministers and advisers), the cost was made much greater than it need have been and the margin for manoeuvre was greatly and quickly reduced. Unfortunately, many of these industries were failing and had, like steel, been supported but not rebuilt by the state over a long period simply because politically their collapse would have been too costly. This was not the dynamic core of a new technologically advanced France, but the declining industries of a previous era faced, by 1981, with a world crisis.[12] By February 1982 they were in public control, new executives had been appointed, for the most part from the state elite, and the guidelines for their action had been set out. It was not yet clear that their situation had been changed positively or transformed.

Decentralization, the other big measure of the septennate and the first transfer of regulatory and financial powers from the state since the Revolution, was pressed with vigour, but its genesis was not straightforward. For Interior Minister Gaston Defferre, no radical, this was an extension of the power of the big cities (mostly socialist since 1977) and local politicians rather than a new dimension for French democracy. It suited the big cities, which would be relieved of the prefectoral oversight of their affairs (*tutelle*), and the departments, which were also given greater autonomy. Regional councils were to be elected but their role was relatively small and certain powers were transferred from the state to them – though these were often a sloughing off of problems rather than a form of 'self-management'. Overall, decentralization was to the benefit of local elites in a part of the state where the left was strong and likely to remain so.[13] Elections to the regions were held simultaneously with the 1986 general elections.

Foreign Policy

Mitterrand's foreign policy was distinctive and over-ambitious from the outset: it had its share of the rhetorical, particularly on the Third World, but it was transatlantic in a way that put it in the old Socialist Atlanticist and European tradition rather than in the gaullist tradition. Likewise, the new President's support for the deployment in Western Europe of Nato's Cruise and Pershing missiles, in response to the Soviet build-up of SS20 missiles, was steadfast. French opinion was broadly hostile to the US deployment, with 47 per cent against and only 33 per cent in favour (20 per cent 'don't knows'), but as none was placed in France it was not of high salience as an issue.[14] However, Mitterrand's view on North–South questions and his verbal support for resistance movements, notably in El Salvador and Che's companion in Bolivia, Régis Debray, who was appointed to the Elysée staff, caused anger in Washington. Mitterrand also spoke out against Reagan's policy in Nicaragua and provided arms for the Sandinista government. This arms sale went ahead, but the ensuing rift with Washington led to the announcement that it would stop.

In Mitterrand's other main sphere of foreign interest, the Middle East, he seems to have come with a determination to make his mark by supporting the Camp David agreement but demanding that the PLO recognize Israel's right to exist. He was seen by many as pro-Israeli (he sent envoys to reassure Arab states that he was not anti-Arab) and did hope for a new relationship with that country, but a 'just' settlement in his eyes involved concessions from Israel leading to the setting-up of a Palestinian state. Israel had been intended for his first state visit, but the Israeli attack on a nuclear power station in Iraq, killing a French worker, caused its postponement. He eventually visited Israel in March 1982 and spoke to the Knesset, taking the opportunity to advocate the creation of a Palestinian state. However, Mitterrand's views were swept aside by Prime Minister Begin and repudiated by the Arab world. Palestinian supporters dangerously increased tension in France itself with terrorist attacks, and French staff abroad were also attacked. Mitterrand's advocacy of dialogue with the PLO found no takers in the Likud government.

Nevertheless, Mitterrand appears to have believed that he had dissuaded Begin's government from their planned attack on southern Lebanon. But Israel's attack took place on 6 June (while a G7 summit was in progress) and went way beyond the 40 kilometres Begin had declared as an objective. Mitterrand condemned the invasion of the Lebanon and the subsequent siege of Beirut. This stance was to the detriment of his entente with Israel, which interpreted his position as one of complicity with the PLF. Mitterrand did see Yasser Arafat as the key to peace in the region and protected him in his withdrawal from Lebanon later on. In August 1982 French troops became part of the international force in Lebanon and stayed until 1984, when the Lebanese President declared that their mission had been accomplished. But there had been a great loss of life, and a further conflict with Tehran, envenomed by France's support for Iraq, had developed. It was an off-key episode for a practitioner of realpolitik. France had proposed a policy to Israel that the Begin government reviled and Mitterrand lacked the power to support Lebanon or to prevent Syrian and Iranian intervention from tearing it apart. Mitterrand had overestimated the strength of his own hand in the Middle East and had not expected the Israelis to take a course that he thought was evidently wrong. By some accounts his confidence was shattered by his misreading of the situation.[15]

Africa

French African policy was traditionally the preserve of the Elysée, but Mitterrand was expected to be innovative here. The French system of power in Africa goes back to the 1950s and the Fifth Republic maintained the continuity through the gaullists and Giscard d'Estaing.[16] Mitterrand himself was in no hurry to change things. African policy, before and under Mitterrand, was part of the 'reserved domain' and was run out of the Elysée by a small team and by the Ministry of Cooperation (in substance, the Ministry for Africa). But there was an initial promise of a change with the appointment of Jean-Pierre Cot as the Minister for Cooperation. Jean-Pierre Cot, a Rocardian radical and hence a peculiar choice for such a sensitive post, was keen to reform relations and to condemn the record of the many petty dictatorships in the area. Cot had started well with a round condemnation of the Apartheid regime in South Africa – though not a trade embargo – but soon settled back into the familiar pattern. As President, however, Mitterrand maintained France's traditional tutelle over these former colonies.[17]

However, Cot's implications that the neo-colonial relationship would change were badly received by government circles in sub-Saharan Africa. There were suspicions in Morocco and Algeria that a new emphasis on human rights would question government practices in Africa and change old relationships. In August, a secret visit to Morocco by Mitterrand to reassure the King of his conservative outlook inflamed their Algerian rivals and he then went to Algeria to reassure President Chadli. In fact, Mitterrand continued to run policy directly with his councillors, his son Jean-Christophe ('papamadit') and Guy Penne. Cot resigned in late 1982, disillusioned at the continuation of the neo-colonial satrapy in Africa. Then the presidentialization of African policy was carried almost to the point of parody when Cot was replaced as Minister by the more amenable Christian Nucci (subsequently implicated in the 'Carrefour du développement' funding scandal) and Jean-Christophe Mitterrand was made special councillor.

Military interventions took place in sub-Saharan Africa as before to support favoured regimes or to evacuate foreigners. In Chad, the French army found itself in a long confrontation with Libyan forces. President Habré of Chad had asked for French aid in June 1983 when rebel forces backed by Colonel Gadaffi had gone onto the offensive, and Mitterrand had sent troops and supplies. It was felt in Paris that the southern part of the country ought to be defended because a domino effect would overturn other 'friendly' states in the region. French troops defended Chad's 15th parallel and a diplomatic solution was sought rather than an offensive to regain the north of the country. After a meeting with Colonel Gadaffi in November 1983 and the conclusion of a much-derided deal, Mitterrand withdrew the French contingent only for Libya to go onto the offensive eighteen months later. This provoked French retaliation and the sending of another contingent which was steadily reinforced. Despite French troops remaining out of the front line, but supported by French aid, the government of Hissène Habré forced the Libyans out of their country. During this trial Mitterrand had defended France's ally but in a discreet and background manner, and he resisted pressure from the USA for a more forceful intervention.

Several reports were produced recommending changes in Africa, but these were all pigeonholed by the Elysée (Ambassador Hessel's in February 1990, for example).[18] Mitterrand's long refusal to envisage a change in the relations of France with sub-Saharan Africa eventually led to one of the most tense confrontations between the President and his associates of the double septennate. Mitterrand's close entourage virtually cornered him into making a change of direction towards a more open and accountable system.[19] (This change of heart did not last.) But the single party states began to meet with increasing unrest and opposition, while their progress (and sometimes regression) since independence gave no grounds for optimism. Over the 1980s there was a switch in diplomatic and informal circuits, but little changed in the relationship between France and its former colonies.

This was the background to the Franco-African summit in June 1990 at La Baule and the need, as seen by other Socialists, to modernize the ramshackle dictatorships in the French sphere of Africa. Mitterrand went along with this pressure, to the irritation of African leaders, many under threat, at La Baule – a shift in French policy towards conditional aid and to modernization was perceived. But there was to be no real change and the brief hope was snuffed out by Mitterrand himself, so that by the Libreville Franco-African summit of October 1992, little remained of the new ideals.[20] Immediately following the summit at La Baule, France appeared to be either bolstering these regimes or acting as a bystander at the worst excesses. Even Hissène Habré of Chad, who had become critical of France, was overthrown in December 1990 with the help of the French secret services and replaced by the one-time dissident Idriss Deby, who, as expected, implemented few changes in government style.

It was in the former Belgian colony of Rwanda that the conduct of French African policy, with its determination to preserve its sphere of influence and to reinforce it in 'Francophone' countries, was most criticized. Rwanda was a predominantly Hutu society but with a small Tutsi minority which had links with compatriots in Uganda who had fought with the Ugandan army and were descendants of those who had fled a generation before. France supported Habyarimana's Hutu regime when the Tutsi Rwandan Patriotic Front started an attack from Uganda in October 1990. Mitterrand acceded to Habyarimana's request to repel a foreign invasion and sent two parachute regiments to Rwanda.

However, the lack of discipline and of government control led to massacres of refugees and when Habyarimana was killed in a plane crash the genocide of Tutsis began. Perhaps as many as 800,000 people died in the slaughter. (The new Edouard Balladur government of the conservative right intervened and then withdrew.) In fact, the genocide of 1994 was being prepared by Habyarimana, who had no intention of modernizing his country and had made that clear at the summit of La Baule. Although events in Rwanda moved very rapidly after the plane crash, France was compromised in the subsequent genocide and it had had warnings from several sources that the situation was deteriorating. Mitterrand was criticized personally for supporting the Habyarimana government (he had, after all, overthrown Habré without compunction) and for not understanding the meaning of events and then for reacting too slowly.

Although internal and not foreign policy, in New Caledonia Mitterrand's election in 1981 was expected by the indigenous Kanaks to bring something close to independence. New Caledonia, in the Pacific, had a population of 145,000 divided into about 41 per cent Melanesians, 38 per cent settlers and 12 per cent Polynesians. Reforms were proposed but when these did not materialize the tensions on the island increased and the elections were boycotted by the Kanak party. But for many settlers, and some conservatives, reform was top of the slippery slope. Edgard Pisani, the former gaullist minister, was made High Commissioner and asked to find a settlement, while the conservative right poured petrol on the flames by accusing the government of preparing to undermine the Republic's authority in the territory. This situation got worse, not better, as Pisani reported back in 1985 and there were demonstrations and violent incidents leading to a state of emergency. In September 1985 the independence parties won three of the four regions, although overall the anti-independence parties won a majority. It was a problem that had to face the next government.

'Euromissiles'

Mitterrand's initial inflection of French alliances away from Bonn and towards London was but a brief interlude (mainly a *mésentente* with

Helmut Schmidt) before the reassertion of the post-war Franco-German entente.[21] Later, in 1982 Mitterrand's support for Mrs Thatcher when the Argentine Junta invaded the Falklands was full hearted and that of a very close ally. When he was told about it, Mitterrand was convinced that Mrs Thatcher would see it through, but the diplomatic 'repayment' was meagre. Mitterrand's intervention in German politics came at a time when the feeling against Nato's new missiles (a response to Soviet SS20s) was growing. Mitterrand went to the West German Bundestag on 20 January 1983 and made a ringing case for the deployment of the Nato missiles and attempted to thwart what many regarded as a neutralist temptation on the German left. His call to restore the balance in Europe was a disavowal of the German Socialists and an implicit endorsement of their conservative opponent Kohl, who won the upcoming general elections. Mitterrand's defence policy otherwise remained in a largely gaullist framework but with additional consultations with the German government and the use of a revived WEU to coordinate defence efforts in Europe.

Mitterrand's relationship with Kohl (who became German Chancellor in October 1982) was by 1984 even more cordial than it had been with Schmidt, and a closer Franco-German security cooperation was initiated. This new closeness was captured by an image of Mitterrand and Kohl at Verdun, but the limits were set by the USA to which Germany was close. France's support in the critical phase of the Cold War was important. In December 1981, Solidarity was suppressed in Poland under martial law by the army. Mitterrand's reaction to this coup was much closer to the USA's than had been anticipated, unlike Giscard's appeasement of the USSR after the invasion of Afghanistan, and was in keeping with France's new coolness to the Soviet bloc. Despite the Communist ministers, whose presence increased his vulnerability to attacks from the right, Mitterrand's views were very forcefully put and left no room for doubt, but along with Germany, the President resisted Washington's calls for sanctions.

There remained considerable problems between Paris and Washington over North–South questions, where France had little influence, but, in particular, over the pipeline taking natural gas from the USSR to Western Europe.[22] This had been in negotiation for some time. However, it became real just after the coup d'état in Poland in December 1981, when the USA feared that it would mean dependence on Soviet supply, would give them hard currency and might mean the transfer of technology to the enemy.[23] At the beginning of 1982, Reagan suspended the export licences for American equipment and then extended the embargo in June to foreign industries that used American licences, and Atlantic relations hit a new low even though the American embargo was revoked in November. Other clashes came over the US Star Wars project (SDI), which, as Mitterrand saw it, undermined the French deterrent. EUREKA, the European research initiative, was Mitterrand's reaction to the research component of SDI and to some extent compensated for the contracts that French firms lost as a result of France's opposition. There was also a long-running disagreement during the GATT negotiations (from 1986 to 1993) but that stretched over five governments, two 'cohabitations' and the two septennates. At issue here were agricultural subsidies and the liberalizing of the trade in film and TV. However, Mitterrand took care to visit the United States in 1984 shortly before he travelled to the USSR.

U-turn

Unfortunately, high American interest rates and the overvalued dollar caused France to put up its own rates, which severely hindered the recovery on which the President depended. Mitterrand and his close associates may have hoped that at the Versailles summit of June 1982 the industrial nations would bring some solution, perhaps by organizing a worldwide reflation or even monetary reforms. In the event little emerged, although there was a decision to smooth out fluctuations in the value of the dollar and US interest rates began moving down somewhat. Not just the USA, but also Germany had refused to heed French demands to reflate their economy. After that rebuff – accompanied by expressions of mutual esteem – the Socialists' change of course was inevitable, though it was still resisted. By June 1982 the decision to change direction had been taken and the first measures implemented, but polls showed that the introduction of restrictions had caused the credibility of the President and the Premier to fall badly.[24] Where Mitterrand's experience differs from his predecessor in 1936 was that he remained in power longer than one year and was backed by a majority after the rout of his initial policies.

Between the Matignon and the Elysée the expansionary Keynesian policy was called into question, mainly by the Premier, the Finance Minister, the Budget Minister, the Elysée Secretary-General and Mitterrand's special councillor, with friends and acquaintances of Mitterrand adding their advice. Bit by bit over 1982, a deflationary policy was introduced, reducing expenditure and abandoning the strategy of expanding the economy out of its problems with its priority of reducing unemployment. After the second devaluation of June 1982 a series of restrictions were put in place, including a wages freeze. At the end of June 1982 a reshuffle saw the arrival from Research of the dirigiste Jean-Pierre Chevènement as the Industry Minister, but at the same time Bérégovoy replaced CERES's Nicole Questiaux at the Solidarity Ministry and brought with him a new determination to master costs. This new policy was contrary to the expectations of the voters in 1981 and the U-turn lost the President support as its effects bore down on the left's traditional supporters through the *désindexation des salaires* and the policy of competitive deflation. In particular, the priority to reduce unemployment was abandoned along the way.

In September 1982, the President's speech at Figeac buried the old policy and praised the spirit of free enterprise and innovation, appropriating conservative themes like battling against inflation and adaptation but without explanation. But it was an uncertain trumpet that sounded from the Elysée from 1982–3. If the Prime Minister and the Finance Minister were determined on a new direction, restraining internal demand and lightening taxes on business, Fabius and others (particularly Jean Riboud, a 'night visitor', and the parliamentary party) still resisted a U-turn. Mitterrand, on the other hand, was not disposed to choose and, although by January 1983 he was talking about 'enterprise', 'initiative', 'investment' and 'reducing the tax burden', no agreement had yet been given to Mauroy's deflation plan.[25]

After the March 1983 local elections, where much was at stake for the Socialist Party, the decision had to be finally and irrevocably taken. There were ten days of hesitation from 13 to 23 March. Premier Pierre Mauroy, who had felt on the verge of dismissal for more than nine months, faced quite a large group, including Chevènement, Bérégovoy and Séguèla, who wanted him replaced.[26] Mauroy was saved by a mobilization of voters that on 13 March retained some city halls thought lost for the PS, on condition that he renounce the policy he had followed with Delors since June 1982. Mauroy refused to comply and Mitterrand again vacillated.[27] Mitterrand's hesitation has been presented as tactical (with the implication that he never intended to leave the European Monetary System – EMS) and the Germans were unlikely to have agreed to revalue the Deutschmark. So it was in the crucial ten days after the municipal elections of March 1983 that the decision was taken, and he turned his back on the voluntarism of the 'alternative economic policy'. In 1983 Mitterrand found that he that he had 'made a mistake' about the steel industry, but that everybody, on the right as well as on the left, had been mistaken about that sector.[28]

It was made clear to the President by Delors and latterly Fabius that leaving the EMS was not the easy option, that the reserves were too small and that high interest rates would strangle many an industry.[29] Their argument was accepted and the stage was prepared for a new deflationary plan

with a devaluation of the Franc and the negotiation (by Delors) of a reval-
uation of the Deutschmark. Maintaining Mauroy had the benefit of giving
the impression of continuity despite the U-turn. Mitterrand's decision after
the devaluation of March 1983 to stay in the EMS was presented as a decision for Europe at the price of 'deflation' and 'spending controls'. But he
had been convinced that leaving the EMS would not have been the cure to
France's ills, and in any case France's European commitment was well
anchored. France had withdrawn from the system before (in 1974 and
1976) without undue damage to its European commitment. EMS was
more the symbol and guarantor of the new policy its advocates wanted to
follow. By the end of 1983, economic growth was negative, unemployment
was rising and the real value of salaries had fallen, though the balance of
payments was coming right. For Mitterrand, 'Europe' became the symbol
and the cover for his change of direction. It was used to give gravity and
weight to the subsequent politics in which, of course, the President would
play the main role.[30] If the Socialist Party, always pro-European, had been
reassured by this justification of the U-turn, the new policy opened up a
gap between the left and its voters. In domestic politics the policy moved
from the 'rupture with capitalism' to financial orthodoxy but without an
explanation being disseminated. For Mitterrand, however, Europe was
personalized, identified with him, and opened up a vista of summits and
symbolism.

Socialist theory aside, in political terms, the President's new affection
for market economics cut the ground from under the conservative right,
which had been promoting a Reaganite free market policy as the alternative to Mitterrand's socialism. In this U-turn was to be found the route to
Mitterrand's victory in 1988 as the centrist President of all the French. But
this was a presidential effect, personal to Mitterrand, and not a shaping of
the Socialist Party. Mitterrand was going to have to find a solution to this
problem even as he maintained the old government of Mauroy and the
Communists to give a sense of continuity. A solution appeared at first
through the praise of the mixed economy, profit, effort and the need to
suffer pains to get the gains: it was translated by Jospin (Socialist First Secretary) as a 'parenthesis' to the PS Comité directeur on 26 March 1983,
with the implication that the bracket would sooner rather than later be
closed. Mitterrand then repeated this view in a prominent interview.[31]
Thus while the government swung round to deflation, it implied that the
programme of 1981 would be resumed. No rethink of Socialist ideology
was undertaken and, although the subsequent congresses moved away
from the strident revolutionary rhetoric that had characterized the party

in the 1970s, the free market thrust of government action swept aside a more modest reformism or social democracy. Mitterrand, the de facto leader of the party, had no interest in having a debate opened out that would expose the unreality of the 'Epinay line', necessitated a recantation by his supporters and shown his opponents to be right.

Europe and Crisis

Mitterrand's commitment to Europe did not, at first, stand out as a priority, and his belief in European integration often had to stand back from other commitments. But with the ambitious economic policy now dropped he decided to revivify his appeal to the centre. Thus he decided to revitalize his European policy in 1984, moving, in the process, the Community out of a rather stagnant phase. His speech to the European Parliament in May 1984 was adventurous, suggesting an expansion of integration and restrictions on the veto. Under France's presidency of the Council of Ministers, Mitterrand took steps, based on solid German support, to resolve the problem of the British rebate and to revise the Common Agricultural Policy, to abolish MCAs (now working to France's disadvantage) and to enlarge Europe to Spain and Portugal. It was also agreed that Jacques Delors would become the next President of the Commission when Gaston Thorn stepped down in January 1985. Delors was, with Mitterrand's essential backing, able to move the Community into a new and dynamic phase of integration with the Single Act as a start, signed in December 1985.

The collapse of the Prime Minister's popularity forced Mitterrand onto centre stage. In a TV interview on 15 September 1983, the President announced that taxes would fall by 1 per cent in the next year, but neither the government nor the Elysée team had been alerted to this possibility.[32] Neither the Finance Minister nor the Premier, who had been preparing a budget with slight tax increases, were pleased at being presented with a fait accompli.[33] Mitterrand, however, had signalled that the assumption of substantial growth was unreal and that the policy would henceforth be one of economic 'realism'. His carefully prepared interview published in the left-wing daily *Libération* was intended to promote the ideas of social justice and social progress as the left's commitment. However, these issues were neglected as the press latched onto the President's exaltation of the 'mixed economy' and the interview was portrayed as a rightward drift.[34]

Laurent Fabius, as the first PA for the new policy, declared that 'modernization' was the objective. Unlike Delors or Chevènement, Fabius was a close associate of Mitterrand's (heading his private office at one time) and was in constant communication with him. What was decided in this instance was a restructuring of the old industries and a refitting of them for the rigours of the international market. This required intervention and funds and it would cost jobs and factories: even branches in sectors essential to the left – steel, coal, shipyards and automobiles – could be shut down, but the books of the nationalized industries would be in balance after two years. As Fabius's star waxed, Mauroy's waned, but never before in the Fifth Republic had a president fallen so low in the polls.[35] Paul Barril's Elysée police unit was involved in a scandal of the arrest of three Irish people accused of terrorism in August 1982. This was a herald of the later scandals; it transpired that the evidence against them was false.

During the process of industrial restructuring, Mauroy frequently found himself defending the weaker industries of his own region against the Industry Ministry's application of government policy.[36] But the plan at the end of March envisaged the loss of about 30,000 jobs and a drastic cut of steel production in Lorraine, and Mitterrand decided to cut the production of coal from 18 million tons to 11 million (a decision taken in December 1983). In April 1984, Marchais joined a march through Paris by steelworkers, although the Communists stayed in the government for a further four months. But until 1983 there had been no obvious replacement for Mauroy, although Fabius fitted the times better and the confrontation between them intensified. Crucially, by 1984, having been completely won over to the new course by Fabius, Attali and others, Mitterrand had decided to change the Prime Minister.

Before plans had matured, 'events' overtook the President and the government and forced a change of personnel. In Mitterrand's 110 proposals, number 90 gave the commitment to a 'great unified public and secular national education system', (the so-called 'Savary law'), bringing the private schools (mainly Catholic) into the state system. Savary had carefully constructed a law in the spirit of the 90th of Mitterrand's proposals acceptable to the moderates on the two sides. As Savary had envisaged it, the law would have been a genuinely progressive reform that would have reduced competition, brought the two systems closer and reformed teaching. Savary's compromise was not within the letter of the 90th proposal, and, worse still, in the three years since Mitterrand's election, feelings on the Catholic schools' side and in the teachers' unions had hardened and the Education Minister struggled to keep any reasonable balance. Throughout 1983 the issue became one that divided France once again. Before the Savary law was sent to the Assembly, Mitterrand seemed satisfied with the draft and congratulated Savary on his work.[37]

Yet Mitterrand had no commitment to the 'Savary law' and did not support it when the crunch came. By 1983, the Opposition, rather than the Church itself, which was conciliatory if vacillating,[38] had scented the political possibilities, particularly amongst the masses of middle-class parents dissatisfied with public provision who might want to opt for private Catholic schools. Very quickly, the protests against the Socialist proposals gathered force and huge demonstrations were organized in the major cities against the 'attack on freedom' that it supposedly represented. Mitterrand, irritated, it seems, by the opposition to the proposals, allowed the parliamentary group to amend the law, giving it a much more anti-clerical aspect than had been envisaged and upsetting Savary's careful compromise.[39] This change brought the Church authorities into outright opposition to the new law, dooming it.[40] Mitterrand had, however, two years in which to effect a recovery.

On 17 June 1984, the European elections were a setback for the left: the Socialist vote fell by 3 per cent to 21 per cent compared with 1979, and the Communists, with 11 per cent, lost almost 10 per cent. But the surprise was the rise of Le Pen's extreme right-wing Front national, which appeared on the national scene for the first time with 11 per cent of the vote. Meanwhile, the opposition to the new schools legislation grew: there was a massive demonstration against it on 24 June, and the President decided to change tactics and to drop the Savary law.[41] There would be a counterattack: Mitterrand used his presidential address on 12 July to take up the conservatives' suggestion of a referendum on the schools legislation, but before that could be done the field of topics on which a referendum could be held would have to be extended – hence a referendum on the referendum was proposed.

Mitterrand's tactical shift was to put the onus on the conservative Senate's refusal to approve a referendum. It enabled an abandonment that was not a humiliation, but sacrificed the short term for the benefits of the long-term reforms crafted by Savary. Whatever the calculation, and perhaps it was at first only in peripheral vision to the President, it deprived Mitterrand of much credit on the issue of freedoms and eclipsed other successes. On 14 July the President dropped the Savary law. Alain Savary, 'hung out to dry', resigned on the spot and so did the Prime Minister.[42] This precipitated a change of government probably intended for the autumn.[43]

The New Fabius Government

Prime Minister Fabius's new government was more than a reshuffle; it was a makeover, with the departure of such strong personalities as Delors,

Mauroy, Cheysson and Savary, as well as that of the Communists and the entry of Bérégovoy, Dumas and Joxe and the return of Chevènement (to education). In foreign affairs the independence of Cheysson (who was pro-Arab, for example) had led to a certain incoherence in French policy, and he was replaced with the reliable Dumas. Fabius, only 38 years old, had been recognized as the President's 'favourite', but he had to make it clear that he was his own man. He had, unusually, Mitterrand's complete confidence and this lasted until late 1985.

While Fabius was rebuilding confidence in the government and 'bringing people together', Chevènement was restoring peace in education ('make no waves') and in the process built himself a statesmanlike stature in public opinion. Meanwhile, Interior Minister Joxe was regaining 'law and order' ground for the left. Bérégovoy, on the other hand, was trapped by the President's promise to lower taxes and found it necessary, because of spending commitments, to increase indirect taxes on some goods. There was very little room for manoeuvre: budgeting had to be severe and the balance of payments righted. But for the President, the important priority was now to lower taxes, not to redistribute or increase social expenditures, still less to subsidize failing industries.

Mitterrand allowed his Prime Minister to move into the front rank in the first year of the new government and, mindful of the misfiring of the interview with *Libération*, took fewer opportunities to explain himself. All the same it was a new President who appeared through the tests of mounting unemployment and social unrest provoked by the lay-offs and closures inherent in the policy of market reform undertaken. Mitterrand now appeared distant from the government (the 'Madonna of the airports', in Poniatowski's phrase) and above the mêlée of social disturbances, a national figure ready for the inevitable 'cohabitation' with the conservative right in 1986. Mitterrand continued to cut the ground from under the conservative right with an emphasis on managerial competence, 'stealing their clothes'. This tactic was evident in the budget for 1986. Unlike the anticipated election 'give-away budget', the Finance Minister was austere. State expenditure was capped, as was the deficit, and ministerial plans were cut back (with the exceptions of research, police, culture, defence and justice), while the number of state employees was also reduced.

Events

Opinion polls registered a new confidence in the President, although this was linked to the 'Rainbow Warrior' affair ('underwatergate'). Greenpeace had embarrassed French naval forces in the Pacific with its protests against French nuclear testing there. On 10 July 1985, Greenpeace's *Rainbow Warrior* was sunk by two bombs in Auckland harbour in New Zealand, killing one crew member. In the Elysée there seems to have been confusion, and the Prime Minister was 'out of the loop' on defence matters.[44] Two days later, the New Zealand police caught a couple posing as Swiss newly weds who turned out to be French secret service officers. Various attempts were then made to escape the responsibility for the sinking.[45] For several weeks, during which it must have been obvious where the origins were to be located, Mitterrand played for time and supported his Defence Minister Hernu publicly. But then in September *Le Monde* published details of the secret service's operation and Hernu resigned.[46] In this affair, which did Mitterrand little damage in public opinion, the Prime Minister could not discover the culprits, for it was in the presidential domain not Matignon's. It was badly executed, incompetent in detail and in conception, and should have been vetoed by anybody with political sense. Yet there remains some doubt as to what the President knew and when he knew it.[47] If Mitterrand had no hand in the sinking of *Rainbow Warrior*, then his own supporters should have brought the operation to him for approval. The demands made by him to know what had happened after details were published in the press show his capacities in a very bad light. Defence Minister Hernu's resignation prevented the affair from inflicting further damage, however.

Fabius's high rating in the polls was abruptly ended with a poor performance in a television debate with Jacques Chirac in October 1985. Mitterrand was not best pleased by the Prime Minister's performance and let him know it.[48] This preceded Fabius's clash with Parti socialiste First Secretary Jospin over who should lead the 1986 election campaign, as both claimed to be the natural leader. Mitterrand came down in Jospin's favour. This rivalry, resembling as it did one between the Blues and the Greens in Imperial Constantinople, concerned the place of the two possible young successors (youngish by the tolerant standards of politics). Then, at the end of November 1985, General Jaruzelski, the suppresser of Solidarity in Poland, paid a visit to Mitterrand. Fabius went out of his way to declare himself 'disturbed' by the President's action. Meeting Jaruzelski was, in public relations terms, a major misjudgement at a time when French opinion had swung strongly against the Communist bloc and its leaders, and its significance had to be downplayed by the Elysée. Mitterrand reportedly fulminated that it was Jaruzelski who, for saving his country from invasion, should have got the Nobel Prize, and not Walesa.[49]

Pre-election Manoeuvres

There followed a flurry of measures intended to set the framework before the 1986 general and regional elections. One of the most important of these was the marketization of the airwaves, breaking up the state monopoly in a way that would make impossible the conservative right's control of the media after 1986. In November 1985, without competitive tendering and ignoring the Audiovisual High Authority put in place to ensure balance, the first private channel (the fifth channel) was awarded to the Franco-Italian consortium of Jérôme Seydoux and Silvio Berlusconi, a decision that ensured a good airing for the Socialist viewpoint after the 1986 elections. Proportional representation was introduced in April 1985 for the 1986 general elections (and Rocard resigned in protest). It was a system of multi-member constituencies based on departments and closed party lists with *suppléants* and a 5 per cent threshold.[50] This system of proportional representation favoured the larger parties, dispensed with the need to form alliances on the second ballot (Communist hostility rendered this problematic in 1986) and potentially limited the conservatives' wins as well as the Socialists' losses. In the event, it also introduced the Front national into the Assembly. Mitterrand over the next few years emerged with the reputation of a master tactician even if, at the same time, he posed as the president 'above politics'. 'Cohabitation', in other words, although a tense situation and a political battle, was to be fought from the high ground.

7

'Cohabitation': 1986–1988

'Cohabitation' was not unexpected. That the President elected by one coalition would face an Assembly dominated by the opposition had always been an inherent possibility in the Fifth Republic. In 1978, when it looked as if the united left was poised to win the general election, President Giscard had envisaged a 'cohabitation' and warned the French voters that to return Mitterrand's left to power in the general election would lead to the ruin of France.[1] In 1978 Giscard's supporters on the conservative right won the general election, but as the Socialist-dominated Assembly came to its close in 1986 it was almost certain that Mitterrand, who preferred the term 'coexistence', would be a constitutional innovator in this respect. Edouard Balladur's article in *Le Monde* showed the evolution of the conservative right on this point.[2] For the RPR leader, Jacques Chirac, it would be the *pons asinorum*, and if he was prepared to 'cohabit' then the other conservative parties would follow. Mitterrand, reportedly, entered Attali's office the day *Le Monde* published Balladur's viewpoint with the comment: 'An interesting article, isn't it?'[3]

Despite appearances, Mitterrand's constitutional position was not greatly different from that of a president of the Third or Fourth Republics. If the backing of a supporting majority is removed from the President, he is constitutionally reduced in status to a 'figurehead' and power moves 'across the Seine' to the Prime Minister in the Matignon. Under articles 20 and 21, the Prime Minister would control the administration, decide the affairs of the nation and also exercise considerable patronage powers. The President of the Fifth Republic had very few constitutional powers and those that he did have were mainly marginal (to delay things), or for emergency (like article 16), or circumscribed by the need to concur with other institutions. Even in foreign policy the President had limited power. Under the constitution his powers were purely formal and the ability of the Elysée staff (which was very small) to deal with foreign policy matters was limited without assistance from the government. There was the control of the French nuclear force, but this was attributed to the President only by a decree (of dubious legality) that could be very easily reversed by a government majority.

In sum, the President, were the elections lost, would find his constitutional position weakened, although he would retain some of the accumulated prestige that the new presidency had established since 1958. In article 5 of the Fifth Republic's constitution, the President is described as an 'arbitrator' (or referee), who maintains the balance between institutions by calling in other powers (like the Constitutional Council or even the electorate) and that would be the legal basis for the President's role in 'cohabitation'. Other constitutional 'powers' sometimes adduced for the presidency were based on a misreading of a constitution that is in reality not so much ambiguous as over-ridden by the politics of the successive presidential majorities that transferred power to the President.

Mitterrand, on the other hand, implied that he had vast constitutional powers and a sphere that he did not intend to abandon, without specifying what these were. This was exemplified by his statement on several occasions that he did not intend to be a mere bystander but that he would 'respect the constitution'. But the President, even in a conflictual 'cohabitation', was not defenceless. In the first place he could not be made to resign. Mitterrand had been elected for seven years and as, in effect, the 'leader of the Opposition' after 1986, he would remain in office – indeed, in the most prominent of offices in the Republic. It would not be possible to ignore the President; anything he said would acquire a force of authority from the institution itself and could not be dismissed as 'just' the observations of another politician. A peculiarity of the constitution was that he would also chair Cabinet meetings and, although this conferred no substantial powers on the President, it would open possibilities for exploitation. It meant that Cabinet meetings under 'cohabitation' were perfunctory, with no debate – one lasted only 12 minutes – and glacial.[4] Mitterrand also controlled the election timetable.

But of course the institution of the presidency had become more authoritative over the first twenty-eight years of the Fifth Republic and the 'Bully Pulpit' was correspondingly more effective. Conservative politicians, whatever their view of Mitterrand, would not wish to see the presidency humbled and hoped to return it to its gaullist dimensions after the incumbent departed. Nobody had an interest in drawing attention to the Emperor's clothes. Because of the status of the presidency, Mitterrand could also stretch the constitutional powers, such as they were, to the limits. There would be battles during the 'cohabitation', but they would be fought on political and not constitutional lines, with the standard political weapons of persuasion and ruse and by raising issues that would appeal to the public: the court that would decide the outcome of the 1988 presidential election.

Of course, Mitterrand had one other important weapon to hand and that was the Parti socialiste. Coordination during the 'cohabitation' was very close, and he communicated on a daily basis with both the party and the deputies.[5] This party had been transformed into a vehicle for Mitterrand's own advancement over the 1970s and in 1986 it was in the hands of his supporters and still well organized. Lionel Jospin, the party's First Secretary, had disputed the control of the campaign with Fabius, but he was still a Mitterrand loyalist: the party could go into the offensive where Mitterrand, as a President supposedly 'above politics', could not.

One factor was proportional representation and another was the Constitutional Council, to which Robert Badinter was nominated as president. Over 1986–8 the Constitutional Council would play a small but significant role in changing or delaying the legislation of the conservative government. With Le Pen's Front national polling strongly, they would serve to divide the conservative right and limit the gains for the mainstream right. Conservatives would be faced with the dilemma of trying to capture the Front national's vote by toughening law and order and clamping down on immigration, while at the same time retaining the floating voters in the centre of the political spectrum. This required a high degree of political skill, but in addition the Front national would serve as a bogey to unite and mobilize the left in the absence of a 'project' to transform society and of the 'alternative' economic strategy. Whether intentional or not, the presence of the Front national in the Assembly was far from being inconvenient to the President during 'cohabitation'. Le Pen, and his supporters, had spent as much time opposing the gaullists (dismantlers of the Empire and sellers-out of Algeria) as the Socialists, and was in no mood to give assistance to a conservative right that cold-shouldered them.

Facing the Right

But the conservative right was riven by more cleavages than just what to do about the Front national. In the first place, Jacques Chirac, the leader of the biggest party, was not the favourite of conservative voters. That position was held by former Prime Minister Raymond Barre. Since leaving government in 1981, Barre's stature had grown with conservative voters. He had, in retrospect, been seen to be correct about the need for France to embrace a more modern political economy and for a deflationary 'austerity' policy to deal with the lack of competitivity, balance of payments difficulties and inflation. It was Barre rather than Giscard who reaped the benefits of this retrospective justification of the – at the time – much disliked economic policy of the 1970s. But Barre belonged to the junior part of the coalition, the weak and internally divided UDF, which was more of an electoral cartel of local notables than a mass conservative party and it could not run a presidential campaign. Worse for Barre was that the UDF contained many different outlooks, ranging from the free market evangelists of the Parti républicain to the more socially minded Christian Democrats. Some of the UDF supported Chirac, and Barre's main support came from the Christian Democrats, while the 'young Turks' of the Parti républicain looked on Jacques Chirac with greater favour. All the same, the polls indicated that, were a presidential election to be held in 1986, Barre would be the choice of the conservative voters and not Chirac.

Jacques Chirac, then 54, needed a spell in government at the head of the conservative coalition to confirm his presidential stature and his position as the leading candidate of the right. Chirac did not want a confrontation with Mitterrand, and that gave the President the upper hand. Chirac had been an ambitious politician in Prime Minister Pompidou's office in 1962 and rose through the ranks under Pompidou's patronage, becoming a minister in 1967. He had been Minister of Agriculture (vital to the rural Corrèze) in 1972–4. He had been mayor of Paris since 1977 and the deputy for Ussel in the Corrèze since 1967, when he had wrested the constituency from the left. As Interior Minister in 1974, he organized support for Giscard in the presidential elections, sinking his own party's candidate in the process, and had been made Prime Minister by Giscard at the youthful age of 42. His time at the Matignon had been used to reorganize the gaullist party, which he transformed into his own instrument, but he resigned after two years in a dispute over policy and power with President Giscard.

Chirac's public image was not of a statesman but of a very ambitious politician and one who had previously resigned as Premier. He thus needed 'cohabitation' to work, but for its benefits to redound to him in an unambiguous manner, promoting him beyond both Barre and Mitterrand in the polls. Barre, on the other hand, could not lead the conservative coalition and would have had to take a subordinate position in Chirac's government. He announced that he would not serve in a 'cohabitation' government and preserved an ability to speak out as well as an independence that would enable him to benefit from the government's mistakes.

Born in 1924 on the island of La Réunion, Raymond Barre had a distinguished academic career as a professor of economics. His contributions to public life tended to be technical – he had been a European Commissioner before he was called to government by President Giscard as Minister for Trade in January 1976. He was and had been closely associated with gaullist circles and had advised de Gaulle on certain economic matters. He was appointed to the European Commission by de Gaulle and was Economic Affairs Commissioner from 1967 to 1972, after which he returned to his academic post and took a seat on the board of the Bank of France. Barre was not a party politician and his economic expertise made him Giscard's choice as Premier in 1976 when Chirac resigned. Barre's managerial capacities were never in doubt, but his political experience was limited. However, as with other politicians, his political abilities grew rapidly when he was in office, but he was charged with the unpopular deflationary policy and market reforms of the late 1970s. In 1978 and 1981 he had been elected as a deputy for Lyons. He started a campaign to become president in the 1980s when his popularity as a conservative politician rose spectacularly.

Jacques Chirac's coalition had put together a free market platform promoting neo-'Reaganite' economics with a 'tough on crime' stance to appeal to the Front national's voters. It was confidently expected that implementation of this platform would put 'clear blue water' between the conservatives and the outgoing Socialists, but it had to work rapidly to launch the 1988 election campaign. To some extent the conservative right had become over-confident, partly because the Socialists' abandonment of their own programme in 1982–3 had left them floundering in the polls and partly because the 'Reaganite' enthusiasts had got carried away. The new platform was advertised as solving the old problems of over-centralization and state-dominated society. This was a tall order for a short two years, during which Chirac was not going to be given a free run by either the centrist challenger or the President. Chirac needed time he did not have for his ambitious programme to work and for it to bear fruit that the electorate would recognize, and haste was one of his main problems.

An Active Presidency

Mitterrand was not inactive. He had started campaigning early to be able, in keeping with the more dignified presidential function, to retreat from the front line when the official electoral campaign started. There were press conferences in November 1985 and January 1986 rallying voters on the left to the defence of the government and intended to set out the Socialists' record and bolster their reviving popularity. There was also a TV interview with Yves Mourousi that was set in a discursive style and showed the President as alive to the problems of society but looking with confidence to the future. In the main, Mitterrand revived the left/right division and put the accent on the social gains of the Socialists' five years, while giving the impression that the conservatives would call these into question. However, this was no crude attack on the 'bourgeois' right but a carefully crafted campaign placing the emphasis on consensus and social solidarity against an impetuous and 'revolutionary' right. These were themes that would enable Mitterrand to claim a centrist position later and to place himself in the immediate frontline as the focus of France's community, guardian of the national interest. His standing in the polls rose steadily from the autumn of 1985 and on the eve of the elections it reached 50 per cent for the first time since 1982.[6]

This in essence was Chirac's problem. He wanted to be President, but there already was a President, and Mitterrand was far from being unpopular so a crude ousting was not possible. Mitterrand had decided to play the presidential role to the full, floating free of partisan attachments and representing the best interest of the country. For this reason he decided to maintain an ambiguity about whether or not he would run for a second term. By keeping his intentions in the dark, by allowing, even encouraging, Rocard to prepare for the candidacy in 1988, and questioning close collaborators and visitors about whether he should run, he guarded his position as a non-candidate, a President of all the people, until the last possible moment. It was a thespian performance of diverting skill, encouraging supporters to act 'as if' he was going to run in 1988 (and hence organizing and financing a campaign) while not relinquishing the presidential ground.

Vigorous campaigning and a series of optimistic figures announcing a fall in unemployment and inflation, and a good balance of payments as well as an increased purchasing power, meant that the 1986 election results were far from being the disaster that was predicted for the Socialist Party. On 16 March the Socialists polled 32.1 per cent (8.8 million votes) and took 216 seats (in an enlarged Assembly of 577). Although the Communist Party's vote fell to 9.7 per cent (2.7 million votes) it still had 35 deputies and an Assembly group. Moreover, the left, with 44 per cent, and without the ecologists' 1.2 per cent, had a slight edge over the conservative right. But if the object of the change in electoral law had been to prevent the conservative right from winning a majority or force them to deal with the Front national, it had failed. The leaderships of the two formations (UDF and RPR) had achieved a harmonious distribution of candidacies, avoiding competition in damaging places and winning an absolute majority of three seats. Front national candidates had polled 9.8 per cent (2.7 million votes) and won 35 seats, but the UDF and RPR (and 10 independents) combined had polled 43.1 per cent (11.8 million votes) and held 291 seats. In the Fifth Republic, 3 seats gave a majority that would enable the new conservative government to rule without undue difficulty in the Assembly.

Rumours circulated about the likelihood of Chaban Delmas, an old associate of Mitterrand's, being nominated Prime Minister, but, like Fourth or Third Republic presidents faced by a determined majority such as the Popular Front or the Cartel des gauches, there was little choice, although Mitterrand liked to imply that there was.[7] He nominated Jacques Chirac as Prime Minister, but having done so he stepped back to make clear the separation between the President and Prime Minister. According to Attali, Mitterrand's special councillor, the President told Chirac that he would let him govern.[8] Any mistakes or unpopular decisions made by the government would be the government's own and not a result of presidential action or imposition. On 18 March, Jacques Chirac, the leader of the largest party in the new Assembly, was asked to form a government.

The 'Stand-off'

'Cohabitation' started a two-year battle between President and Prime Minister. However, it was confined within a fairly restricted framework because an open clash at the summit of the state over significant matters would not be tolerated by the French public, who expected their politicians to cooperate. There were therefore few open confrontations and the public aspect was formal and polite, as were private meetings – indeed they were sometimes even friendly. There was little public slanging although there were a few occasions when ministers did not listen to Mitterrand, and on one occasion the President let his view of Chirac out to the press. But there were public policy disagreements at crucial points and these marked the two years even though they were exceptional in tone.

On the composition of the government itself much has been said. Chirac had his own internal 'cohabitation' to deal with, bringing the various components and personalities of the conservative right into the same team. But between Mitterrand and the Prime Minister the principal difficulties were foreign and defence affairs. Here Jacques Chirac needed to build up his presidential stature and world diplomacy was the most important area of policy in which to do that. Carving out potential presidential status required, in most candidates' view, a presence on the international stage but not as a mere factotum. Foreign and defence affairs would see a vigorous clash between Mitterrand and Jacques Chirac, although the Prime Minister held the effective power.

Mitterrand, however, was to use the traditional presidential prerogatives to advise, to encourage and to warn to full effect, using his understanding of the public mood to wrong-foot the government. At various times he criticized most of the policies of the government, but he was able to amplify a disagreement on the changes to the nationality laws and to the repatriation of immigrants in a manner that appealed to the younger voters. A presidential statement could put something on the agenda and set the terms of debate as, for example, Mitterrand did when he criticized the programme of prison privatization started by the Minister of Justice.[9] At the end of 1986, during the general strike in the public sector, Mitterrand had a meeting with striking railway workers. Nothing was actually said, but, while the government was under siege, this gesture to its opponents could hardly have been more obvious.

Before becoming president, Mitterrand had frequently pointed out that the idea of the presidential 'reserved domain' of defence and foreign policy was not constitutional and was incoherent. But he needed to protect this 'reserved domain', even though he had often repudiated it, and to retain his public priority in it. For this reason he defended the presidential pre-eminence in defence and foreign policy in Le Point.[10] As Head of State, Mitterrand could hardly be excluded from decisions about the choice of Defence and Foreign Ministers but this was a delicate issue and it suited both President and Prime Minister to allow it to be thought that the candidatures of Lecanuet (as Foreign Minister) and Léotard (as Defence Minister) had been vetoed by the Elysée. Eventually a career diplomat, then Ambassador in Moscow, the gaullist Jean-Bernard Raimond went to the Quai d'Orsay, while the rumbustuous André Giraud became Defence Minister. This was not the fruit of a last-minute search: Raimond had been sounded out six months earlier by Balladur (with whom he had worked previously on Pompidou's staff). Mitterrand conceded that Jacques Chirac would accompany him to G8 and European summits, but warned the Premier that not all decrees would be automatically signed. Chirac was closely supported by a combative Minister of the Interior, Charles Pasqua, by Finance Minister Balladur (who was Chirac's 'prime minister') and by his supporter Alain Juppé (Chirac's Chirac). Balladur was expected to work the economic transformation and Pasqua was to transform law and order, two key areas whose success would propel Chirac into the Elysée.

Mitterrand had prepared for 'cohabitation' and for the possibility that he might be cut off from information by ensuring that the Elysée had its outposts in different ministries and kept him informed of developments. He also depended on informal sources of information.[11] In fact, after Chirac's arrival at the Matignon, diplomatic telegrams, messages and top secret foreign briefings were no longer passed on to the Elysée, and there was no constitutional obligation to do so.[12] But Mitterrand had 'friends' in place who were able to keep him informed. In addition, he had a small team of experienced and reliable staff at the Elysée. These included Attali, Bianco, Colliard, Bredin, Védrine, Royal, Salzmann, Glavany, Charasse and others. European affairs were under the remit of the Secrétariat général du comité interministériel and that was led by the President's Europeanist Elizabeth Guigou, an appointment that ensured regular information as well as knowledge of the government's own deliberations on Europe.[13] This technical sounding committee was in reality the key to European developments and to European meetings, and the conservative right was slow to recognize its importance – just as they were to realize that the summits had been prepared and practically negotiated before they came to power and little could be done to undo them.

The Crucial Test

In April 1986 came the first test of 'cohabitation'. On the 12th the USA asked for permission for American bombers to overfly France to bomb Gaddafi's headquarters in Libya. This was refused by both Chirac and Mitterrand and for much the same reason: that it would only serve to consolidate support behind Gaddafi.[14] Although much pressurized, Mitterrand did not change his view and nor did Chirac, and a communiqué was issued by the Quai d'Orsay in agreement with the Elysée. But the difficulty came from Chirac's attempt to take the credit for a decision generally applauded by French public opinion by declaring on television that he had 'taken the decision'. This statement that a key foreign policy decision had been taken by the Prime Minister alone enraged the President, who arranged for a series of counter explanations to be made in the press (notably Le Monde) to defend his position.[15] Chirac's supporters did not, of course, allow this to pass without riposte and an infernal dialectic took place.

A struggle for the pre-eminent place in The diplomacy of the Republic continued over the G8 summit meeting due in Tokyo in May and to be followed by the European summit in The Hague in June. It was unfortunate for Chirac that the Tokyo summit was the first, for the Japanese, sticklers for protocol, would ensure the prominence of the President. Mitterrand had no intention of backing down from his decision to attend, even though Chirac, contrary to the usages of the Fifth Republic, had also decided to go. They therefore both went, with the result that the President was given priority by their meticulous hosts and also that either the Finance Minister or the Foreign Minister would not attend. Because Chirac would not be included in the opening dinner, he was due to arrive on the following day and he stayed away from meetings where France was represented by the head of its delegation. A discussion about international terrorism that had emerged onto the agenda was more or less concluded before the Prime Minister's arrival. But the Foreign Minster, Raimond, who had also been kept in the dark, saved face when he obtained, from Mitterrand, the concession that decisions would not be made public until Chirac had seen them.[16] For the final press conference, Mitterrand gave the views of the French delegation, while the Prime Minister sat apart, below the stand, thus reinforcing – pictorially – the President's pre-eminence. Because the summit had been prepared in advance, and because little was changed while it was under way, it was essentially a battle for status between Chirac and Mitterrand, which Mitterrand won.

European conferences were more relaxed, but the Hague proved to be another battle for status between Mitterrand and Chirac, particularly as the technical nature of the subject and the detailed work conducted by the government made them prime ministerial material. European summits were led by Prime Ministers and Foreign Ministers, with the exception of France which sent the Head of State and Foreign Minster. Europe was willing to accept a French delegation of three: President, Prime Minister and Foreign Minister, but Mitterrand would have none of it. He brusquely informed Raimond that Chirac should sort out who, between the Premier or Foreign Minister, was going.[17] Franco-German relations also continued through the Elysée, even though the Prime Minister tried to displace the President and Chancellor Kohl was frequently put in a difficult position between the two. There were further confrontations over protocol, and attempts to play off one against the other, but after these two meetings in Tokyo and the Hague the conduct of foreign delegations was settled to Mitterrand's advantage.

Foreign Policy

On the substance of foreign and defence policy there were similar disagreements, but more often than not these were behind closed doors. Jacques Chirac had tended towards Euroscepticism and the conservative right had opposed the 'Southern enlargement' of Europe to included Spain and Portugal. They were also against the system of milk quotas, and criticized the Single Act. On these matters the Prime Minister abandoned his initial hostility. However, at the Madrid summit of March 1987 Chirac attacked the European enlargement agreed by the Socialists for the damage it had done to French interests (agricultural) and added, for good measure, that the prosecution of Basque terrorists had been insufficiently vigorous. Mitterrand's response was immediate and magisterial. Jacques Chirac was rebuked for opening a dispute on foreign territory and for reneging on France's commitments.

In defence matters, the President confronted a minister who was more Atlanticist than the, by now gaullist, stance of Mitterrand's Socialists. These positions were set out in somewhat academic speeches to specialist audiences, but they ran through the differences between Mitterrand and the government throughout the 'cohabitation', although on essentials Chirac was manoeuvred into backing down. Mitterrand artfully played on Chirac's weakness on this issue, above all others, because his position had departed from gaullist orthodoxy, because he could not afford for 'cohabitation' to fail and because the public would not understand (he thought) an open dispute on matters within the President's supposedly 'reserved domain'.

On 12 September 1986 Mitterrand laid out his powers – as he saw them – as head of the armed forces and the gaullist doctrine on defence at the Institut des hautes études de défense nationale (IHEDN) and supplemented this in a speech at a parachute regiment headquarters in southern France a month later. He placed himself in the mainstream of the gaullist tradition on defence policy and took the high ground of orthodoxy against a Prime Minister and Defence Minister disposed to innovate on this. André Giraud, in particular, was keen to shift French defence policy in a more Atlanticist direction, and that was known from the outset. This position as guardian of the conservative orthodoxy against the conservatives themselves enabled Mitterrand to win the 'cohabitation' battle over defence.

Defence Policy

One dispute, abstruse in its appeal to nuclear theology, was over the modernization of France's nuclear forces: should priority go to the undetectable submarine force as the President insisted, or to the terrestrial missiles? Missiles on the plateau d'Albion, as Giraud noted, were vulnerable and he proposed instead to create a mobile force ('SX') that would travel around France undetected and would thus be invulnerable to first strike.[18]

Accordingly, Giraud proposed to cut the budget for modernizing submarine missiles and use the savings to create a mobile missile force – and this was seconded by Jacques Chirac. Given the determination of the government, the President accepted the new missiles but remained adamant that the submarine systems had also to be modernized, and he was ready to bring the dispute out into the open. This was a prospect that Chirac could not entertain and he backed down and asked Giraud to do likewise. Although Giraud was reluctant to cede the point, he was not supported by Chirac who, at the time, could not afford a squabble on this particular (remote) issue.

But there was a further clash between Mitterrand and Giraud before the Defence Minister gave up attempts to assert his views. This time the problem was the French view of the United States' doctrine of 'flexible response' to threats in Europe. It was the doctrine that replaced the massive retaliation of the 1950s. Flexible response, as elaborated by J. F. Kennedy's Secretary of State McNamara, replaced the idea that thermonuclear warfare should be unleashed when deterrence failed with the idea that there could be limited exchanges – some nuclear – before the choice between apocalypse or capitulation. This doctrine was never accepted by the French, but Chirac, in his speech to the IHEDN on 12 September 1986, envisaged the use of French missiles as part of a flexible response. This distinction between tactical and strategic arms was at serious odds with French orthodoxy, as many gaullists pointed out, and, of course, contradicted the President.

Mitterrand affected to ignore the change in the government's position, but took care to recall the gaullist orthodoxy. However, André Giraud returned to the idea of flexible response in a discussion of disarmament in Europe.[19] Mitterrand made it clear to Chirac that this was unacceptable and Chirac concurred. Giraud's ideas were similar to those of many centrists and to those influenced by the Christian Democrat persuasion of the 1950s, and he was supported by UDF deputies as well as by Raymond Barre. It was a difficult situation for the Prime Minister to manage and it widened a split in his increasingly fragile coalition. Mitterrand, no doubt seeing this crack, decided to reiterate the orthodox French doctrine dismissing flexible response, as well as confirming the French one of 'dissuasion'. Giraud backed down.[20]

On the withdrawal of all nuclear weapons from Europe, the so-called 'zero option', which became serious after the Reykjavik meeting between Reagan and Gorbachev of October 1986, there was another disagreement. Many allied leaders were worried by what might have been a near abandonment of Europe by America, and this included Chirac, Giraud and Raimond, but not Mitterrand. When the Foreign Ministry issued a statement warning of the dangers of a denuclearization of Europe, this displeased the President. Mitterrand wanted France to support the Gorbachev proposals and to get a European view on the issue and he persuaded the Prime Minister to silence critics for the time being in the interests of unity, leaving Giraud alone to express the 'Atlanticist' viewpoint with his condemnation of a 'European Munich'. This point resurfaced again when another proposal from Gorbachev caught the Europeans unprepared and Chirac warned of the dangers of a denuclearization of Europe. Mitterrand had no such qualms, and once again the neo-gaullist Prime Minister backed down, reluctant to challenge the President's championing of gaullist nuclear doctrine, leaving Giraud impotent. This set Giraud and Chirac at odds to some extent, despite the Prime Minister's continual suspicion of disarmament initiatives that seemed to him to detach the USA from Europe. A last public display of this difference came over the modernization of the Lance missile system, which the Premier and his defence and foreign policy ministers approved and Mitterrand did not. This time, two months before the elections of 1988, Chirac chose to make his disapproval known only by letter and Mitterrand successfully called his bluff by threatening a public debate.[21]

Foreign Affairs

Jacques Chirac's foray into Middle East politics in August 1986 also ran up against Mitterrand's new gaullist stance. Mitterrand had supported Arafat's desire to see a Palestinian state created, but Chirac dismissed this idea out of hand and added that the PLO was of doubtful legitimacy in any case. These views, given to an Israeli newspaper, were in turn repudiated by Mitterrand, who announced that French policy had not changed. Chirac had also disclaimed his part in supplying the nuclear reactor to Iraq that the Israelis had bombed, and situated the responsibility with Giscard d'Estaing. This subject, at Mitterrand's behest, was raised by the Assembly's Chair of the Foreign Relations Committee and Chirac was rebuked by the former President for his attempt to rewrite history.[22]

But Chirac's démarche in the Middle East was different from that of the Socialists because he tried to conciliate Iran while remaining a supporter of its enemy Iraq. One major change was the attempt to normalize relations with Iran (seven French hostages in the Lebanon might then be released with Iranian intervention). There was a degree of success, including the visit of the Iranian deputy Prime Minister in May 1986, but he came demanding the satisfactory conclusion of the financial 'Eurodif affair' and the cessation of opposition activity in France. These problems began to be resolved by diplomats and a month later two hostages were released in what was assumed to be a gesture by Iran. However, at the same time the Interior Minister Pasqua was also using his own networks to get the hostages released.

In October, when the President was in Indonesia, there was a wave of terrorist attacks across France linked to the Iranian revolutionary regime and diplomatic normalization was then abandoned in favour of using Pasqua's network. Wahid Gordji, one of the people thought responsible for the September explosions, took refuge in the Iranian Embassy. The Elysée was informed neither of the accusations, nor of the proof against Gordji, nor of the negotiations. Because he was kept uninformed, Mitterrand made mistakes in public statements and at one point was sending his own agents to discover what was happening. He had constantly refused to allow an exchange of terrorists in France for embassy personnel in Tehran who had been taken hostage, but he was presented with the exchange of Gordji for French hostages in Iran as a fait accompli. In July 1987 France broke off diplomatic relations with Iran, but Iran, keen to return to respectability, exchanged the hostages in return for Gordji, who was bundled out of the country without being interrogated. However, negotiations for the return of the remaining hostages continued, with the Iranians aware that Chirac was increasingly demanding their return in time for the presidential elections. There was more than a suspicion that Chirac's policy in the Middle East was shifted to get the hostages back and it enabled Mitterrand to hint that something had been conceded.

There was also the serious accusation made in Le Matin in January 1987 that Jacques Chirac had intervened with Iran in the negotiations to free hostages, effectively ensuring that they would not return home before the 1986 elections. Le Matin, faced with Chirac's denial, published the diplomatic telegram from the Ambassador in Teheran and the affirmation by the Foreign Minister in 1986, Dumas, that the negotiations had been expected to be concluded before the elections. This report was based on material that must have been sanctioned by Mitterrand and the newspaper repeated its allegations with further evidence on 5 February, but none of it was conclusive. This affair was never resolved, but the accusation was astonishing and, of course, hotly denied. Chirac's supporters continually maintained that it was false, and some saw in it an attempt by Iran to poison the French political waters (accusations that were repeated by the

Speaker of the Iranian parliament, Rafsanjani), but numerous top Socialists continued nevertheless to make the allegations.[23]

'Affairs'

Scandals were part of the weaponry of the two sides during 'cohabitation'.
First, through the leaking of Defence Minister André Giraud's investiga
tion, came the revelation of the sale of shells to Iran – then at war with
Iraq – by the armaments company Luchaire. A leak of the investigation
report went to the conservative newspaper *Le Figaro*. It was alleged that
sales of weapons to Iran were embargoed, but these had been authorized
by Mitterrand's Minister of Defence Hernu and they had enriched politicians and, it was alleged, the Socialist Party. Mitterrand denied knowledge
of the arms traffic, but, in keeping with Chirac's new policy, arms sales to
Iran were restarted in July 1987, the scandal fizzled out and charges were
discreetly dropped in 1989.

More serious was the 'Carrefour du développement' affair, so-called
after the name of a company set up in 1983 to train African managers. This
company's treasurer was Yves Chalier, who was head of the private office
of Minister for Cooperation Christian Nucci. An inquiry by the new Minister for Cooperation revealed some rather gamey accounts. Money from
the firm had been used to subsidize a Franco-African summit in 1984 and
also to fund Nucci's election campaign as well as for personal expenses. A
dossier of the accounts was handed over to Interior Minister Pasqua implicating the Socialist Party in the siphoning of money from it (information
was drip-fed to *Le Figaro* throughout 1986). Meanwhile, Chalier had fled to
Latin America, from where he continued to denounce his former associates. His departure had been made possible with a 'true-false' passport
provided by the Interior Ministry, and he alleged that Pasqua had been
manipulating from behind the scenes. Allegations and counter allegations
muddied the waters and the Minister of the Interior refused to answer
questions, citing 'defence secret', but the 'Mitterrand system' was again
severely damaged.

Returning fire from Mitterrand was aimed at the Minister of Justice
Albin Chalandon and proved to be an effective counter even though it had
none of the dimensions of the Carrefour scandal. This time it came from
Le Monde, which revealed that Chalandon had an account with the bank-
rupt jeweller Chaumet. Jacques and Pierre Chaumet had been charged
with bankruptcy and fraud, and even though it was private – not public –
money, Chalendon was, as Minister of Justice, involved as an official and a

witness.[24] As an affair, it lacked the punch of the Luchaire or Carrefour scandals and was not as lavish, but as a diversion from the other affairs it did its job.

Privatization

There were, however, clashes on other matters, and the first of these was about privatization. Privatization was the flagship of the new government as much for what it symbolized as for its real impact on the economy, and it was one of the few deliberately public confrontations of the 'cohabitation'. In its determination to get its programme through, the government wanted to use decrees to privatize 42 banks and 13 insurance companies in the first tranche. An enabling law had been rapidly drawn up and was passed by the parliament by 2 July after a vote of no confidence had been defeated, and Chirac hoped to use the decrees to implement it. How he could have believed that decrees could have been used without impediment is a puzzle, given Mitterrand's warning, but possibly he was misled by the strict legal reading that led him to believe that the President could not refuse to sign.[25]

On Bastille Day 1986, using the prerogative of the presidential address, Mitterrand announced that he would not sign the decrees implementing these privatization laws. (Mitterrand argued that the nationalizations of the Liberation were the work of the CNR and hence part of the national heritage, although those of 1982 were not.)[26] As reasons, Mitterrand gave the need for such measures to go through parliament and that French interests were insufficiently protected by the process the government had engaged. This refusal dramatized the President's situation and his ability to act, even though he was walled up in the Elysée by hostile forces. It established his authority and reminded people that Mitterrand was not part of the government and was opposed to its flagship measure. But, although public opinion was broadly sceptical of the privatizations, Mitterrand was taking a risk: the refusal came with the price of public disapproval of a clash at the summit of the state. No compromise was possible and, at the Cabinet meeting of 16 July, Jacques Chirac accepted the need to resubmit the text to parliament for approval. Chirac had backed down to avoid a confrontation and Mitterrand had gained in authority as a result. What was more important was that the passing of its key measure had become a setback for the government. Chirac's majority in the parliament ensured speedy passage of the bill and it made no substantial difference to the timetable, but the rebuff inflicted by the President transformed the symbolic meaning of the measures. Mitterrand was able to portray the privatizations as an Ali Baba's Cave open to the elite. Later in October 1987 the pace of privatization had to slow down because of the stock market crash, but already the edge had been taken off the government's authority.

New Caledonia

New Caledonia, which became an explosive problem during the elections of 1988, was an immediate point of discord. This dossier had been handed to Bernard Pons, a Chirac supporter who was made Minister for Overseas France, and who had been charged to put into effect the election promise to impose order on the island. Conservatives started with the intention of changing many of the institutions the Socialist Pisani Commission had set up; they stopped the movement that could lead to independence and slowed down the land reforms – all to the pleasure of the neo-gaullist movement and the settlers, but opposed by the Kanaks. Mitterrand used the Cabinet meeting to point out the dangers of the course on which they were engaged, but his objections were rejected by Pons in a long address to the President in front of his colleagues.[27] Chirac's majority voted for the changes in New Caledonia. Violence resumed on the island in November, resulting in three deaths, and the situation rapidly worsened as a 'dialogue of the deaf' took place between the government and the Kanaks. This deteriorating situation had its dénouement during the election campaign in 1988, but Mitterrand's view that the 'Pisani plan' should be implemented was invariant.

University Reform

Mitterrand knew how to draw strength from his opponents' blunders and how to extend his presidential stature in the face of the government's difficulties. It was not Mitterrand's presence but Jacques Chirac's impetuousness that led to a series of mistakes in the first year, the most damaging of which was university reform. Chirac's government had made it a badge of honour to repeal the university legislation drafted by the Socialist Education Minister Alain Savary in January 1984. This task fell to the junior minister Alain Devaquet who, like Savary, found himself in charge of an issue on which the more extreme views outbid the moderates. Devaquet's law would have decentralized admissions (introducing selection and what started the problem in 1968) and increased fees. It slipped unnoticed onto the agenda in the summer of 1986, when attention was turned to the dispute over privatization and was barely registered in the universities, although small groups were alerted. It looked as if the reforms might succeed; they had passed the Senate and they were scheduled to go before the Assembly in December.

But student opposition had been steadily building up and it was led by students who had links with the Socialist Party (Dray and Thomas). Mitterrand was kept informed by liaising with politicians like Jack Lang.[28] On 22 November Mitterrand gave a speech in Auxerre commemorating the centenary of Paul Bert, a Third Republic educationalist and politician, at which he gave a wink and a nod to the protestors. On the same day there was a massive demonstration against the law in Paris and some suggested changes came from the government. However, tension mounted, demonstrations continued, universities went on strike, calls were made for the law to be scrapped and the proposed changes to the code of nationality to abolish the right to citizenship of anybody born on French soil were condemned. There followed various mishandlings of relations with the students and further demonstrations in Paris and the provinces.

Then, on 5 December, a second-generation immigrant student was killed in a police charge and opinion in the conservative ranks began to turn definitively against the Devaquet law. Mitterrand visited the bereaved family three days later. Jacques Chirac, meanwhile, returned hastily from a European summit in London and dropped the bill along with the proposed nationality code and the controversial plan to privatize prisons. Mitterrand's touch was to have indicated to the student protestors that he 'felt their pain' without presenting himself as the opposition's politician. He also managed to imply that he had brought about the scrapping of the Devaquet laws and then stepped in to 'congratulate' the government on having the grace to withdraw the bill. Although the nationality code was stalled, it was not dropped, but opposition to it in the new year led to Chirac prudently setting up a committee in March to examine it, thus allowing sufficient time for it to be removed from the agenda. Devaquet became the scapegoat for the failure of the university proposals, although Chirac suffered a severe blow to his prestige on the right and in public opinion. This was probably the point at which Chirac's presidential bid failed.

Chirac's ascendancy over his coalition was badly undercut by the student protests and the various climb downs and splits shown in the Cabinet. François Léotard, the Minister of Culture, felt particularly aggrieved and criticized his Prime Minister in an outspoken manner, which, had Chirac been in a position of strength, would have led to his dismissal. In New Caledonia the situation had become much worse. The violence had restarted in November 1987 and Mitterrand had condemned, by implication, the government as well as the separatists. A referendum on independence had been decided for September 1987 but, as the result would be known in advance given the balance of forces, it solved nothing and provoked the Kanaks. Chirac's supporters (RCPR) had gained the upper hand on the island and the army had become more active in its attempt to impose a solution on the Kanaks. Then, on 22 February, nine policemen were taken hostage by separatists.

Towards a Second Term

Jacques Chirac had run out of time. Nothing, not even spectacular government coups (of which there were a few) could retrieve the situation for the Prime Minister who had more or less lost the presidential elections. However, he still needed to set himself up as the principal conservative politician if he was to have a future after a lost election, and that made the situation particularly tense. Mitterrand, who was remarkably placed, could afford to be serene but could not relax. He too had to look beyond the immediate elections to the next septennate, in which he would have to retain his authority. He had to avoid the slippage of that authority to other personalities in his own camp and to retain the loyalty of his coalition despite the ending of his presidential term. Though simple, the answer to these problems was not easy and would be worked out over the septennate starting with the presidential elections.

The Second Term: 1988–1992

At the beginning of 1988 Mitterrand, although not declared a candidate, was predicted by the polls to be the winner on the second ballot by a good margin of 3 or 5 per cent. In 1981, he had said on several occasions that the septennate should be non-renewable.[1] While Mitterrand remained ambiguous about his intentions to run as a candidate in 1988, Jacques Chirac and Raymond Barre had no such reticence. Jacques Chirac's RPR machine was galvanized by Chirac's announcement on 16 January and his ratings immediately shot up past Barre's. On 8 February Barre announced his candidacy, but lack of money and of party backing meant that his campaign flagged and never took wing. Chirac, moving onto the Front national's territory, declared that, while reproving xenophobia and racism, he 'understood' the reactions of people to immigrants. This brought the left out in force and helped mobilize Mitterrand's voters.

Although Mitterrand's hesitation waltz continued despite personal tragedy (the loss of a grandson), it is likely that he believed himself cured of cancer.[2] He continued to ask coquettishly of visitors and acquaintances (though not his doctors, who would have given a definite 'no') whether he should stand.[3] Mitterrand's declaration came on 22 March in a TV interview, only a week before Easter and the public holiday, with the assertion that he wanted a 'united France' and not one 'taken over by intolerant spirits' or run by 'clans and bands'. It implied a short, carefully crafted campaign to the benefit of the ageing president.

The 1988 Campaign

Mitterrand's 20,000-word manifesto, his *Lettre à tous les français*, was published on 7 April. It was long and rambling and gave little away on future intentions and little was concrete on policy, although it included the RMI, but two million copies were printed and it was published in two Parisian and twenty-three regional dailies. Its tone was 'father of the nation' presidential; it eschewed doctrine, and there were no verbal pyrotechnics;

and the end to nationalization and privatization ('ni-ni') was announced though without replacing belief in the virtues of active state intervention in industry and business with anything else. His aide Attali thought he had lost all faith in the ability of the government to transform the country.[4] Mitterrand laid out his vision of foreign policy and defence (with a sideswipe at his Prime Minister) and set out the priorities as European unity, education and research. This, as with the campaigns of 1965, 1974 and 1981, replaced the party's manifesto voted at its Lille Congress in April 1987.

There then followed a planned rather than a vigorous campaign of four meetings, two radio broadcasts and the face-to-face debate between rounds. Mitterrand's first meeting at Rennes was staged on a podium with a tricolour flag gently agitated by a wind machine; it portrayed the message of unity and consensus and was pitched to appeal to the centre and floating vote that were both vital for the second round, not always to the pleasure of the activists. He went out of his way to praise 'some excellent people' (they were unnamed) in the conservative government, but prudently noted that France would not be unified if inequality and injustice were allowed to flourish. He did find issues to which the centre could rally, such as Europe, immigration, nationality and New Caledonia, and the intensity of rivalry on the conservative right moved some politicians closer to the President than to Chirac. It was a feature of this campaign that the work of trying to enthuse his own electorate was undertaken by the PS itself, and thus he had the luxury of trying to woo centrist voters on the first round and the Socialist Party was kept in the background.

Mitterrand's move to the centre may have been strategically astute, but on the left it was a demobilizing factor (this had been recognized late in the campaign). This explains why, although well ahead and a certain winner, the first-round votes were a disappointment. He had been expecting to poll over 35 per cent but on the first ballot on 24 April he fell slightly short of that ideal with 34 per cent.[5] Raymond Barre had polled 16.5 per cent, Chirac 19.96 per cent, Le Pen 14.5 per cent, and the Communists had polled only 6.8 per cent. Le Pen's high poll was the shock of the first round, but Chirac could only tap this mass of right-wing support at the expense of losing the centrists. This poor showing by the Communist Party deprived Mitterrand of the reservoir of votes needed for the second round and made the centre voters the more vital to his success, but he did not need to make any concessions to the Communist Party in order to gain that bloc of votes.

Mitterrand's victory in the second ballot on 8 May was anything but certain. There was still the debate between ballots on 28 April in which the

President would confront his own Prime Minister. Watched by 30 million people, Mitterrand courteously called his opponent 'Monsieur le Premier Ministre', underlining the relative status of the two. There was an exchange of accusations about the freeing of terrorists, but the main contention was about the conduct of the government faced by Iranian terrorism. But this quickly escalated when Mitterrand brought up a subject from a confidential meeting. Chirac was accused by Mitterrand of freeing the Iranian Wahid Gordji despite a substantial dossier of evidence implicating him as the author of the attacks in Paris at the end of 1986. Chirac was taken aback. Behind his eyes, panic swirled like paisley. He reposted that the meeting had been confidential and demanded whether Mitterrand could 'look him in the eyes' and state that he had ever said that they had proof of Gordji's complicity in the attacks. Mitterrand replied that he did, but the revelation of the confidential meeting was an error. Mitterrand was in such a dominant position in the polls that the debate probably had little influence on the final vote.[6] On 1 May, Le Pen said the choice was between 'le pire et le mal' ('the worst and the bad'), but not without denouncing both candidates.

But the Prime Minister was not finished and things happened rapidly in the last week of campaigning. On 4 May, Mitterrand learned from President Assad of Syria that the last three French hostages in the Lebanon had been released. What, Mitterrand is reported to have asked, did they pay to Iran to obtain that?[7] This looked too much like an electoral ploy by Chirac to be really usable in the elections, as Mitterrand noted. New Caledonia, where the policemen (and a local judge) had been taken hostage, now had a menacing aspect. A negotiated settlement was thought possible by many of those involved, though not by Chirac's representative. On 5 May, Chirac ordered the kidnappers to be stormed by troops and in this action two soldiers and 19 Kanaks were killed. Mitterrand, as President, had been informed of this operation and had eventually given his go-ahead, although the Elysée had not been informed of it while it was actually happening.[8] Mitterrand's calculation may have been that it was impossible to prevent the operation given the political damage that the shooting of hostages would have meant.[9] Finally, Captain Prieur, one of the agents who had been involved in the Greenpeace affair and who was confined to an atoll in the Pacific, was brought home to France.

On 8 May, Mitterrand was re-elected handsomely by a margin of two and a half million votes. He was the first President to be re-elected by universal suffrage to a second term by 54 per cent of the voters. It was a truly national victory with an even spread of votes in the first round, and in the second he made progress in areas that were not normally socialist (Catholic areas like Brittany and the Loire). He polled well amongst the working class (74 per cent), those aged 24–34 (65 per cent), teachers (70 per cent) and non-practising Catholics (74 per cent). On the second ballot, 20 per cent of Le Pen's voters switched to Mitterrand, as did 14 per cent of Barre's, 79 per cent of the ecologists and most of the Communists (87 per cent) and extreme leftists (80 per cent). Mitterrand had a majority in every region of France except for PACA, Corsica and Alsace. On the first ballot he had a recognizably Socialist electorate, taken from the working class, public service workers, the young and the secular. His support also increased in traditionally non-Socialist categories, like the older generation (amongst whom he was rivalling Chirac), farmers (a third) and business, and whereas 45 per cent of women had voted for him in 1974 this was now 55 per cent. On the second ballot this non-traditional support increased even further to, for example, the Vendée and the west, although his support did not increase as much in some of the old socialist bastions. Chirac resigned as Prime Minister on 9 May.

The Rocard 'Mortgage'

At various points in the campaign Mitterrand had paid tribute to Michel Rocard, whom he perhaps believed to be honest to the verge of simplicity, but with his habitual teasing of the pretenders, Mitterrand kept up the uncertainty about the next Premier. There is evidence of real hatred for Rocard, and the Wednesday dinners of 'Mitterrandists' became denunciations of the Premier.[10] Mitterrand dismissed him as 'not up to the job', although he deprecatingly remarked that he did not hate somebody who never really stood up to him.[11] Michel Charasse reports Mitterrand as saying that 'after six months people will see through Rocard like a cigarette paper' and Mitterrand's attitude to his Prime Minister contrasts, for example, with the indulgence he showed to the rogue business entrepreneur Bernard Tapie.[12] Mitterrand was later to comment that the nomination of Rocard was his 'only mistake'.[13] Yet Rocard had helped the President to be re-elected and he was a key figure in the move to the centre that Mitterrand had thought necessary to win the presidential elections. Moreover, an extension of the Socialist Party's coalition to the centre would be necessary to compensate for the lack of Communist support. As Mitterrand's radical commitment had fallen away in the mid-1980s, the practice of Socialist government had come more to resemble Rocardian social democracy than the radical 'Common Programme', and this made Rocard the obvious choice.

Rocard was officially nominated Premier on 10 May. Mitterrand composed the government himself and brushed aside, for example, Rocard's preference for a career diplomat as Foreign Minister. In the new government of 42 there were 27 Socialists, but 4 centrists, and the 11 non-party ministers, including Brice Lalonde, the first Ecologist Minister, counted in Mitterrand's 'united France'. Five of Rocard's supporters became ministers, but the tenor of the government was given by the Mitterrand loyalists who included Lionel Jospin as Education Minister and Pierre Bérégovoy as Finance Minister, as well as Pierre Joxe as Interior Minister and Roland Dumas as Foreign Minister. Yet Mitterrand took a detached stance towards Rocard's government and at certain times would deliver public lessons to it – as he had done under 'cohabitation'.[14] For example, Mitterrand criticized the deterioration of the social climate during a strike of nurses in November 1988 and deplored the timidity of the government on social questions. Direction from the top was lacking in the second septennate that never answered Jospin's question: 'a second term, to do what?'[15]

Bérégovoy, however, emerging as a Mr Pinay of the Left, operated a freeing-up of the market through deregulation and changed the financial institutions as well as winding down the state's role in the economy in keeping with the trend of the times. In 1980, two million were employed in public sector industries but this fell to one and a half million by 1995, while Renault became a private company, France Telecom was separated from the postal system, and banks were privatized. Partial privatizations of Elf, Rhône-Poulenc and Total took place in defiance of Mitterrand's promise to keep the status quo. There was a change in the French economy that pushed the balance towards business and finance and a slow-down in the rise in wages and salaries. Unemployment remained stubbornly high and at the end of the double septennate it was, at 12 per cent, the highest in Western Europe. Markets were freed up with the suppression of the need to have job lay-offs agreed by the state, ending exchange controls and allowing prices to be decided freely. Bérégovoy's deflationary policy also had its effects in turning round a balance of payments deficit of fourteen million dollars in 1980 to a surplus of eleven million in 1995. These were accepted by the Socialist Party but they were not what Mitterrand had promised in 1981.

There was also the problem of the Socialist Party's leadership. On 11 May, three days after humiliating Chirac, Mitterrand entertained close supporters making it clear that he wanted Laurent Fabius. To Mitterrand's fury this was refused.[16] Party archons preferred to make Lionel Jospin's nominee, the former Premier Pierre Mauroy, First Secretary rather than Fabius who, they feared, would run the party as his personal machine. This was a highly significant revolt. It meant that a post-Mitterrand phase had already started and that the President was entering what the Americans call the 'lame duck' presidency. A president with no further prospect of re-election (Mitterrand would be 79 at the next election and could not be expected to run again) lost much of his hold over the party. Mitterrand's succession crisis spiralled downward into catastrophe without his being able to impose order.

General Elections

But Mitterrand had decided on a dissolution and this would be under the two-ballot electoral system on 5 and 12 June. This general election would capitalize on his big victory in May and the belief was that the voters would replace the conservative Assembly as had happened in 1981 – if not with quite such a big majority. However, there was a spirited conservative campaign unified under the Union du rassemblement et du centre. Mitterrand, rather complacently, noted to journalists after his annual pilgrimage to the Roche de Solutré that 'it is not healthy for a single party to govern', and that it was necessary for other political 'families to take part'.[17] It was a continuation of his view during the presidential campaign that *ouverture* to the centre ought to be managed, but it was badly received by Rocard. No Premier, he said, could be expected to mobilize to win the general elections if Mitterrand gave the impression that he was calling on people to vote for the right. It was an uncertain trumpet and a lacklustre campaign, and there was a degree of voting fatigue after the presidential election; the abstention rate was 34 per cent on the first ballot.

Mitterrand's landslide victory in the presidential elections was not repeated. Candidates of the presidential majority (Socialist, MRG and some independents) polled 37.55 per cent, but they had to face the hostility of the Communist Party and the centre as well and that meant an uncertain second ballot. UDF candidates had polled 18.49 per cent and RPR candidates polled 19.18 per cent, but although the Front national took 9.65 per cent it was in a weak position because the single candidacies of the URC did not enable it to get onto the second ballot in many constituencies. On the second ballot, the Socialists and MRG emerged with the largest numbers in the Assembly but without an absolute majority. With 276 deputies to the UDF's 130, the RPR's 128 and the PCF's 27, with 1 Front national and 13 independents, it was possible for the Socialist government to be defeated and the narrow majority made the Assembly difficult to handle.

During the second septennate Mitterrand launched a building programme on a scale to rival previous presidents. These included the Institut du monde arabe, the movement of the Finance Ministry from the Louvre to the Quai Bercy to free up museum space and the new entry hall designed by Pei, the Bastille Opera House, the Arch at La Défense, La Villette and the Library. These were criticized for their extravagance at a time when the public sector was being reined in, though there is no evidence that they were unpopular. Most of the new buildings were tied into the bicentenary celebrations in some way and although these, too, were not without their critics, they were popular both in France and with visitors.

German Reunification

Mitterrand's attention in the second septennate turned to foreign affairs, and these, as it happened, were momentous in the years 1988–95. They included the end of the Cold War, the reunification of Germany, the collapse of the USSR and of the Communist system, European integration and, of course, the Gulf War. In particular, the end of the Cold War, and with it the end of France's careful positioning, required a rethink of traditional certainties. Mitterrand was no more farsighted than anybody else about the trend of Gorbachev's reforms and the implications for the world of the change in the structure of world politics, although he had to manage France in the transition from the bi-polar world to the hyper-power of the United States. In the new conditions of post-Wall Europe, none of the old maps was a guide and Mitterrand, like other leaders, wavered on key issues during a time when it became difficult to interpret events, but he also exploited opportunities as they arose. There remain, however, big questions about Mitterrand's judgement of events and his role in them.

When the Communist regimes collapsed in 1989, Mitterrand underestimated the speed of events.[18] His problem was that he was the first postwar president to face the prospect of a united Germany that was real and not just an aspiration. A united Germany could be the dominant continental power once again and, especially with the USA, then in isolationist mood, there would be no counterweight to the reunified state. Mitterrand

and the British Prime Minister met on 20 January 1990 and agreed – it seemed – on the necessity to slow down or prevent reunification (Mrs Thatcher seems to have felt that Mitterrand reneged on his commitment).[19]

Reunification was an affair in which German internal politics were dominant and the United States was the principal outside power, although Mitterrand did play a small role.[20] It was, for example, Secretary of State Baker who determined the conditions.[21] In public, Mitterrand's reaction to the prospect of reunification (just before the Wall came down) was supportive of Chancellor Kohl, who in turn gave the President much credit. However, in other accounts he was hostile to reunification until the meeting with Gorbachev at Kiev and then, when it became unstoppable, he reacted by accelerating European integration.[22] He was asked at a press conference on 3 November whether he was afraid of reunification and he gave the direct reply: 'No. I am not afraid of reunification', but, he added, it should happen within a European framework.[23] Reunification could not, of course, go ahead while one half of Germany was Communist, but on 9 November 1989 the Berlin Wall came down. Mitterrand may also have expected the East German state to be more durable and was unconvinced of the East German desire for unity.[24]

Mitterrand was concerned to have the East German frontier ratified and he tried to push Chancellor Kohl into that confirmation. Kohl was doing nothing to rein in demands for border changes to the 1937 boundaries at that time. In 1975, all parties had accepted the Oder-Neisse line, but Mitterrand, like other leaders, was worried that there might be changes now that the reunification was under way. Mitterrand was consistent in insisting on this. On 9 March 1990, he received the Polish leaders in Paris and supported their demand for a treaty confirming the borders before the reunification. This was received in Germany with annoyance. President Bush nearly caused a cabinet crisis in Western Germany (when Genscher threatened to resign) by pressuring Kohl to endorse the Oder-Neisse line.[25] As Secretary of State, James Baker wrote to Chancellor Kohl on 12 December forcefully stating that there could be no change in the Eastern borders.[26] Kohl at first refused to give any guarantee, presumably because of the weight of opinion at home, but eventually did so when he felt it to be the right time.[27] Mitterrand, however, seized the moment to promote integration by bringing the transformation of the European Community into the equation.

But things were moving fast. Chancellor Kohl could see his place in the pantheon of the greats being set up if he could achieve reunification under his aegis. There was no real opposition to it; there was a great deal of pressure for reunification and the West German general elections were due in December 1990. All the same, Mitterrand was taken aback by Kohl's announcement on 4 January of a ten-point plan for reunification and was reportedly furious that he had not been informed.[28] A meeting had been set up with Gorbachev in Kiev on 6 December at which the Soviet leader expressed his worries over the pace at which reunification was proceeding. Mitterrand concurred.[29] Gorbachev was worried at the repercussions that hasty reunification might have in the USSR and voiced fears that it might threaten his own position.[30] But shortly afterwards Gorbachev met Kohl and stated that he did not intend to prevent reunification although he had told Germany that the Communist GDR should both continue and remain a member of the Warsaw Pact. Mitterrand may have feared the break-up of the Soviet Empire into small ungovernable fragments and wanted a counterbalance to the East as well as to maintain the 'great power' control of reunification.

From 20 to 22 December Mitterrand visited the GDR, a miscalculated encounter. The regime was collapsing and there were diplomatic recriminations about who had or had not been informed. This visit was again used to announce publicly that he did not oppose reunification but he warned against excessive haste.[31] Mitterrand may have believed that the East German state was viable and that could explain his praise of its last ephemeral leader Hans Modrow as well as the conclusion of an economic agreement with it. This is a plausible motive though why, given the collapsing of the absurd structures of the Eastern bloc and the inability of the USSR to support its satellite, he came to that conclusion is not clear.

By January 1990 the instability of East Germany was very evident and with Washington, Bonn and Moscow agreed on reunification, there was little room for manoeuvre, although Mitterrand continued to insist to Kohl on the confirmation of the borders.[32] Then, after the East German elections of 18 March returned a parliament eager for unification (and a strong support for Kohl), the die was cast. Mitterrand wished Germany 'Good Luck' and dropped objections to the simplified reunification process. On 3 October 1990 Germany was unified within Western Europe and Nato. Mitterrand had moved with the flow. It is true that he could not have prevented it, but he could have taken a line of active opposition and he did, indeed, wrest some advantages from the process of German reunification.

The Maastricht Trick

Most important of these moves was the quickening of the pace of European integration (already under way before the collapse of the GDR) that led to the Maastricht Treaty. Mitterrand had linked the two and, in a dialectic familiar in European political relations, a German move eastward was balanced by a move to reassure the Western states. It was on the basis of this dynamic that the Community was transformed into the European Union. In this, Mitterrand was aided by Jacques Delors who, as President of the Commission, wanted to push ahead. Mitterrand himself, as his objection to extending the powers of the European Parliament revealed, was wedded to the inter-governmental institutions and wanted to keep the Council of Ministers, where the states made the decisions, as the locus of power in Europe.

In the event, the Maastricht Treaty in December 1991 lacked the political dimensions but moved economic integration ahead in a major initiative. Germany had been persuaded to back a common currency (the 'Euro') to be implemented by 1 January 1999 at the latest. There would be a European Central Bank and criteria were set for public deficits (at a maximum 3 per cent of GDP). Stringent convergence criteria of economic and fiscal orthodoxy were set for admission to the EMU, including inflation rates and currency fluctuations. Mitterrand had developed the idea of the 'three pillars' of economy, diplomacy and social affairs for the structure of the Treaty: the economic measures were technical but were implemented, the common security and foreign policy was feeble and the social aspect of Europe undeveloped. However, Mitterrand had achieved the taming of the Deutschmark by integrating Germany into the European framework.

But it proved difficult to get public opinion to accept the Maastricht Treaty because it involved the abandonment of traditional features of sovereignty like the franc. Mitterrand decided to opt for the ratification of the Treaty by referendum. This appeared to be a way of strengthening the President's position; Europe, it was thought, was a popular cause and the referendum would confirm Mitterrand's authority while splitting the right.[33] It would also anchor the European policy for the future, show France's commitment to the new Union and legitimize the replacement of the franc by the euro. But there was a substantial opposition to European integration and that found a new voice in the referendum campaign. In addition to the Communists and the Front national, who could be relied on to oppose integration, the conservative right was split: the RPR was not supportive and in its ranks there was Philippe Séguin who provided a new tone and a credible opposition.

When the Maastricht referendum was announced, in June 1992, the polls showed that 52 per cent of voters were in favour of the Treaty, but the campaign was intense and Mitterrand, now suffering badly from cancer, was not as active as he had once been. Opponents of the Treaty proved more effective and more astute than had been anticipated and they capitalized on a widespread rejection of the political elite and its lack of appeal. A desperate last-minute effort was made to swing public opinion and the leaders of the Opposition also campaigned for a 'Yes', while the President used a television debate with Séguin to help turn things round. On 23 September the 'Yes' vote had a slight advance over the 'No': the referendum was won by 51.3 per cent and, as Giscard noted, it was extraordinary that anything the President proposed was accepted. But this narrow victory opened a fissure. It divided anti-Europeans like the Communists and Chevènement from the Socialists, but also put the Socialists and the President on a different line from their working-class supporters who had voted 'No'.[34]

Yugoslavia

While the Eastern bloc was collapsing, the state of Yugoslavia was also falling apart. In the component republics of the federation the nationalists were stirring and they began to assert themselves. This was another of these intricate Balkan problems whose significance was not immediately apprehended by outsiders and which quickly degenerated into killing fields that required intervention. Slobodan Milosevic was elected President of Serbia at the end of 1989 and had started to create a 'Greater Serbia' using the Yugoslavian army. This Serbian aggression was at the origins of the conflict (a factor not recognized by Mitterrand), but it precipitated a reaction and in April Franjo Tudjman was elected president of Croatia and the break-up of the federation was under way. Croatia declared its independence on 23 June and Serbia and Slovenia declared theirs on 25 June 1991. There were many complications to this, but one was that the Serbs had been allies of the West for a long time and this delayed the understanding of the nature of Serbian aggression by Mitterrand.[35] There was also a very intricate pattern of interlinking religions with nationalities that could not be separated geographically, and in Yugoslavia, as elsewhere, Mitterrand had fears of a generalized creation of mini-states each with their own subnational minorities and a resurgence of what he saw as ancient national rivalries.[36]

Europe sought for a negotiated compromise that would bring peace and stability to the region, but Mitterrand had at one point hoped to send troops to separate the combatants. There was a tension here between the Germans, who wished to recognize the secessionist Croatian republic, and

Mitterrand, who wanted a coordinated European response to obtain a peaceful settlement that guaranteed minority rights and the maintenance of Yugoslavia.[37] In Germany, however, there were pressures in a different sense from those who saw the right to independence from a Communist regime as legitimate and as a defence against Serbian aggression. On 23 December 1992 Kohl's Germany, ignoring Mitterrand and the EU's desire for a common policy on Yugoslavia, recognized Croatia and Slovenia, although this had no restraining impact on the fighting, which the Serbs then spread to Bosnia. Serbian ethnic cleansing and the fighting in Bosnia, as well as their march into other 'ethnic areas' with the aim of creating a Greater Serbia, led to an outcry, and in France (as elsewhere) public support for the victims. But by recognizing, on 6 April, Bosnia's independence, and a 'marble cake' of different groups, a new impetus had been given to the settling of scores. In the UK, Douglas Hurd and John Major dismissed a peacekeeping force. Mitterrand himself went to Sarajevo, then under siege, in a diplomatic 'coup' in June 1992.

Rocard's Trials

Rocard's first test had come in 1988 with the New Caledonia problem, passed to him by Mitterrand for solution. Rocard used the occasion to define his own style, a form of consensus to reach agreements. The elections had been boycotted by the Kanaks' FLNKS, leading to a landslide for the settler RCPR party, but, even so, the settlers threatened that they would take up arms against any Socialist government that tried to constrain them or that tried to move the island to independence. A team of negotiators composed of church leaders and experienced officials was sent to mediate a solution between the factions on the island. These led to a meeting between Jean-Marie Tjibaou and Jacques Lafleur, the leaders of the two sides, at the Matignon, where an agreement was concluded. There was to be a redistricting on the island, dividing it into three regions: two with Kanak majorities and one with a Caldoche majority. In addition, more public money was to be made available and a referendum would be held on the island in ten years. This compromise ended the immediate crisis.[38] On 6 November there was a referendum in France ratifying the agreement and there was a very high 'Yes' vote of 80 per cent, although the exercise was undermined by the record abstention rate of 67 per cent.

Next, for Rocard, came the institution of the *revenu minimum d'insertion* (RMI) announced in Mitterrand's *Lettre à tous les Français*, but it was an idea he had had in mind before the elections. It was announced on 29 July and passed unanimously on 12 October. By re-establishing the wealth tax abolished by Chirac it would be possible to deliver a social wage to those poorest people who were excluded from society to enable them to subsist until they found work. In the final version, unemployed people over the age of 25 could get a payment for three months to a year through their local councils. It was intended to enable people to find work, but the level of unemployment remained stubbornly high in a 'growth recession' and it became a more or less permanent feature of the social security system. More controversial was Rocard's imposition of a new tax to pay for social security: the *contribution sociale généralisée* (CSG).

Problems with Associates

Also in November the nationalized company Péchiney put in a bid for American National Can, in that way intending to make itself the world leader in the field. This was supported by Rocard, but the Elysée was not keen as it would mean a partial privatization of the firm, which would be going back on earlier commitments.[39] This was the beginning of a chain of scandals that, by the end of the septennate, gave the impression that Mitterrand's associates had been wallowing in a jacuzzi of cash. In this case the associate was the businessman and former POW Roger-Patrice Pelat. Pelat had helped Mitterrand financially over their long association, had bought property for him and had paid him a retainer as a lawyer. It was not the first occasion on which rather gamey deals had been done by Pelat and in connection with the Elysée (there had been the case of Vibrachoc, for example, on shock absorbers).[40] American investigators noticed unusually large transactions in the stock of American National Can just before the sale and traced these to Pelat and others who had made a killing (Pelat, who affirmed that he had bought only 10,000 shares, probably made over £250,000).[41] Forced onto the defensive, Mitterrand devoted nearly half of a long *Sept sur sept* TV interview to the affair and to lauding the incriminated Pelat. Pelat and another of the President's friends – Max Théret, the owner of FNAC, a former bodyguard of Trotsky who had become a millionaire – were indicted for insider trading in February 1989, as was Bérégovoy's head of office Alain Boublil. Pelat died on 7 March before he could be brought to trial. Mitterrand's reaction was that 'the press had killed him' and that Pelat had done nothing wrong.[42]

A month after the affair there were municipal elections (12 and 19 March). These showed no evidence of the 'Pelat effect' and, resisting as they did the usual mid-term ebbing of the Socialist tide, were a success for the left and hence for Rocard's government. The Socialists won ten city halls and confirmed their place as the principal party of local government. A Rocard supporter, Catherine Trautmann, won Strasbourg from the conservatives, in Marseilles Robert Vigouroux was helped win against the official Socialists by Defferre's widow (and possibly Mitterrand as well) and former Communists led the left to victory in Le Mans and Orly. If the Communist Party was sliding down faster and Chirac had won every Paris district, the conservative right was still in disarray and leaderless after the trouncing of 1988. One sign of a new force was the breakthrough by ecologists in a number of towns. This ecologist wave was repeated at the European parliamentary elections at which they polled 10.6 per cent and won nine seats in Strasbourg. But the Socialist European list, led by Fabius, was less of a success and its vote fell to 23.6 per cent. It was another setback for Fabius, but the elections were a torpid affair with an abstention rate of 51 per cent.

Social security finances have been a major problem for French governments since the system's institution after the war. Rocard was determined to plug the deepening hole and for that a new tax would be needed – the CSG. Rocard's new tax had the advantage of being socially just and of expanding the base of those who would pay, but it was a new tax and would not be received with rapture. It had the President's support when the law was reviewed by the Cabinet on 3 October, but it was violently opposed by the Communist Party, which voted against it in the Assembly. Only by dragooning in deputies from overseas France and a few supporters of Barre was the government able to pass the legislation (by five votes). At the end of 1990 Rocard was popular, defying the 'Parodi curve' of declining prime ministerial popularity and considerably more so than his Socialist predecessors at the same stage, but Mitterrand also remained popular.

In April, however, another financial scandal started. A front company (Urba-Technic) was uncovered skimming off money from public works for the Socialist Party's benefit. One of the directors had scrupulously noted these operations, and that became the basis for a police inquiry. An inquiry would have revealed an extensive system of dummy companies and public contract exploitation that would have done substantial damage to political reputations and probably have destroyed the PS. In fact, because of an 'arms race' in campaigning, all of the parties employed these methods to finance their lavish campaigns. Rocard's suggestion that the party should admit its wrongdoings was brushed aside. Mitterrand made one of his habitual denunciations of 'easy money', but the affair could not be shrugged off. A law giving amnesty to people involved in funding scandals, but not to national politicians or those who had made personal gains, was eventually passed in April 1990, though not before the Communist Party and the conservatives had made political capital out of the President's discomfort. Mitterrand's reputation, as the head of the party's finance system, suffered in the polls. Financial scandals, however, continued.

Rennes Conference

But there were other problems associated with Mitterrand's waning authority. In the Socialist Party there was turmoil. There were several 'players' in this game of 'après Mitterrand'. Most important were the possible 'présidentiables' of Fabius and Rocard, but Delors, Chevènement, Jospin and other 'barons' like Mermaz, Joxe and Mauroy were also significant. None of the 'présidentiables' could allow the party to be led by a rival contender (as it would then become their machine), but the leadership at that time lacked the authority to bring other factions into line. Implicit in the entry of Rocard to the Matignon was the deal that he should leave the party alone, but Mitterrand saw his Premier's hand in all the manoeuvres.[43] In addition to the lack of power at the centre, the main factions divided the activists roughly equally between them: 30 per cent for Rocard, 30 per cent for Fabius and 30 per cent for Mauroy, with the rest going to Chevènement and minor figures. This strategic impasse was added to the rivalry between Jospin and Fabius, but became manifest not in a heroic battle of ideas (as at Metz) but in a clash of egos at the 1990 party Congress at Rennes.

Little or nothing substantial divided the contenders for the leadership and the Party Congress was treated to what Freud called the 'narcissism of minor differences' in which trivial points were elevated into major disputes. This spectacle of naked ambition was presented to an astonished public and for Mitterrand it was important to prevent the Prime Minister's faction from taking control as well as to promote Fabius's prospects. Jospin also stood resolutely in the way of Fabius and may have paid the price with Mitterrand. But no agreement was possible and the quarrel moved to Paris, where the party's leaders thrashed out a mediocre compromise leaving a weary Mauroy at the top but keeping the balance between the faction leaders. Mitterrand had lost control, seen his dauphin rejected, his rival Rocard confirmed and been severely damaged in the polls. After the Rennes Congress it was only a matter of choosing the moment to 'drop the pilot' of the new consensus and '*ouverture*'. It was another warning to

Rocard when, in a speech in May 1990, Mitterrand called for greater vigour in social policy to tackle the inequalities, which had worsened under Rocard's government.[44]

The Gulf War

Rocard was about to be replaced as Prime Minister even though he remained popular, but his tenure on the Matignon was prolonged by the Iraqi invasion of Kuwait on 2 August. It was not possible to replace the Prime Minister at that juncture, but the Matignon was sidelined as attention turned to the foreign stage. Mitterrand took command of French foreign relations with a certainty and an attention to detail and nuance, while he left his Prime Minister, on a sailing vacation in the Adriatic, 'out of the loop', telling him not to return (Minister of Defence Chevènement also remained on vacation).[45] It was a concentration of powers in a small group, a presidentialization of policy, of the 'personal power' Mitterrand had denounced in the *Coup d'état permanent*.[46] One indication of this 'reserved domain' was the immediate despatch of twelve presidential envoys to key capitals to explain France's position, but during the war itself there was an unprecedented centralization by the Elysée.

France's position was carefully balanced: Mitterrand was to make clear that France was not an enemy of the Muslim world but at the same time that it wanted to see international law respected. It was able in this way to support the USA but also to keep friendly with the Middle Eastern states. But in both the Gulf crisis and the long agony of Yugoslavia, Mitterrand's attitude to the USA was again tested. France's long-standing policy of building up Europe as a counterbalance to American power had no more success under Mitterrand than under previous presidents. De Gaulle, the author of this policy, had been successful to the extent that there had been no crisis and no call on his loyalties. Europe had been promoted by Mitterrand; the Force d'Action Rapide was a Franco-German core to what might become a new capacity and in June 1987 a joint brigade was created and a defence council was also created. The WEU had also been revived but this did not duplicate Nato's planning and command structure and was no more than a talking shop. Neither in the Franco-German core nor in wider Europe was there the military capability or the will to make a real difference to Europe's capacity. In the Balkans Europe's response was inadequate in the 1990s until the United States became involved. Much the same lesson could have been drawn from the Gulf war but Mitterrand continued to insist on the importance of Europe.

As with other Western states, France had been friendly to Iraq in the early years of Saddam Hussein's presidency when the ruling Baath party was seen as a modernizing and secular force in a backward society. Iraq was regarded in the 1980s as a counter balance to the Ayatollahs of Iran, who had declared their hostility to the West and indirect aid went to Saddam in his war against Iran. There were many examples of French links with Saddam Hussein's regime, like the sale of arms to the building of nuclear power stations in the desert and the indulgence of the substantial debts that he had run up. This surreptitious arming of Iraq had gone on through the first Socialist governments and may have been one reason why Iran had chosen to put pressure on France.

But after the invasion of Kuwait there was, for Mitterrand as for other Western leaders, no question of allowing Saddam Hussein's adventurous regime to control the vast oil wealth of Kuwait and to become the major power in the Gulf. Mitterrand declared that the situation was one that would lead to warfare and the country would have to be at America's side without delay and join the forces that would be sent to the Gulf.[47] However, while supporting the United States, Mitterrand also kept open links to Baghdad and continued attempts to get a peaceful settlement, and there were contorted arrangements to show that France was not under US command. This was almost 'gaullist' in approach: Mitterrand wanted to mark out France's special role in the crisis in some way and to ensure that its weight was evident in international relations. Most of Mitterrand's Cabinet wanted United Nations support for any action taken in the Gulf by America, and the search for a peaceful settlement was intended to reassure Arab allies of France's independence.

On this crisis, public opinion proved to be difficult to manage, although people were favourable to Mitterrand's stance at the outset. An emergency session of the Assembly was called to condemn the invasion and to declare an embargo of Iraq. There were splits in the Cabinet and there was a range of opinion in France itself that was opposed to sending French soldiers (many of whom were conscripts). The Communists found themselves on the opposite side to Moscow for the first and last time and the Front national, in a bizarre twist, also supported Iraq. Mitterrand decided that it was better to have his anti-American Defence Minster Chevènement inside the Cabinet, keeping marginal forces behind the government, than to have him outside causing trouble and also, perhaps, as a sign that France's foreign policy had not moved in an anti-Arab direction. In the same spirit, in the United Nations on 24 September, Mitterrand raised the possibility of a negotiated solution 'if Iraqi troops were withdrawn and the hostages released and the solution was linked to a settlement of the Palestinian question'.[48]

In the United Nations Security Council, France had voted for the immediate withdrawal of Iraqi forces from Kuwait, and Mitterrand had despatched French forces to the region. These forces remained under French command and were not integrated into the American command structure so that there was considerable uncertainty about the French position. This was also in part a result of the reluctance of Defence Minister Chevènement to place French forces under US command, but after the passing of resolution 648 in the UN this was done.[49] American planners seem to have been alert to the need to accommodate French sensibilities and their deployment was both militarily and politically astute.[50]

Yet Mitterrand's policy came up against the same constraints as de Gaulle's had done: although he had the ambition to play an independent role, the means were lacking. For this reason his suggestion of a possible negotiated solution if Iraq was prepared to declare its willingness to withdraw at the UN on 24 September was without follow-up. There was a reaction neither in Iraq nor amongst other states in the region that might have been tempted by such a solution, but it annoyed the Americans who thought that it made Iraq less likely to comply with the UN.[51] There were, though, promising openings, notably with Gorbachev, and frantic diplomatic activity through Mitterrand's emissaries at various times (Cheysson, Vauzelle and Pisani) and visits from states of the region.[52] These may have encouraged Saddam Hussein to believe that he could divide the allies (and he may have seen France as a weak point), but the bridge to the United States that would be necessary was not in place.

Positions, however, hardened on the Western side as the military build-up was prepared. On 29 November the Security Council voted unanimously to allow the allies to 'use all means necessary' to free Kuwait from Iraq if Saddam's troops had not left by 15 January. What counted was America's vast force and its logistic capacity as well as its financial and diplomatic resources at home and in the region. Mitterrand's France had to content itself with symbolic participation and the conscript soldiers who comprised most of the army could not take part in the Gulf War for political reasons and because this was a specialist operation for professional forces. It revealed the ill-adapted nature of the largely conscript French army and its lack of equipment, as well as stretching the professional section of the army to its limits (and perhaps beyond).[53] On 14 September, 5,000 soldiers of the 6th Light Armoured Division were the first troops to be sent to Saudi Arabia along with 50 aircraft (more than 12,000 eventually went to join the 500,000 allied troops). On 15 January an emergency session of the Assembly was called and it approved of the use of force and French participation by 523 votes to 43. Operation 'Desert Storm' to remove the Iraqis from Kuwait started on 17 January and was over in five weeks. France had participated in the UN's American-led operation, but its political weight was insubstantial.

Rocard Dismissed

Rocard, as Prime Minister in May 1992, was far from played out and was still popular in the polls. However, the confidence that the Fifth Republic executive President needs to have in his lieutenant was not there, and if Mitterrand was going to make a mark during the last years of the legislature a replacement had to be found quickly. There were several possible candidates, including Bérégovoy. Given his experience and commitment to the new Socialist policies, Bérégovoy would have been expected to be the main contender. There were others, including Lionel Jospin, who had been an impressive interim Prime Minister and was number two in the government, and there were also Michel Delebarre and Jean-Louis Bianco.[54] Mitterrand had not liked Rocard's method of government and returned to the early Socialist Party method of imposing solutions more in Zorro than in anger. However, using the pretext of social deficits, he brusquely dismissed Rocard and nominated Edith Cresson to be the first woman Prime Minister of France. This decision was to prove a disaster.

9

The Last Years: 1991–1996

On 5 May 1991 Edith Cresson was appointed Prime Minister. She was a long-time supporter of Mitterrand who had started in 1965 working for the presidential campaign as a member of the Convention des institutions républicaines, before joining the Socialist Party in 1971 with the others in the CIR. Cresson's ascension had been steady but not spectacular. She had been a not very successful Minister of Agriculture in the first Socialist governments (1981–3), where she had provoked the farmers' organizations. In Rocard's government of 1988 she was Minister for Europe, before resigning in October 1990 in protest – she said – at Rocard's failure to promote French industry sufficiently.

Cresson was Mitterrand's choice and he made it against the advice of most of his councillors.[1] He was determined to have a committed cipher in place as Prime Minister. There was a certain shock value involved in nominating France's first ever woman Prime Minister to cover Rocard's dismissal. Although the first response was welcoming, Cresson soon became an object of derision and there were many anti-feminist reactions. Edward Balladur said:'You can't give that job to a woman!'[2] and she was dismissed as a 'Pompadour'.[3] But it was perhaps Cresson's abrasive and, in tenor, left-wing style that made Mitterrand appoint her.[4] Cresson's rhetoric was leftist but nothing in her past predisposed people to believe that she incarnated the grass-roots left. Didier Pineau-Valencienne, Cresson's employer at Schneider, was brought in to ponder 'Europe's industrial future'.[5] At the Matignon, Cresson's principal aide was a gaullist, Abel Farnoux, who ran a network of conservative *groupes d'études et de mobilisation* (lobbies), which was suspect in Socialist eyes and which was rumoured to direct policy on some issues.[6]

All of Rocard's supporters (Le Pensec apart) were removed, as were the ministers from the centre parties (except for Jean-Pierre Soisson).[7] Cresson failed to have Bérégovoy moved to become Governor of the Bank of France.[8] Hence, this all-powerful Finance Minister, who was now in charge of a super ministry of the Economy, Finance, Industry and Trade, remained at the centre of the government. With four junior ministers, Bérégovoy's super ministry created a countervailing power to the Prime Minister at the heart of the government and Bérégovoy himself, who had hoped to be Prime Minister, did not conceal his campaign against the Premier.[9] Aligned against her too were the Rocardians, who did not appreciate being evicted from power, Fabius's supporters as well as others who thought that they should have been nominated.[10]

That Cresson's appointment was a mistake became evident from the moment she gave her speech of investiture to the Assembly. Some reason had to be given for the replacement of Rocard, but Cresson misjudged the Assembly and gave a rambling, badly enunciated and imprecise address that failed to communicate a sense of direction. This speech, apart from outlining a more active industrial policy, even seemed to reconfirm the priorities of the outgoing Prime Minister.[11] Cresson's unhappy tenure of the Matignon cast an even better retrospective light on Rocard's premiership – the opposite of Mitterrand's intention. As has been noted, when it proves necessary to execute someone, it is best to make sure that there is a proper justification and manifest reason for it.[12]

By June, the benefits of the 'shock nomination' had dissipated.[13] At the beginning of July the proportion of those who approved Cresson's action were at 38 per cent (11 per cent down according to a Sofres poll)[14] and by March of the next year that number had fallen to 22 per cent the lowest point of any Fifth Republic Premier.[15] Edith Cresson quickly became a liability, and this was not helped by a continuing inability to master the technique of public communication.[16] Her language was brusque and slang-laden, syntactically contorted and, as far as the public were concerned, not prime ministerial.[17] There were many gaffes including denegration of the stock market, absurd comments about the English,[18] and remarks that compared the Japanese to ants and proposed to send illegal immigrants home by chartered aircraft. As the new Prime Minister's position weakened, so did the President's, and as she went down in the polls, attempts to shore her up only reflected badly on Mitterrand himself.

At the end of May there were riots in Mantes-la-Jolie, a small town with many immigrants just outside Paris. A young '*beur*' (second-generation immigrant) died while under detention in the police station. This resembled the events of 1986 rather too closely, and in response the Prime Minister visited the family of the bereaved and criticized the police. Two days later a policewoman was killed and so was a young immigrant, but this time the police were angry and accused the Prime Minister of lack of support and incomprehension of their position. This came at a time when the conservative right were competing with the Front national and both Chirac and Giscard had criticized the immigrants' culture.[19] Cresson's staffer, the Prefect Ivan Barbot, took a law-and-order line and the Premier's own declarations led people to expect this despite generous intentions (facilitating integration) and the promotion of Togolese-born Kofi Yamgnane as Minister for Immigration. Cresson's version of giving it straight from the shoulder did considerable harm to her own cause. In particular, her television declaration that military aircraft would take people back to their homelands created confusion on the issue of the forced and bulk repatriation of illegal immigrants.[20]

The USSR Collapses

On the morning of 19 August there was an attempted military coup in Moscow. It seemed that the anticipated reaction to the reforms had happened. Mitterrand's response was far from sure-footed and he gave the impression of not having supported Gorbachev sufficiently and of accepting the coup. By some accounts, however, Mitterrand had anticipated a military coup by hard-liners in the USSR, but when it happened its exact prospect was unknown.[21] It was not until Mitterrand's television interview that evening that it was condemned and there was a circumspection about his response to it that left doubts. Mitterrand read out a letter by the putsch leader Gennadii Ianaiev and he may have been comforted in his belief that the USSR would be preserved intact while Gorbachev's reforms were enacted.

But Mitterrand's attitude seemed to be that the putsch had succeeded and that there had been a change of leadership in Moscow, whether this was liked by the West or not. Mitterrand's critics in the Opposition were quick to point out that the President's reaction to the coup (reading the letter from Ianaiev and not denouncing the illegality of the coup) and discounting Gorbachev and Yeltsin had been a misjudgement. (Giscard had his revenge by describing Mitterrand as 'Ianaiev's postman'.) Still, even after the coup Mitterrand persisted in hoping that the Russian confederation would, in some form, continue as a counterweight to Germany and the USA and tried to support the newly formed Commonwealth of Independent States (CIS) in this.[22] Mitterrand wanted to bring the new Russia into the international system and to avoid triumphalism after the Cold War.

On 20 August Mitterrand's stance changed, though this did not wipe out the first impression given of indulgence to the coup leaders. A joint declaration from Europe forcefully condemned the coup d'état and an emissary from Yeltsin was met at the Quai d'Orsay and in the Elysée. When the putsch had clearly failed, Mitterrand returned to the television to deplore the 'unrealistic and superficial' coup.[23] As the military coup collapsed, the man of the hour, Boris Yeltsin, emerged to eclipse Gorbachev, who had been the favourite of the West. Mitterrand phoned Yeltsin in the partially blockaded White House the next day asking what could be done for him. In fact, the failure of the coup brought about the collapse of the Soviet Union and the movement of power in Russia to Boris Yeltsin (Yeltsin dissolved the Communist Party). A break up of the USSR would mean uncertainty and possibly war, but Mikhail Gorbachev no longer had the power to restrain the centripetal forces of local nationalism and ensure an orderly transition. He resigned as President of the USSR on 25 December 1991.[24]

Government Failures

Edith Cresson's difficulties sometimes came from the mistakes of the Elysée. This was the case with the affair of the Palestinian terrorist Habache, who was taken to hospital in Paris in January 1992. Given his implication in terrorist acts, including those in France itself, this was bound to cause an outcry and international protests unless conducted in the highest secrecy – which it was not. Both the President and Foreign Minister were abroad, but the visit had been authorized by somebody in high authority. Mitterrand rejected Cresson's demand that Foreign Minister Dumas should resign, but the opposition called for heads to roll.[25] Eventually, Georgina Dufoix was made to pay the price for this mistake along with several members of staff in government ministries, and Habache was bundled out of the country despite demands from the investigating judge, but it still damaged the prestige of the President and the failing Cresson premiership.

Mitterrand's authority, and that of the government, was falling beyond recovery. In the autumn of 1991 there had been open squabbles between government ministers, and one resignation (Roger Quilliot). Farmers' demonstrations were disrupting the countryside, and nurses, doctors and other social groups were also demonstrating or on strike. Dockers' strikes over the closed shop policy continued into 1992. Confronted with this disorder, Mitterrand, in presidential style, proposed to increase subsidies to farmers and set up a series of reforms in order to pacify the rural world. This undermined the Prime Minister (and the Agriculture Minister),

created problems for the budget and confirmed the impression of incoherence. In December 1991 on *Sept sur Sept*, the television programme,
Mitterrand backed the Prime Minister, but with tepid words. For Cresson,
this was a warning of imminent replacement. In the Socialist Party itself
there were changes. Pierre Mauroy had decided that it was time to leave
the party leadership and Mitterrand was finally able to ease Fabius in.[26]
Fabius's entry into the party headquarters was followed by a search for documents about illegal party funding carried out by Judge Van Ruymbeke
and the bailiffs.

But before Cresson left the Matignon there were the 1992 regional and
local (cantonal) elections, at which the Socialist Party was destined to be
trounced unless there was a complete change of heart in public opinion.
Despite showing considerable courage, Cresson was unable to effect such
a change. In the regional elections on 22 March the Socialists polled only
22 per cent and lost control of all their regional councils except Limousin
(though the Nord was kept from the right by supportive ecologists). For
the Socialists, the only bright spots were the successes for Lang in Loire-
et-Cher and Emmanuelli in the Landes, although the Elysée's favourite, the
Radical Bernard Tapie, was elected in the Bouches-du-Rhône. On the other
hand, the ecologists, split between Génération écologie and the Verts,
polled 13.9 per cent and took 212 seats, while the Communist Party polled
8.03 per cent which was only 2 per cent below its 1986 figure. On 29 March
the Parti socialiste polled a mere 18.9 per cent of the vote, a pitiful result
that condemned the Socialists to certain opposition after the 1993 elections, and with only a year to the general elections there was no time to
do more than limit the damage.

Mitterrand's judgement had clearly been at fault here. On the one hand,
he had chosen a Prime Minister against advice who turned out to be an
inexperienced and ill-organized candidate for the Matignon.[27] Prime ministers in the Fifth Republic in normal times have to expect that people will
try to get round their decisions by appealing to the President, but Cresson's
team of staff in the Matignon also seem to have been particularly argu-
mentative and sometimes disloyal. Mitterrand was both too supportive and
not supportive enough. When Cresson's shortcomings became evident, he
continued to support her beyond what was prudent for either himself or
the government. On the other hand, Cresson had not been given a free
hand and had been unable to deal with the baronies in the government
and the party. In addition, she was expected to radicalize the government
but without changing its policy, which was an impossibility. Over the span
of a legislature two prime ministers can normally be expected; Mitter-

rand's next choice was a year late and timing was crucial. In a move unusual in these cases, Cresson's letter of resignation criticized the President – she clearly felt hard done by.

Bérégovoy's Year

Pierre Bérégovoy had been the Prime Minister in waiting in 1991 and had run the Finance Ministry in the governments of both Rocard and Cresson. After Savary's eviction in 1971 as Socialist leader, he had been a loyal Mitterrand supporter in the Socialist Party's internal battles and then one of the feral left, but he had re-emerged as the Marat of capitalism, championing the 'franc fort'. He was also was one of the few Socialist leaders of genuinely humble origins. He had been Secretary General at the Elysée from 1981 to 1982, before becoming Social Security Minister (1982–4), then Finance Minister (1984–6) and again Finance Minister in the governments of Rocard and Cresson (1988–92).[28] However, Bérégovoy was a technician and not a political star, although he made a virtue of his probity and modesty. He operated on a short fuse and although he had no quarrels with Mitterrand he felt under-appreciated in government.

On his appointment as Prime Minister, Bérégovoy was greeted with approval by the public and the polls were good at first. At his investiture he committed his government to deal with unemployment, crime and corruption (the three 'Cs' in French). This was to be a government, it seemed, with mendésiste 'frankness, explanation and decision'. Bérégovoy's government included the big names but also some of the new post-Mitterrand generation: Dominique Strauss-Kahn, Aubry, Bredin and Sapin, as well as newcomers like Vauzelle, Royal, Glavany and Tapie. Tapie, just on the windward side of honest, had run a sparkling campaign against Le Pen. It was Bérégovoy's idea to make him Minister for Cities to deal with the burgeoning crisis in the suburbs and he seems to have fascinated Mitterrand.[29] But Lionel Jospin was missing, frozen out, possibly for having been too active in his campaign against Fabius, and he had been critical of Mitterrand's politics in a book published the previous year.[30]

But Bérégovoy's three 'Cs' began to go wrong from the outset when the Prime Minister brandished a paper which he claimed was a list of politicians who had been corrupt. Then the government was hit by scandal. Bernard Tapie had to resign in May, indicted for embezzling thirteen million francs from his company, although Mitterrand used a Cabinet meeting to praise him for his energy. Charges against Tapie were dropped, and he returned to the government in December, but he was eventually jailed in 1996. In July the former Minister Henri Emmanuelli was indicted on charges related to financing the party. On more basic matters, the numbers of jobless continued to rise despite Mitterrand's promise to eliminate long-term unemployment by finding a job or a training or a public service activity for these people. Economic growth had been expected to pick up strongly, but it was sluggish and the budget deficit worsened as a result.

In his investiture speech Bérégovoy had rejected a return to proportional representation for 1993, a last chance for the Socialists to limit the extent of the defeat looming in the general elections. This time the Socialists in the Assembly, fearing that they would be accused of sharp practice, were reluctant to take this route to salvation. Bérégovoy had also announced that the President wanted a moratorium on French nuclear testing in the Pacific. As a result, on 15 April, nuclear tests were suspended by Mitterrand. This was condemned by the conservative right and by the army leadership, but Mitterrand insisted that they would only be restarted if other countries did not follow suit.[31] Mitterrand also decided to hold a referendum to ratify the new Maastricht Treaty on European integration. When he announced this decision to the Cabinet on 3 June there was a 'glacial silence'.[32]

Sarajevo

On 27 June, the President absented himself from the EU summit in Lisbon with his Humanitarian Aid Minister Bernard Kouchner and flew to the city of Sarajevo, which had been besieged by Serbian forces. The Serbs were allowing flights into Sarajevo airport under United Nations control because that freed the Serbian armies to attain their main objective of partitioning Yugoslavia. However, the exact nature of the negotiations is unknown. It was a visit that had been organized in haste (though the meeting with the Serbs had been planned on 29 May)[33] and neither Mitterrand nor the team were fully sure of the position in the country.[34] France's policy was pro-Serbian and Mitterrand's visit to Sarajevo does not seem to have materially altered that, although the visit has been subsequently redescribed as a farsighted recognition of Serbian aggression.

Mitterrand and his group arrived, after a forced stop-over in Split at which Mitterrand tried to evade the Croatian representatives, on the symbolic anniversary of the assassination of the Archduke Ferdinand: 28 June. Coming from a supposedly pro-Serbian President, this visit was a coup d'éclat.[35] But it had no further consequences other than to weaken the

Bosnian position.[36] Mitterrand was informed by the Bosnian leader Alija Izetbegovic of the concentration camps and mass murders in the country, but chose to do nothing with the information, and he also met Serbian leaders at the airport (including Ratko Mladic and Radovan Karadzic).

In late July and August the truth about Serbian concentration camps became known through the English-language media, and it can be said that the French authorities were not active in verifying these reports nor in disseminating Bosnian reports.[37] At first Mitterrand continued to support the Serbian cause, alarmed, possibly, by German intervention in Croatia (in this Mitterrand was not alone) and the break-up of Yugoslavia into petty and warring statelets. In this instance it was not France that was the impediment to action. There was little inclination internationally, or in Washington where it mattered, to intervene and although France had mooted the sending of peacekeepers to Croatia and Bosnia in 1991–2, the country had neither the means nor the desire to do so alone.[38] Mitterrand was far from alone in incorrectly judging Milosovic and in not understanding the drive to create a greater Serbia, nor in appreciating the damage that inactivity (presented as 'non-intervention') was doing. This was ultimately, however, a failure of European collective will to undertake the necessary intervention against Serbia and a poor assessment of the military position (less hazardous than it was believed to be).

What was the meaning of this visit by Mitterrand to Sarajevo? In domestic politics it was an *image d'Epinal* which swung the spotlight onto one of the more popular ministers (Kouchner) but its effect was short lived. Ultimately, this was another symbolic gesture – but symbolic of what? To the French public it provided a dramatic sound-bite of a President on a daring mission to a surrounded city escaping under fire and bringing humanitarian aid. In strategic terms it symbolized French isolation and Europe's impotence and division. To the Serbs it was also a symbol of French and international support and the absence of any intention to intervene. For the Bosnians it was only symbolic. It did not change their conditions: the killing did not stop and the city remained besieged for a further three years. Mitterrand's strategy of encouraging negotiation, but refusing to back this up with force ('War should not be added to war') did not lead to a solution, and in all probability greatly worsened the situation by allowing Serbians to temporize while using their army with impunity.[39] On the ground the Serbians saw that nothing would be done. This is an unedifying story in which Western Europe failed to react. This failure allowed ethnic cleansing and prevented the victims from defending themselves and nobody in the West emerges with much credit. At basis for Mitterrand – as for others – was the inability to assess the drive to a greater Serbia or to distinguish between aggressor and victim.

Health Problems

By the summer of 1992 Mitterrand's health was conspicuously failing. Misleadingly anodyne bulletins on the subject had been regularly issued. Problems had started during Mitterrand's visit to Mexico in October 1981 when he had complained of back pains, and in November he had been diagnosed as having a particularly invasive prostate cancer and given only three years to live.[40] Rumours about his illness had circulated even in 1981 but, apart from his doctors, those in the know were limited to his brother Robert Mitterrand, his partner Anne Pingeot and possibly Pelat and Rousselet. Passing references to cancer were removed by Mitterrand from Attali's *Verbatim*.[41] Mitterrand's Doctor Gubler was gagged with the brusque injunction that the President's health was a 'state secret' and he was instructed to issue false medical bulletins.[42] Dr Gubler's book on Mitterrand's illness was suppressed and its revelations were furiously denied.[43] When Mitterrand suffered, he had it put about that it was a 'golfing injury' and that the secrecy resulted from the popular view of golf as a 'bourgeois' game inappropriate for a left-wing president.[44]

The cancer had been treated with a new drug, with the result that it had appeared to have gone into remission from its discovery until about 1991, and Mitterrand was apparently healthy. He then completed the first septennate and embarked on the second (without asking the doctors' advice).[45] During the debate on the Maastricht Treaty on 4 September 1992, Mitterrand's ill health could no longer be kept secret and it was shockingly evident to the public and the participants.[46] Mitterrand underwent an operation at the Cochin Hospital in Paris on 12 September. However, he stipulated that the word 'cancer' could only be used if it was announced that it had been cured and it was duly stated that it had been caught in its nascent stage.[47] This first operation in 1992 was part of the arduous battle against a debilitating illness that showed the extraordinary will-power central to his political life. Mitterrand made known his intention to continue at the Elysée – health permitting – until the end of the septennate, though he, and nobody else, would decide if his health permitted or not. After July 1994, although his capacity for analysis was undiminished, his physical state became incapacitating and he could no longer work intensively. According to his doctor, the President should not have continued in office after November 1994.[48] Medication also had effects on his personality.[49]

Bérégovoy's Calvary

Bérégovoy had to work not only with a seriously ailing President; he had also to struggle against the ebbing tide. Nowhere was this more evident than in the Maastricht Treaty referendum, which was won by a whisker. But Bérégovoy, 'Mr Clean', soon had his own scandal to deal with. This began at the beginning of February 1993 with the revelation by *Le Canard enchaîné* that he had been lent one million francs interest-free by the business entrepreneur and friend of Mitterrand, Roger-Patrice Pelat, in order to buy a flat in Paris.[50] It was Bérégovoy who, while at the Elysée, had demanded that the nationalized Alsthom buy Pelat's company Vibrachoc at 20 per cent above its quoted value.[51]

Judge Thierry Jean-Pierre, investigating some of Pelat's deals, had discovered this loan dating back to 8 September 1986 during the first 'cohabitation'. This was above board and had been declared to the tax authorities, but although Bérégovoy claimed to have paid it back (so it was claimed, in books and objects of vertù), there was no proof that it had been so. If it was a gift, what was it for? This is where it became doubtful. Instead of opening the books and stating what the financial link with Pelat was, Bérégovoy chose to allow the Ministry of Justice to stifle the proceedings. Bérégovoy was completely undermined by this 'affair'. As somebody on good terms with doubtful characters his reputation as 'Mr Clean' was in tatters. The affair preyed on his mind to such an extent that he became convinced that he was responsible for the left's crushing defeat in 1993.[52] In the *Common Programme* (Pt 3, ch. 1, line 6) it had been asserted that these dubious practices would end under the left.

But the defeat of 1993 was not Bérégovoy's fault and had been inevitable since at least Edith Cresson's appointment as Prime Minister and the President's inability to tackle unemployment. (Charles Salzmann told Mitterrand as much in a note of 4 December 1991.)[53] In 1993 unemployment was mentioned by two-thirds in an exit poll as the reason for their vote against the Socialist Party.[54] (Inequality had also increased since 1982.)[55] Unlike the defeat in 1986, the situation in 1993 was hopeless; the only unknown was the size of the conservative landslide. Mitterrand's intention of splitting the right over the Maastricht Treaty referendum (if that is what was expected) had failed.

The Right

Reading the polls, the conservative right had to decide what to do about the next 'cohabitation'. Jacques Chirac's presidential ambitions had revived and he was again the conservative's front runner with, this time, no competition from Barre (or Giscard). He did not want to jeopardize his 'presidential' status and was willing to let his close ally Edouard Balladur become Prime Minister in 1993 for what would be, at the outside, two years in the Matignon. Moreover, if the second 'cohabitation' did not work out too well for the Prime Minister, it would benefit his party leader and he would be rewarded later.[56] Edouard Balladur was more a technocrat than a glad-handing politician and a lesser figure in Chirac's RPR party. Chirac saw no drawbacks in allowing him the ingratitude of the daily grind as Prime Minister governing in prose, while he, Jacques Chirac, campaigned in poetry. But he had underestimated Balladur's ambition, independence and determination.[57]

On the left the Socialist Party was in disarray and the First Secretary, Fabius, was in no position to lead a campaign, tied up, as he was, with the affair of the AIDS-contaminated blood. To the left, the Communist Party was refusing to change with the times and the ecologists were squabbling with each other. Centrists, of course, had returned to the conservative right and there was no possibility of an alliance there. Michel Rocard was the principal figure left standing in this shambles and he entered the field in February by calling for a 'Big bang' on the left to rebuild the alliances with ecologists, centrists and dissident Communists and create a new party. This was well received by the left in general, but it was an implicit attack on Mitterrand and a warning of an intention to rebuild the Parti socialiste on a new basis.

In the general election of 21 and 28 March 1993 the Mitterrand era ended. Bérégovoy was re-elected from his constituency, but the Socialist Party was in the same shambolic condition as Cresson had left it. Rocard, Lionel Jospin and fifteen ministers were defeated, while some twelve thought it prudent not to stand again, a wise move given the rout of the Socialist Party, which was reduced to 67 out of the 577 seats. Together, the left took 30.76 per cent of the votes (as against 49.2 per cent in 1988), the Socialists took only 20.13 per cent (32.65 per cent in 1986) and the Communists 9.87 per cent (11.31 per cent in 1988); the ecologists polled 10.71 per cent, but their divisions were deep. Conservatives polled 44.10 per cent on the first round and 57 per cent on the second, but the Front national managed to get 12.5 per cent of the vote, an improvement on its 9.76 per cent in 1988. This Assembly, with its huge conservative majority, recalled the right-wing Chambre bleu horizon of 1919: the UDF had 207 deputies, the RPR 242 and others on the right held 36, but the extreme right had no seats. Yet the result was more a rejection of Mitterrand and his collaborators, his financial affairs and the unemployment rate than it was an affirmation of the conservative right, which had only just recovered from its drubbing in 1988 and was 1 per cent below its level of that year.[58]

Jacques Chirac, consolidating his reputation as the most aggressive of the conservatives, called on Mitterrand to resign, but this view was not seconded by other eminent conservatives.[59] Mitterrand had declared that any new Prime Minister would have to respect the constitution and support the Maastricht Treaty, two conditions that did not narrow the field to any great extent.[60] Faced by a massive conservative majority, with the RPR preponderant within it, Mitterrand had little choice other than to nominate Balladur as Prime Minister.[61] This second 'cohabitation' would be less confrontational because Mitterrand would not stand again and the Socialist Party had collapsed. Edouard Balladur was a more relaxed and less combative figure than Jacques Chirac. Thus the competition at the summit of the state would be less intense and limited to skirmishes over points of principle (mainly foreign policy). All the same, Mitterrand had prepared for the second 'cohabitation' by ensuring that there was an information network in place that could prevent him being 'out of the loop'. There was also a flurry of nominations before the elections, one of which, Pierre Joxe's elevation to the presidency of the Cour des Comptes, caused protests.

Balladur's Government

Once nominated, Balladur rapidly put in place a small government of twenty-nine ministers composed in consultation with Chirac, one of whom was challenged by Mitterrand.[62] Balladur's government included a number of old personalities, like the pugnacious Charles Pasqua who again became Interior Minister, Chirac's closest ally Alain Juppé as Foreign Minister, and the rising star, Nicolas Sarkozy, as Finance Minister. However, Balladur's government also included Veil (Social Affairs), Léotard (Defence), Douste-Blazy (Health) and Bayrou (Education), and was more centrist than neo-gaullist in composition, and it was soon divided into the partisans of the Prime Minister and of the RPR leader. This government was well received and Balladur's rating went high and stayed high.

He was aided politically by Mitterrand's illness, which by 1993 had become serious. Balladur had lived through President Pompidou's ill health and so knew how the system could work. But neither Mitterrand nor the conservative Cabinet had any interest in revealing the extent of his incapacity. Mitterrand was reported as saying that he 'could not go on' in October 1994.[63] But he did continue to work although his inaction spoke louder than words and his anticipation and planning were probably minimal, as was his ability to carry the battle to the adversary.[64] Prime Minister Balladur had every interest in keeping the 'cohabitation' going and to enable Mitterrand to continue, and in this he was ably assisted by the Elysée's Hubert Védrine, with Nicolas Bazire as Balladur's contact man. The Elysée began to resemble Haydn's *Farewell Symphony*. Mitterrand, with superhuman effort, was capable of giving long speeches at times and one of these was given in the open air at the Socialist Congress of Liévin. He was also able to meet foreign emissaries at the Elysée for stretches.[65]

Socialist Collapse

Inside the Socialist Party there was dismay at the election débâcle. This was regarded by the opponents of the First Secretary Fabius as the moment to depose him and a combination of Rocard's and Jospin's supporters passed a motion of censure at the Directing Committee meeting on 3 April and elected an interim leadership to be in place until the next Congress. Thus the defeat saw the President's rival Rocard take over Mitterrand's party from his 'dauphin'. Mitterrand was displeased at what he took to be a personal repudiation and let it be known that he would freeze the party out.[66] In truth, this was as much a manoeuvre of desperation than anything else. Rocard needed the party to launch his presidential bid in 1995 and in its contemporary state it would not serve that purpose.

On 1 May there was the dramatic suicide of Pierre Bérégovoy, who shot himself in the head.[67] He had been deeply depressed and, although the inquiry into the Pelat loan had been dropped by the judiciary, he would have been called to give testimony in the Péchiney affair in June.[68] Mitterrand's response to this was to declare in the funeral oration that Bérégovoy had been hounded to death by the press and the judges. This attack on the press functioned like the burglar's bone, which keeps the dog of public opinion engaged while the miscreant escapes. Bérégovoy had been compromised and Mitterrand himself was accused of refusing to take calls from his anguished former Premier.[69] Nothing emerged from the autopsy, or the inquest, and Bérégovoy's diary disappeared. A year later, on 7 April 1994, François de Grossouvre, who had been frozen out of the presidential entourage for not knowing a placeman's place, but who retained an office in the Elysée 'looking after the presidential hunt' (hunting was an activity Mitterrand disliked), committed suicide in his rooms.[70]

Michel Rocard's position at the head of the Socialist Party and as the 'presidential candidate in waiting' was severely damaged by the June 1994 European election campaign. There had been no need for him to head the PS list, but he did so and himself took the opprobrium for the 14.48 per cent result, the Socialist Party's worst ever. Rocard had had difficulties with the continuing divisions in the Socialist Party but also with the barn-storming campaign run by Radical's Bernard Tapie, which polled 12.03 per cent. Tapie had appealed to voters from the left, and this was believed by many to have been encouraged by Mitterrand.[71] Mitterrand himself was under attack in this campaign for a policy in Bosnia that was deemed insufficiently supportive of the Muslims. Intellectuals, led by B. H. Lévy, wanted in particular an end to the arms embargo. Rocard's weak response to 'BHL' and his conduct of the campaign are, it must be said, explanation enough of his defeat without the Elysée's intervention. His resignation plunged the PS into another crisis: one year before the presidential elections it had no leader and no candidate.

Mitterrand's way of managing the Socialist Party had been to juggle its warring factions but to use the energy and commitment of the younger generation (who presented no threat to him) to run the party and government. There was, however, the king over the water: Jacques Delors who, in the opinion polls, was bound to be the certain winner of the 1995 elections. But on 10 December 1994 he announced that he would not run.[72]

Foreign Policy

Mitterrand's health did not prevent a clash with the Prime Minister over the recommencing French nuclear tests, provoked by President Clinton's decision to prolong the test ban moratorium until September 1994.[73] Clinton wanted to start a process of test banning and wrote to the French President to propose a treaty. This Mitterrand approved and he discussed it with Balladur, who was, however, reluctant. Furthermore, the conservatives had been particularly critical of this moratorium in opposition. Mitterrand assured Clinton that France would not restart tests before the end of the US moratorium, only to be contradicted by the Defence Minister. Supported by a team of defence experts, who also recommended ending the moratorium, Balladur put pressure on the President to renege on his decision and he was in turn pressurized by Chirac's supporters who asserted that modernization could not take place without testing. They were making the reintroduction of nuclear tests a touchstone for Balladur's capacity to lead the conservative camp. Mitterrand imposed his view with a threat to 'take his decision to the French people'.[74] Balladur's article in *Le Figaro* claiming responsibility for France's foreign policy was reproved by Mitterrand, who stated that the President was the authority in that area. There was no follow-up to this quarrel.

Mitterrand and Posterity

In July 1994 there had been a second operation on Mitterrand's cancer. This left him more incapacitated, weak, in pain and unable to find a comfortable stance, and the doctors did not think he would survive the year.[75] How badly he was affected was clear to people who saw him behind the scenes at a television interview later in the year.[76] He was unable to keep on with his usual activities and the Prime Minister took on additional tasks, but Mitterrand was determined to complete his second septennate as President.[77] Taking part, indeed, seemed to revivify the President and give him an extra energy.[78] Mitterrand was still, even in his last months in office, going to official events and conducting the ceremonial functions of the presidency. Whether a fit Mitterrand would have had some effect on French policy in Rwanda, where the French were accused of being complicit in attempts to frustrate humanitarian intervention to prevent a genocide, is an unknown. Nothing in Mitterrand's record, and certainly not his comportment over the Yugoslav crisis, points to that conclusion.[79]

There was a flurry in the 'affair' of Mitterrand's Vichy past touched off by Péan's book on the subject.[80] This was one of the aspects of Mitterrand's career well-known amongst the '*tout Paris*', but Mitterrand may have underestimated the ensuing storm. Younger people probably did not know the details of this career and had been led to imagine something different about the 'President of the left'. Péan laid out, however, Mitterrand's close relationship with Vichy milieux and Mitterrand was forced to defend himself (denying any affinity with the extreme right),[81] although, in one response, on television on 12 September, he commented on his Vichy and right-wing past without serious embarrassment. What was less expected was the continuing closeness of his relations with former Vichy leaders like Jean-Paul Martin and the Vichy Police Chief who organized the round-up of the Vel d'Hiv, René Bousquet.[82] Mitterrand refused to dissociate himself from Bousquet, who was not a particular friend.[83] 'Anybody can be mistaken', said Wiesel, 'even God'. 'Not me', said Mitterrand.[84]

One other revelation was to come before Mitterrand's septennate ended, though this was also an open secret, albeit known to fewer people. Françoise Giroud had published a *roman-à-clef* in 1983, and Jean-Edern Hallier had threatened to publish a book about Mitterrand's 'morganatic' marriage with Anne Pingeot and their daughter Mazarine. After fourteen years of self-restraint by the press, the story was revealed, with photos of Mazarine with Anne Pingeot, who was a museum curator at the Orsay, published in the *Paris-Match* of 10 November 1994 and more or less authorized by the President himself.[85] The first that Mitterrand's sons knew of Mazarine was when they stumbled across her at Mitterrand's bedside at the hospital in July 1994.[86]

Mitterrand's ménage was presented as a veritable second family that had displaced the 'First Lady' Danielle, and Anne now lived with him in an open marriage – his wife was never reduced to squawish subservience. But the two families were kept apart and hospital visits were staggered so that they would not meet. Mazarine and Anne Pingeot were housed in an annexe of the Elysée (somewhat irregularly).[87] As a result, Mitterrand's lickerish private life, with his refurbished chateau, epic promiscuity and envelopes of cash, were eclipsed.[88] To adapt Watkins, he lived in a permanent state of what the Calvinists call 'concupiscence': 'If the old music halls had still been in existence, there would have been derisive though admiring songs about him.' Françoise Giroud said about this aspect: 'For a month, for a year, it is impossible to say how many fell under his charm and remained, sometimes devastated, even though, they always reported, he broke off with delicacy. But he broke off to move on to somebody else.'[89] What Mitterrand had conducted, by and large, was a successful exercise which presented the 'second family' as part of an open 'modern' marriage, but as an intimate one.

It was also revealed in December 1994 by an investigating judge that Mitterrand had a bulimic appetite for telephone tapping.[90] There had been over two thousand telephone taps during Mitterrand's time in the Elysée, and these had included journalists, actors, lawyers and ordinary people.[91] Mitterrand was given print-outs of the transcribed conversations and cannot reasonably be said to have been 'unaware' (as he claimed, for example, in the Greenpeace affair) of the extent of this activity or its nature, the purpose of which (probably) was to protect his private life.[92] Mitterrand's staff formed an investigating unit who, to put it bluntly, were not fussy about whom they took information from, collecting it on potential or actual opponents.[93] This was all executed by one who, in Opposition, had been a fierce defender of the right to privacy and who had declared in 1993 that the 'Elysée did not listen in to anybody', and that he had 'never personally seen a tap'.

Mitterrand Steps Down

Mitterrand made his farewell to the Socialist Party at the Liévin Congress of 18–20 November 1994 when Delors was presumed to be the PS's virtual candidate. On 4 January Lionel Jospin seized the opportunity of Delors's withdrawal and declared himself a candidate. Although there was no serious opposition, not all of the Socialist leadership – and probably not Mitterrand either – were keen on Jospin's candidacy, which would, if successful, create a new power in the party, so Emmanuelli (pushed by Fabius) also entered the ring. After three weeks of a sometimes bad-tempered campaign Jospin was supported by 66 per cent of the party activists in their 'primary'.[94]

It was far from evident in February 1995 that Jospin could go to the second ballot, let alone win, but from his point of view it must be remembered that by this time Mitterrand's name had become voter-toxic. Glavany, Mitterrand's right-hand man, had a plan to eject Jospin from the leadership if, as expected, Balladur faced Chirac on the second ballot.[95] (Glavany, later one of Jospin's ministers, denied such intentions.)[96] Jospin was critical of Mitterrand and had supported Mauroy against the President's wishes in 1988, and by 1992 had quit the government barely on speaking terms with Mitterrand who, he believed, had not supported him and even intrigued against him.[97] Jospin had been latterly critical of Mitterrand's politics and had said during the Péan revelations that he thought the left needed a leader with a rather more clear and simple itinerary.[98] There had been some reconciliation over the years, but some of Mitterrand's closest associates still regarded Jospin as a traitor and his son Frédéric Mitterrand (like Pierre Bergé and Claude Brasseur) supported Chirac.[99] Mitterrand did support Jospin (and even affirmed that 'obviously' he would vote for him), but his contribution to the campaign was the 'minimum minimorum'.[100] In one sense, in his belief that the pantomime horse of the alliance of the left should still be central to the show, he was Mitterrand's residuary legatee.

On the right, the Prime Minister was taken to be all but elected president. Despite several mistakes by his government (like the attempt to pass new Falloux laws, which threatened a clerical monopoly on education), the suspension of three ministers under investigation and a poor economic record, he led in the polls. Mitterrand, for reasons of his own, decided to prompt Chirac to start campaigning. Chirac was a formidable campaigner and declared his candidacy in *La Voix du nord* on 4 December 1994. Mitterrand intervened to further dramatize the 'Schuller-Maréchal affair', much to Balladur's discomfort. This had come about through the Interior Minister's determination to prevent the magistrate Eric Halphen from investigating RPR party funding. After a meeting with the Premier and the Justice Minister, Mitterrand demanded that the change of judge be decided by the High Council of the Magistracy, chaired by the President. This was of dubious constitutionality (a point the pugnacious Sarkozy did not hesitate to make) but was artfully chosen, as the government could not defend its right to interfere with the course of justice in this case. Mitterrand's intent was probably more to assert presidential authority than to affect the presidential elections, but the ramifications of the affair in the New Year proved to be the beginning of Balladur's slide in the polls.

Jospin's campaign, carefully balanced, turned attention away from the ailing President. There was no political reason for Jospin to refer to Mitterrand, who would only have served to remind voters what they were turning their backs on.[101] Mitterrand, for his part, was not overly enthusiastic about Jospin, declaring at one point that the campaign was a 'bit lifeless'.[102] (There was an unhelpful call for the President to intervene to save the campaign.)[103] Jospin visited Mitterrand on 3 April – the President having expressed his intention to vote for him – but there remained a distance between the two men, and this was not bridged during the campaign.[104] Unexpectedly, Jospin topped the first round ballot with 23 per cent. It made him the leading figure of the left and the leader of the Opposition to Jacques Chirac, who defeated him with a solid 52.63 per cent on the second ballot. After a long delay, Mitterrand phoned Jospin when the results were in and congratulated him, saying 'you have picked up the gauntlet'.[105] (Mitterrand also commented that a 'donkey with a label would have got between 46–48 per cent'.)[106] But Jospin to a great extent moved the Socialist Party on from the Mitterrand years, leaving Mitterrand's closest collaborators to one side.

As President, Mitterrand had one official ceremony to perform before leaving office, accompanied by the president-elect: the fiftieth anniversary of VE Day in Berlin and Moscow. This, too, was not without its controversy. While in Berlin, apparently putting the prepared speech on one side, Mitterrand vibrantly praised the ordinary 'patriotic' and 'courageous' German soldiers who had 'accepted that they would lose their lives' even if it was for a 'bad cause'. This homage to Hitler's army provoked another outcry in France. In Moscow the next day he tried to recover the situation but emotions had been too deeply stirred for him to row back easily.[107]

Post-Mitterrand

President Mitterrand handed over powers to the newly elected Jacques Chirac on the morning of 17 May. The delay was almost unbearable, but he was determined to finish the second septennate to go down in history as the only President to finish two full seven-year terms. It was a courteous hand-over and the new president kept in touch. In mid-morning, immediately after the hand-over, Mitterrand went to the Socialist Party headquarters where there was a reception to which he gave a short speech and he was given a small car as a present by the party. He returned not to the old flat in the rue de Bièvre but to a state apartment in the avenue Frédéric-Le-Play. It was shortly after revealed that he had bought a plot for a grave for a song on the scenic Mont Beuvray, though the subsequent outcry led to an abandonment of this plan.[108]

François Mitterrand lived on in increasing pain and under ever more intrusive chemotherapy to deal with the aggressive cancer. He had been given a 'death sentence' in November 1981 and had lived with the knowledge since that date, although he may have come to believe that it was beaten. He had had time to contemplate death and his reflections became more intensely morbid as he grew more ill.[109] Public opinion appears to have empathized with him in his last fight. He rejected final treatments that would have deprived him of reason.[110] Thus, until the end he was lucid, capable of giving interviews and of finishing two books (one in interview format) as well as of talking to people at some length on the phone. He joined former President George Bush for the inauguration of the American's presidential library in the USA in October and then visited Venice and Egypt in December. On 8 January 1996, François Mitterrand died in his Paris apartment.

Mitterrand lost his faith some time after the war and had not (by several accounts) regained it; but although he had no certainties, he retained a vague New Age spirituality.[111] There were, all the same, two Catholic services. His attempt to arrange a burial in a reserved plot in the protected site of Mont Beuvray had been rejected and the public had not been sympathetic to his seeking a special dispensation.[112] On 11 January a funeral ceremony was held in Notre Dame de Paris, attended by powerful former associates and a tearful Helmut Kohl. While this ceremony went on, he was quietly buried by family and close friends in the family plot in Jarnac.

There was a touching image of his 'three women' (Anne, Danielle and Mazarine) united in their grief, but absent were his Swedish girlfriend, his child and his other paramours.[113]

President Chirac, in a remarked-on oration, declared: 'François Mitterrand, he was a will . . . his choices were always clear and he always made them in the name of France. . . . Ultimately the only thing that counts is that one is faithful to one's truth and what one can do for France . . . at the moment at which François Mitterrand enters into history, I hope that we can meditate on his message.'[114]

Conclusion: 'A Character from a Novel'[1]

Mitterrand set up and ran his own political sub-system: 'with two hundred well-placed men, you hold France'.[2] This was the close entourage who went through the furnace with him and with whom he used to govern the country. In general this system of personal relations can be likened to a solar system, with Mitterrand as the sun and the other individuals in orbit around him. Only Mitterrand knew who was who and where each person fitted, and they were not encouraged to get together (in fact they were discouraged from developing joint viewpoints). But Mitterrand's system was secretive and without the controlling rules of the Newtonian solar system. People would be raised up, promoted or demoted, and their advice sought or employed because Mitterrand wanted it, and for no reason discernible to them. Once in the Elysée, he would ignore his ministers and the official circuits (at the cost of upheaval) and make his own choices.[3]

Individual members might not be aware of other associates and might be quite surprised to see one of the outer comets passing close by; as Jacques Attali was taken aback to see Bousquet at dinner with Mitterrand one evening and was told, 'don't worry he is a friend. He has helped.'[4] Each element remained separate from the other, but Mitterrand was still the centre. This was, no doubt, a development of the Resistance method of separate worlds in quite distinct relations with the centre. There was, in any case, very little in common between Dalida, Lang, Dr Gubler, de Grossouvre, Rousselet, Pelat, Dayan and so on. What mattered was the entourage's commitment to Mitterrand and their use to him. Thus people were picked up and incorporated in the course of a long career. Many were unpartisan (like the pollster Charles Salzmann or Dr Gubler) or even active in opposed parties. In keeping with this practice, Mitterrand refused to make moral judgement of his collaborators (life is 'grey on grey'), but it was a testing experience to be incorporated into the entourage and those who were not pliable did not stay.

Character

One aspect of Mitterrand's *chiaroscuro* was that nobody knew him. André Rousselet commented of him that one person could only know 30 per cent of him and that that 30 per cent was not the same for everybody but that even so, putting all these together, a good third would invariably remain in the dark.[5] Other acquaintances have commented on the 'Zelig-like' personality of the man.[6] Nobody entered the 'secret garden' of Mitterrand's personality, although many thought that they had done so. He would be closed and open at the same time to the same person and would reveal some things to some people and other things to others, but would always conceal something from everybody. Mitterrand, in what was perhaps another Resistance legacy, was permanently on his guard and alive to chicanery. When there were setbacks he could see plots, and in 1981 he drew parallels between himself and Salvador Allende (Chilean President, assassinated in 1973) and this in turn fed the paranoid creation of the phone-tapping presidential 'police force'.

Mitterrand had, when he wanted it, considerable charm. This is how most people were brought into the entourage. There are many descriptions of the exercise of this charm (anybody who had been flattered by Mitterrand remembered it), including from people who were not disposed to like him or to follow him later. An exercise of authority from the outset of his relationship with people was wrapped into a genuine understanding of problems and of situations. On the other hand he could amuse himself by provoking people in his close entourage or with petty humiliations, and he remembered slights.[7]

Distance

Mitterrand's distance from associates was maintained by his invariable use of the formal 'vous'. He would refer to most people by their last name: Jean Glavany was always Glavany (for example).[8] (The story of the Socialist activist, who bounced up and said that, as they were both socialists, they would use the 'tu', only to be met with the glacial 'comme vous voulez, Monsieur', is probably apocryphal but is *ben trovato*.) Any change in address indicated displeasure. Even the devoted brother-in-law Roger Hanin was still 'vous' after twenty years. It is sometimes said that the only exception to this rule was Georges Dayan (an associate from before the war and the army) – but that is another of the unknowns of the Mitterrand system. What Mitterrand did have was an elephantine memory for people and their foibles as well as for their anniversaries, children, animals, favourite books and so on. This, it has to be said, was beyond normal measure (he never forgot significant dates) and not unknown with politicians, but his range of network was formidable. (It also casts doubt on his assertion that he 'did not know' about some people's background.) Mitterrand was also to use posts to augment and reward this network in Africa and the veterans' associations and elsewhere, and his liberal distribution of decorations was a joke in the Nièvre.[9] Once in the Elysée, Mitterrand's 'obsession' (to use Attali's phrase) was to get his people into position and to expand his clientèle. Using the Elysée a vast spoils system, and replacing, of course, the conservative right's nominees, was put in place to reward those who had followed him through good times and bad and to augment his team.

Purpose

Mitterrand's system was designed to get him into power, into office in the Fourth Republic and into the presidency in the Fifth Republic, but it was carefully maintained through nominations and recognition when he was at the Elysée. It was an intricate and shifting system, in its own terms a success. Mitterrand achieved supreme office in the state and had an unprecedented series of election victories (presidential and legislative). To a not inconsiderable extent he had luck ('All success is due to luck. Ask anyone who has failed'), but the robust nature of the system he had created was to no small extent behind his long career at the summit of the state.

Yet, Mitterrand's own personal political entourage was created to gain power and to defeat opponents (internal as well as external) and not for exercising power. He gave little in the way of precise direction to policy and even in key areas such as Europe and education he was content to remain at the level of generalities. He was not interested in ideology or in ideological debate, and was equally uninterested in policy formulation and expert discussion. Hubert Védrine, whom nobody would accuse of disloyalty to the President, said that it is not possible to imagine any system more divorced from deliberative decision-making.[10] Mitterrand was not an adept of the new disciplines of sociology or economics, although he was conversant with the main issues and could make a formidable case for the action he was about to pursue. He was a technician of power who may have concluded that the clashes between experts was so much froth on the surface of the political process which could be safely ignored. In any case, he would never rely on one councillor or one source of information and ensured that he had several viewpoints on even the smallest questions.

Competition

Antagonisms could be stimulated, and if the surrounding entourage was too peaceful would be created. This led to his entourage being in permanent disequilibrium and meant that Mitterrand himself was unpredictable and his use of anger was also psychologically destabilizing.[11] Stable conditions would have deprived him of the ability to choose and an off-balance group avoided a sector being 'captured' by somebody and made Mitterrand the ultimate decision-maker at all times. (Usually decisions were put off but sometimes things were left until a decision had to be taken willy nilly.) Mitterrand, like President Roosevelt, would ask two or perhaps several people to undertake a task or to prepare a position paper. Thus, for example, Attali was working on a deflation plan even while Mitterrand made up his mind between leaving or remaining in the EMS in 1983 and while Jean Riboud prepared a protectionist 'Albanian plan'. These people, often not entirely familiar with the subject and without being aware of the others, would prepare and submit to the President who would then choose between them. Often this annoyed the collaborators, but it was a refined way of ensuring that the President decided.

But Mitterrand was also indirect in asking for information in order to check on its authenticity. When he wanted to know something he would put the question in such a way that people often did not know what he was asking. In delegating tasks he would be unclear and left it to his interlocutor to divine what was wanted. Symptomatic of this, in Mitterrand's Elysée, was the fluid line of division between the Secretary-General (Bérégovoy, then Bianco) and the post invented for Jacques Attali of *conseiller spécial auprès du Président*. By the same token the demarcation between the public and the private also became porous in Mitterrand's Elysée and from that resulted a number of affairs (insider-trading in American National Can, notably).

As befits the French presidential system, Mitterrand's own constellation of power was essentially personal and side-stepped the more common standards (Claude Allègre asserted that 'La morale pour François Mitterrand c'était pour les autres . . .')[12] as well as going outside the state and party structures.[13] De Gaulle, and after him Pompidou and Giscard d'Estaing, ran their own individual systems based on their own personality and Mitterrand was no different. This was possible because of the weakness of the political parties in France and because of the fundamental importance of the presidency as the keystone institution of the Fifth Republic. A system of personal power, which would be difficult to construct and run in political systems controlled by parties, slipped easily into the mould of the Fifth Republic built by de Gaulle and created a presidential court.[14] It was also, with its secrets and clandestine aspects, something both developed under and inherited from the Resistance, although not confined by that.

Firstly, then, Mitterrand created a series of personal bilateral relationships of an eclectic and wide-ranging nature. People who became involved were devoted to Mitterrand personally whatever their own political career or subsequent route. They might be called upon to undertake assignments or to take responsibility, but their relationship to Mitterrand was the essential point and they in no sense formed a unit (though they did feel a belonging to a 'family').[15] They might not have been aware of the nature and numbers of other collaborators, and Mitterrand was willing to ignore the constraints placed on more run-of-the-mill politicians. Thus he had a close relationship with the lawyer for the FLN's 'porteurs des valises', Roland Dumas, as well as with the Vichyite Jean-Paul Martin and the 'leftist' Leccia. But these people themselves would have been, except perhaps in Dayan's case, only dimly aware of who else constituted the Mitterrand group.

Political Use

Having a diverse group of associates and confidants enabled Mitterrand to speak with many voices and to quite specific interests with tailored messages. Contacts could be made through, for example, de Grossouvre, that could then be used or even disavowed as Mitterrand's politics dictated. There was very little that could not be covered in this way but on the other hand the real Mitterrand, the core personality, was known to few people, if to any, after Dayan's death. By the same token, only Mitterrand knew the real shape of his connections, commitments and contacts. It was also based on secrecy and only Mitterrand himself would divulge the decision, to the extent that sometimes collaborators did not know what had been decided. Silence was also demanded from his collaborators because, by the nature of their functions, they would know much that was damaging and the talkative (like de Grossouvre) would be downgraded.

This was a system based on personal loyalty to Mitterrand himself and disregarded formal hierarchies and organizations. Mitterrand's entourage in and out of office was more 'Gaullian' than 'Pompidolian' or 'Giscardian'. De Gaulle demanded personal loyalty, but in his case there was an overarching 'great cause' to which collaborators committed themselves through gaullism. De Gaulle's genius as a politician was to identify himself with the cause at the darkest hour and to retain that identity. Mitterrand was, in contradistinction, not identified with one cause until relatively late in his political career, by which time his constellation of personal relations was already set and in a pattern of mutual reward. Only a few of the younger members of his close associates were brought into the circle.

Fidelity

Mitterrand, it was said, could not separate himself from people. Once having accepted somebody as a friend, there would be no subsequent separation. He would remain loyal to people long after the association had ceased to become politically rational.[16] He had friendships with former 'Cagoulards' and with Vichyites like Bousquet when these were politically risky, but that was but an illustration of his 'talent for friendship'.[17] That description of 'friendship', however, underestimates the essential political contribution made by these various associates who were able to give assistance at crucial points in his career and they would be repaid.[18] The offspring of his associates like Hubert Védrine, Paule Dayan and Nathalie Duhamel (Mendès France's daughter-in-law) were found places, as was his dentist Guy Penne (as African Affairs aide).

Perhaps Mitterrand never succeeded with the 'benign asperity' of downgrading people with the best of intentions. He adopted one of his favourite author's maxims and never refused things point blank, as that deprived dependants of all hope – something he was able to avoid doing.[19] If, as was said, he could never separate himself from people he could, nevertheless, cast them into the outer darkness and uncertainty. This was an aspect of how Mitterrand handled collaborators. Humiliation was one of the resources he used to establish an ascendancy. Charles Salzmann, after twenty years of dedicated service, was simply cast aside, and Dr Gubler was summarily dismissed.[20] Many people were cut off from the source of their commitment, the man himself, to their acute discomfort and this *dynamique affective* was harrowing.[21] In fact, in the last three years of his life his doctors were sacked with astonishing abruptness, and some were destroyed in the process. Being abruptly cut out may have contributed to the downfall of both Bérégovoy and de Grossouvre, although Mitterrand was a master at knowing just how far to push people before readmitting them to grace. The suicides of two people close to the President may have been a coincidence, but his hold on subordinates involved fraught psychological games.[22]

Mitterrand's superiority was demonstrated in many ways.[23] As the centre of the 'solar system' of orbiting individuals, he had to be the dominant person and there were a number of means to this end. How these traits developed is a mystery, and where they came from is also unclear, but the family, and the father, are described as cold and as calculating.[24] Mitterrand's dominance could be established in other ways than the withdrawal of approval: by never arriving on time (even lingering in bookshops until he was suitably late), not wearing a watch or by not carrying money. When shopping, he would signal to a member of his entourage who would then buy the desired item.[25] His indifference to money did not go as far as to refrain from spending it, but he was interested in power not pelf. There were also his pilgrimages to chosen spots. Although the annual visit to the Roche de Solutré is well known, there was also the annual dinner of 10 May and he also had rites in various parts of France to which an invitation to join was much sought after.[26]

Gratitude

Mitterrand rarely, if ever, thanked people – Salzmann noted that he was thanked only once – and he would not give complements, 'not even a slap on the back'.[27] Savaran said that he was never disappointed by Mitterrand because 'I never expected anything from him'.[28] Likewise, Mitterrand would get people to undertake menial errands, using them as a 'runner'.[29] On one occasion Mazarine's cat ran away at the end of a holiday weekend, and an army helicopter was despatched to pick it up the next week. Although presidential displeasure was usually indicated by a change in tone of voice or a phrase rather than in words, tantrums and dressings-down in front of third parties did happen. On one occasion the escape of a family dog from the Elysée led to Hubert Vedrine's being bawled out and then to a mobilization to find it.[30] Yet Mitterrand had perfected the political art of getting into a rage on several occasions when it was politically astute to lose patience.[31]

Hence he was not an easy man, and cultivated tricks and traps for his entourage, but manifestations of the President's regard could also be made in small presents, a conversation or an enquiry after children or personal circumstances. He would not give compliments to his staff and, while he would not scold them either (he could be scathing in private), he would leave no doubt as to his displeasure with an apparently mild remark. Loyalty was maintained by withdrawing approval or even ignoring collaborators for an indeterminate time to show who was the dominant person in the relationship. In this sense, all collaborators were subordinates, nobody was indispensable and fear of disapproval was used to animate relationships. 'There are few pleasures in life so piquantly addictive as being feared. His was a compound of avuncularity, brutality and clarity of mind.' Mitterrand, for whom the word supercilious is inadequate, dealt capriciously with people so he could not be 'read' and gained himself a reputation for being enigmatic. As he said: 'Everyone has their drug. Mine is silence'[32] – in keeping with the advice of one of his preferred authors Graciàn y Morales who asserted that 'reticence was the hall-mark of ability'.[33]

Associates

Central to the system was Roger-Patrice Pelat, an old friend of Mitterrand since the days of the camps and the Resistance, who would take postprandial walks with the President almost daily.[34] This was a close relationship (their wives were the Gouze sisters). Pelat the 'Vice-President', as he was called, rose from very humble origins to a substantial position in industry through the Vibrachoc company. He had supported Mitterrand in the wilderness years with a secretary as well as an annual honorarium as 'legal councillor'.[35] His politics were not on the left and he supported Marie-France Garaud in 1981, but he still became a member of de Grossouvre's Presidential Hunt Committee and was an important councillor and go-between for the new President.[36] Pelat died on 1 February 1989 before his full implication in insider trading became a subject of judicial investigation. His criss-crossing the boundaries of politics (left/right) and the public and private helped to support Mitterrand's political career and his own fortune.[37] Funding of political parties by business is now regarded as offending the finer ethical sense, and, to a considerable extent, it has been suppressed by the law of 1992.

Other financial and industrial personalities who formed part of the Mitterrand system included André Bettencourt and François Dalle (Chief Executive of l'Oréal) as well as Pierre de Bénouville (an executive of Dassault) and Jean Riboud (Chief Executive of Schlumberger). Given the milieu within which Mitterrand passed his early life up to and including the Resistance, it is not surprising that many of them were on the right or extreme right and that few (Halin and Dayan excepted) were on the left. But to this list of associates should probably be added the African interests of his son Jean-Christophe Mitterrand (and his associates) who, however, stepped down as African councillor in 1992.[38]

Mitterrand's association with René Bousquet also falls into this pattern. Bousquet was an important aid at certain points in Mitterrand's career and provided backing.[39] He had been a Radical left-wing civil servant before the war and afterwards maintained an array of contacts. After 'twenty minutes of national disgrace' at the Liberation (as judged by the High Court) he went into the Banque d'Indochine and finance and became a UDSR candidate in the Marne (where he had been a prefect) in 1958 and – after 1959 – was on the board of *La Dépêche du Midi*. This relationship, dated by most back to 1949, was maintained and was mutually beneficial. Of course, Mitterrand was no more inclined than de Gaulle or Pompidou to reopen the question of the Vichy regime or to enquire into the treatment and amnesty of those who served Pétain and Laval. Mitterrand, often depicted as a man of intense loyalties, kept old friends who had proved themselves to be an embarrassment or dishonest, but he could be a poor judge of character. Retaining close contact with Bousquet, whose past was an insult to a large section of the population, was disdainful.

Whatever his intentions, Mitterrand, having seen off the challenge from Rocard, remained during his double septennate pre-eminent on the left (Prov, xiv: 15). There was no cohort of potential successors. As Pope said: 'Be like the Turk, bear no brother near the throne.' Mitterrand's failure to appoint or anoint a successor may have been intentional, for he had no rivals. On one occasion he listed his chosen successors in order: Delors, Léotard, Barre, Giscard, Chirac, My Dog, Rocard.[40]

Final Things

In the final years, Mitterrand conducted many interviews with writers and biographers in an attempt to lay out his record and to justify it. Given the revelations about his past and the continuing unfolding of scandals, naturally enough the predominant note struck was one of self-justification rather than self-satisfaction. Politics does not allow for final answers. But, as usual, something can be said. Mitterrand is the subject of a very large number of books of personal memoirs and testimony (even by his dog), to the extent that it is difficult to imagine that much more will emerge by way of 'revelation'.

However, what emerges is a *homo politicus,* a man whose life was devoted to politics in spite of the setbacks that on many occasions would have daunted a lesser spirit. Mitterrand lived in a hinterland of books and of nature (his speeches are rich with allusions) and effected not to esteem politics, but the extent of that other life remains unknown. His own writing displayed what is politely known as 'heightened literary sensibility'. What emerges from the multiple testimonies is a series of 'pooterish' observations passed over to a usually admiring entourage who would then buff these off to a fine gloss. But then, of course, nothing a President says is going to be wholly without interest – even when it is without interest. In political terms emphasis was placed on Mitterrand's reading by people 'in the know' and on his communion with the literary and philosophical greats, but there were no indications of the seriousness of this activity.

But, from a political point of view, and whatever Mitterrand's literary merits, bookishness served a very useful political purpose and a reputation for impenetrable wisdom was recycled. Books would be strategically pointed up (or left lying where they could be seen). Marx and Engels were read on a visit to the Soviet Union in 1975, for example, and literary dinners at the Elysée were organized and literary figures were invited on presidential voyages. (Mitterrand once declined to see Reagan on the pretext that he was re-reading Lamartine.) It gave the impression that Mitterrand knew something, that he was the President of the Republic of Letters, that he had some insight denied to other people – a mystical communion with nature and the spirit of the great literature of the past. Cultural allusions, visits to places and embellishment helped develop the literary aura of the President for political purposes.

By the same token, Mitterrand's two septennates and the munificent increase in spending on the arts to 1 per cent of the budget enabled him to leave an architectural legacy that is grandiose and that was an ambition announced early in his socialist career. But whatever its aesthetic merits, the Louvre, the Bibliothèque and the Arch are pharonic and the Institut du monde arabe and the Cité de la musique are attractive (and the Bastille Opera is curious) and these buildings are a mark on contemporary Paris. Mitterrand kept a close watch on ten or so projects in Paris and, although teams would review submissions by architects, Mitterrand set the guidelines and always had the last say.[41] But it was Mitterrand himself (not a competition judge) who chose Ieoh Ming Pei for the Louvre and decided in favour of Otto Van Spreckelsen for the Arche and he pushed to get the Bibliothèque built.

But Mitterrand, who constructed a system to enable him to have freedom, did not like to choose and he took refuge in ambiguity and abstraction – what Fabius called his '*sidérante* ambivalence'. This was even carried to the extreme of avoiding making choices in government, giving instructions that were contradictory, refusing to set out the major policies in the big departments, and distancing himself from his own ministers.

Thus the two terms of Mitterrand's presidency floated between decisions, as the President proved to be a procrastinator of Godotesque proportions, and matters moved fast mainly when the situation became irreversible. In this way, and notwithstanding the continuing public fascination with the man, Mitterrand exemplifies Sidney Hook's 'eventful' politician.

Notes

Preface

1 W. Riker, *The Art of Political Manipulation* (Yale University Press, New Haven, 1986).
2 Ibid.
3 P. Riddell, *Honest Opportunism* (Hamish Hamilton, London, 1993), p. 15.
4 *L'Express*, 12 November 1959, p. 40.
5 R. Caro, *Master of the Senate* (Cape, London, 2002).
6 *L'Express*, 5 November 1959, p. 40.
7 C. C. O'Brien, *The Great Melody* (Sinclair-Stevenson, London, 1992).
8 *Le Monde*, 1 October 1997.

Chapter 1 1916–1944

1 See, for example, *L'Aurore*, 22 September 1965.
2 P. Péan, *Une Jeunesse française: François Mitterrand 1934–47* (Fayard, Paris, 1994).
3 Baltasar Graciàn y Morales, *The Hero* (Dent, London, 1953), p. 181.
4 F. Mitterrand, *Ma Part de vérité* (Paris, Fayard, 1969), p. 20.
5 Ibid., p. 10.
6 Ibid., pp. 20–4.
7 R. Mitterrand, *Frère de quelqu'un* (Laffont, Paris, 1988), p. 47.
8 Ibid., p. 225.
9 C. Moulin, *Mitterrand intime* (Albin Michel, Paris, 1982). Mitterrand repudiated any suggestion of anti-Semitism in this attachment.
10 *Le Point*, 15 January 1973.
11 Péan, *Une Jeunesse française*, pp. 28–9.
12 On De La Rocque and his movements, see P. Rudeaux, *Les Croix de feu et le PSF* (France-Empire, Paris, 1967).
13 J. Lacouture, *Mitterrand: Une histoire de français*, vol. 1 (Seuil, Paris, 1998).
14 *Le Figaro*, 2 February 1935.
15 E. Faux et al., *La Main droite de dieu* (Seuil, Paris, 1994), p. 105.
16 C. Nay, *Le Noir et le rouge* (Grasset, Paris, 1984), p. 69.
17 *L'Echo de Paris*, 4 July 1936, quoted in Péan, *Une Jeunesse française*, p. 58.
18 Ibid.
19 Péan, *Une Jeunesse française*, p. 109.
20 Mitterrand, *Frère de quelqu'un*, p. 202.
21 Ibid., p. 75.
22 Péan, *Une Jeunesse française*, p. 294.
23 J.-M. Terrasse, *Catherine Langeais* (Fayard, Paris, 2003), ch. 7.
24 F. Mitterrand, *Politique I* (Fayard, Paris, 1977).
25 Mitterrand, *Frère de quelqu'un*, ch. 13 passim.
26 Péan, *Une Jeunesse française*, p. 97.

27 For example in *Le Monde*, 10 May 1981.
28 Mitterrand, *Ma Part de vérité*, p. 21 (author's translation).
29 Péan, *Une Jeunesse française*, pp. 101ff.
30 Mitterrand, *Politique I*.
31 Terrasse, *Catherine Langeais*, ch. 10.
32 Moulin, *Mitterrand intime*, p. 50.
33 Mitterrand *Frère de quelqu'un*, p. 191.
34 P. Laborie, *L'Opinion française sous Vichy* (Seuil, Paris, 1990).
35 Péan, *Une Jeunesse française*, p. 179; *L'Express*, 5 November 1959.
36 *New York Review of Books*, 3 November 1994.
37 Georges-Marc Benamou, *Le Dernier Mitterrand* (Plon, Paris, 1997), p. 76.
38 Péan, *Une Jeunesse française*, p. 187.
39 Ibid.
40 Ibid., p. 193.
41 Ibid., pp. 178, 182.
42 J. Lacouture and P. Rotman, *Mitterrand, le roman du pouvoir* (Seuil, Paris, 2000), pp. 27–8.
43 Mitterrand, *Politique I*.
44 *Le Monde*, 9 October 1994; but see also *Paris Match*, 22 October 1994, where a witness asserts that the acquaintance went back to Vichy times.
45 *Libération*, 12 October 1994.
46 P. M. Williams, *Crisis and Compromise* (Longman, London, 1964), p. 55.
47 E. Conan, *Le Procès de Papon* (Gallimard, Paris, 1998), p. 56.
48 Simon Arbellot de Vacqueur, *Eau de Vichy, vin de Malaga* (Editions du Conquistador, Paris, 1952); on Mitterrand's request for the *francisque*, see *Ecrits de Paris*, 244 (January 1966).
49 R. Rémond (ed.), *Le Gouvernement de Vichy* (FNSP, Paris, 1972).
50 F. Mitterrand, *Mémoires interrompus* (Odile Jacob, Paris, 1996), p. 82.
51 Mitterrand, *Frère de quelqu'un*, p. 199.
52 Ibid., pp. 201, 205.
53 H. Verity, *We Landed by Moonlight* (Ian Allen, London, 1978).
54 Péan, *Une Jeunesse française*, p. 392.
55 F. Mitterrand, *La Paille et le grain* (Flammarion, Paris, 1975), p. 165.
56 C. Manceron, *Cent mille voix par jour* (Robert Laffont, Paris, 1966).
57 H. Frenay, *La Nuit finira* (Laffont, Paris, 1974), vol. 2, pp. 108–9.
58 Moulin, *Mitterrand intime*, p. 61.
59 E. Faux et al., *La Main droite de dieu*, p. 143.
60 Péan, *Une Jeunesse française*, p. 422.
61 Ibid., p. 439.
62 Frenay, *La Nuit finira*, pp. 202–3.
63 Ibid., p. 315.
64 *Libération*, 1 October 1996.
65 *L'Humanité*, 30 March 2001.
66 Faux et al., *La Main droite de dieu*, pp. 170–6.
67 *L'Express*, 9 July 1992.
68 R. O. Paxton, *La France de Vichy* (Seuil, Paris, 1973), pp. 330ff.

Chapter 2 The Fourth Republic

1 P. M. Williams, *Crisis and Compromise* (Longman, London, 1964), p. 175 and E. Duhamel, *François Mitterrand: l'unité d'un homme* (Flammarion, Paris, 1998).
2 Williams, *Crisis and Compromise*, pp. 174–6.

3 J. Barsalou, *La Mal aimée* (Plon, Paris, 1964) p. 29.
4 P. Péan *Une Jeunesse française: François Mitterrand 1934–47* (Fayard, Paris, 1994), p. 523.
5 R. Cayrol, *François Mitterrand* (FNSP, Paris, 1967).
6 E. Faux et al., *La Main droite de dieu* (Seuil, Paris, 1994), p. 148, and J. Pataut *Sociologie de la Nièvre au XXe siècle* (Cujas, Paris, 1956).
7 Péan, *Une Jeunesse française*, pp. 526 and 504.
8 F.-O. Giesbert, *François Mitterrand, une vie* (Seuil, Paris, 1996), p. 331.
9 Quoted in *Libération*, 9 January 1996.
10 F. Charmont, *François Mitterrand et la Nièvre* (L'Harmattan, Paris, 2001), pp. 37–8.
11 Faux et al., *La Main droite de dieu*, p. 149.
12 C. Nay, *Le Noir et le rouge* (Grasset, Paris, 1984), p. 148.
13 Charmont, *François Mitterrand et la Nièvre*, pp. 100–1.
14 R. Mitterrand, *Frère de quelqu'un* (Laffont, Paris, 1988), p. 233.
15 *France-Soir*, 19 March 1949.
16 J. Terrasse, *Catherine Langeais* (Fayard, Paris, 2003), pp. 301–2.
17 Y. Benot, *Massacres coloniaux, 1944–1950* (La Découverte, Paris, 2001).
18 F. Mitterrand, *Présence française et abandon* (Plon, Paris, 1957), pp. 182, 237.
19 C. de Gaulle, *Memoirs of Hope* (Weidenfeld, London, 1971), p. 68.
20 F.-O. Giesbert, *François Mitterrand ou la tentation de l'histoire* (Seuil, Paris, 1977), p. 112.
21 E. Duhamel, *François Mitterrand, l'unité d'un homme* (Flammarion, Paris, 1998), pp. 39–41
22 Williams, *Crisis and Compromise*, p. 11.
23 Nay, *Le Noir et le rouge*, p. 173.
24 *L'Express*, 17 October 1953.
25 Duhamel, *François Mitterrand*, pp. 83–8.
26 F. Mitterrand, *Aux Frontières de l'union française, Indochine-Tunisie* (Juillard, Paris, 1953), p.170.
27 P. M. Williams, *Wars, Plots and Scandals in Post-War France* (Cambridge University Press, Cambridge, 1970), pp. 53ff.
28 *Journal Officel*, 4 December 1954.
29 Duhamel, *François Mitterrand*, pp.152–3.
30 Faux et al., *La Main droite de dieu*, p. 213.
31 Assemblée Nationale, *Journal officiel*, 12 November 1954.
32 Ibid., 4 February 1955, p. 744.
33 *L'Express*, September 1953, 5 October 1953 and 22 January 1954.
34 Ibid., February 1958.
35 Assemblée Nationale, *Journal officiel*, 14 December 1954.
36 B. Droz and E. Lever, *Histoire de la guerre d'Algérie* (Seuil, Paris, 1982), p. 63.
37 Faux et al., *La Main droite de dieu*, p. 212.
38 Giesbert, *François Mitterrand, une vie*, p. 131; Droz and Lever *Histoire de la guerre d'Algérie*, p. 62.
39 Duhamel, *François Mitterrand*, pp. 139–49.
40 Ibid., p. 166.
41 *Le Monde*, 5 April 1956.
42 *Le Monde*, 8 October 1957.
43 C. Moulin, *Mitterrand intime* (Albin Michel, Paris, 1982), p. 121.

Chapter 3 De Gaulle's Republic

1 *Le Monde*, 13 April 1958.
2 G. Martinet, *Cassandre et les tueurs* (Grasset, Paris, 1986), p. 168.
3 F. Mitterrand, *Ma Part de vérité* (Fayard, Paris, 1969), p. 120.

4 F. Mitterrand, *Mémoires interrompus* (Odile Jacob, Paris, 1996), p. 189.

5 J.-R. Touroux, *Secrets d'état* (Plon, Paris, 1960), p. 399; F. Mitterrand, *Le Coup d'état permanent*, 2nd edn (Paris, Juillard, 1984), p. 73.

6 J. Lacouture and P. Rotman, *Mitterrand: le roman du pouvoir* (Seuil, Paris, 2000), p. 65.

7 *Le Monde*, 5 June 1958.

8 P. M. Williams, *Wars, Plots and Scandals in Post-War France* (Cambridge University Press, Cambridge, 1970), p. 74.

9 C. Nay, *Le Noir et le rouge* (Grasset, Paris, 1984), p. 256.

10 *Le Monde*, 28 October 1959.

11 R. Dumas, *Le Fil et la pelote* (Plon, Paris, 1996); R. Pesquet, *Mon vrai faux attentat contre Mitterrand* (Lafon, Paris, 1995); *L'Express*, 19 November 1959, no. 44.

12 J. Mossuz, *Les Clubs et la politique en France* (Colin, Paris, 1970).

13 Nay, *Le Noir et le rouge*, p. 272.

14 F.-O. Giesbert, *François Mitterrand ou la tentation de l'histoire* (Seuil, Paris, 1977), p. 203.

15 Ibid., p. 128.

16 Mitterrand, *Le Coup d'état permanent*, p. 84.

17 *Le Monde*, 13 March 1965.

18 M. Brulé et al. (eds), *Sondages*, no. 4 (IFOP, Paris, 1965).

19 Mossuz, *Les Clubs et la politique en France*, p. 177.

20 *Cahiers du communisme*, June–July 1964, pp. 52 and 56.

21 R. Dumas, *Le Fil et la pelote*, p. 156.

22 *L'Humanité*, 21 September 1965.

23 Ibid., 24 September 1965.

24 *France Observateur*, 28 October 1965.

25 C. Estier, *De Mitterrand à Jospin* (Stock, Paris, 1995), p. 26.

26 Lacouture and Rotman, *Mitterrand: le roman du pouvoir*, pp. 80–1.

27 *France nouvelle*, 26 May and 1 June 1965.

28 *Combat*, 24 October 1965.

29 Estier, *De Mitterrand à Jospin*, p. 35.

30 *France observateur*, 29 October 1965.

31 P. M. Williams, *French Politicians and Elections, 1951–1969* (Cambridge University Press, Cambridge, 1970), p. 195.

32 E. Faux et al., *La Main droite de dieu* (Seuil, Paris, 1994), p. 34

33 Mossuz, *Les Clubs et la politique en France*, p. 185.

34 Williams, *French Politicians and Elections*, p. 198.

35 *Le Monde*, 10 December 1965.

36 Williams, *French Politicians and Elections*, p. 196.

37 *L'Humanité*, 7 January 1966.

38 *Le Monde*, 5 November 1966.

39 *Cahiers du communisme*, February–March 1967, p. 50.

40 *Le Nouvel Observateur*, 22 November 1967.

41 Mitterrand *Ma Part de vérité*, p. 98.

42 Estier, *De Mitterrand à Jospin*, p. 216.

43 *Paris-Presse*, 24 May 1968.

44 Estier, *De Mitterrand à Jospin*, pp. 230–3.

45 *L'Humanité*, 29 May 1968.

46 Estier, *De Mitterrand à Jospin*, p. 245.

47 P. Grémion, *Paris/Prague* (Julliard, Paris, 1985).

48 Estier, *De Mitterrand à Jospin*, p. 252.

49 Ibid., p. 254.

Chapter 4 The Common Programme

1 J. K. Galbraith, *The Anatomy of Power* (Hamish Hamilton, London, 1984), p. 41.
2 *L'Express*, 21 October 1968.
3 J. Lacouture and P. Rotman, *Mitterrand, le roman du pouvoir* (Seuil, Paris, 1990), p. 92.
4 F. Mitterrand, *Un Socialisme du possible* (Seuil, Paris, 1970).
5 P. Alexandre, *Le Roman de la gauche* (Grasset, Paris, 1977), p. 219.
6 Ibid., p. 212.
7 S. Hurtig (ed.), *Alain Savary* (Presses de sciences po, Paris, 2002), p. 106.
8 A. Savary, *Pour le nouveau Parti socialiste* (Seuil, Paris, 1970).
9 F. Mitterrand, *Politique I* (Fayard, Paris, 1977), p. 542.
10 Lacouture and Rotman, *Mitterrand, le roman du pouvoir*, p. 96.
11 *Politique I*, p. 532.
12 Lacouture and Rotman, *Mitterrand: le roman du pouvoir*, p. 97.
13 Archives nationales, Archives Guy Mollet.
14 F. Mitterrand, *Ma Part de vérité* (Fayard, Paris, 1969), p. 535.
15 *L'Humanité*, 17 January 1971.
16 Ibid.
17 E. Fajon, *L'Union est un combat* (Editions sociales, Paris, 1975).
18 *Le Nouvel Observateur*, 15 March 1973.
19 Archives nationales, Archives Guy Mollet.
20 G. Marchais in *Le Monde*, 11 February 1974, and *L'Humanité*, 4 April 1974; René Piquet in *Le Monde*, 10 March 1974.
21 C. Estier, *De Mitterrand à Jospin* (Stock, Paris, 1995), pp. 82–5.
22 *L'Humanité*, 13 April 1974.
23 *Le Nouvel Observateur*, 29 March 1974.
24 *L'Humanité*, 8 May 1974.
25 P. Robrieux, *Histoire intérieure du parti communiste, 1972–1982* (Fayard, Paris, 1992), p. 188.
26 *Le Nouvel Observateur*, 11 March 1974.
27 In Graciàn's words from *The Hero* (Dent, London, 1953), pp. 3 and 5.
28 *Le Point*, 2 May 1981.
29 See G. Le Gall, 'Le déclin du Pcf', in SOFRES. *L'Opinion Publique 1986* (Gallimard, Paris, 1986) and table 6, 'Le bilan des pays socialistes'.
30 C. Moulin, *Mitterrand intime* (Albin Michel, Paris, 1982), p. 247.
31 *France-Soir*, 22 August 1975.
32 C. Salzmann, *Le Bruit de la main gauche* (Laffont, Paris, 1996) and *L'Unité*, no. 156, 2 May 1975.
33 *L'Humanité*, 11 May 1977.
34 Alexandre, *Le Roman de la gauche*, p. 401.

Chapter 5 Alliance Problems: 1978–1981

1 P. Alexandre, *Le Roman de la gauche* (Grasset, Paris, 1977), p. 403.
2 C. Moulin, *Mitterrand intime* (Albin Michel, Paris, 1982), p. 265.
3 *L'Humanité*, 13 January; see also issues of 26, 27, 28 and 30 January.
4 *L'Humanité*, 6 April 1978.
5 P. Savaran, *Mitterrand, les autres jours* (Albin Michel, Paris, 1997), p. 48.
6 J. Lacouture and P. Rotman, *Mitterrand, le roman du pouvoir* (Seuil, Paris, 1990), p. 109.
7 J.-P. Chevènement, in *Le Monde*, 4 January 1979.
8 J.-P. Chevènement, *Les Socialistes, les communistes et les autres* (Aubier, Montagne, 1977), p. 232.

9 Lacouture and Rotman, *Mitterrand, le roman du pouvoir*, p. 111.

10 *Le Monde*, 8 March 1980.

11 *L'Humanité*, 10 November 1980.

12 *Le Monde*, 14 March 1981.

13 F. Mitterrand, *Ici et maintenant* (Fayard, Paris, 1980), p. 23.

14 R. Cayrol and J. Jaffré, in *Le Monde*, 1 December 1978; C. Salzmann, *Le Bruit de la main gauche* (Laffont, Paris, 1996).

15 Moulin, *Mitterrand intime*, p. 355.

16 J. Glavany, *Mitterrand, Jospin et nous* (Grasset, Paris, 1998), p. 28.

17 *Le Monde*, 5 December 1980; *France-Soir*, 21 February 1980.

18 Moulin, *Mitterrand intime*, p. 299.

19 Savaran, *Mitterrand, les autres jours*, p. 81.

20 *Le Nouvel Observateur*, 18 April 1981.

21 C. Estier, *De Mitterrand à Jospin* (Stock, Paris, 1995), p. 150.

22 *Le Matin*, 2 February 1981.

23 See, for example, *L'Humanité*, 14 and 28 January 1981.

24 *Le Monde*, 25 April 1981.

25 *Valeurs Actuelles*, 19 January 1981.

26 D. B. Goldey and A. F. Knapp, 'Time for a Change: The French Elections of 1981', in *Electoral Studies*, 1(1), April 1982, pp. 3–42 and August 1982, pp. 169–94.

27 E. Conan, *Le Procès Papon* (Gallimard, Paris, 1998), pp. 142–3.

28 J. Frears, *Parties and Voters in France* (Hurst, London, 1990), p. 157.

29 S. Hoffmann and G. Ross, *The Mitterrand Experiment* (Polity, Cambridge, 1987).

30 *Le Nouvel Observateur*, 15 May 1981.

31 V. Giscard d'Estaing, *Le Pouvoir et la vie* (Compagnie 12, Paris, 1991).

32 *Le Monde*, 6 February 1978.

33 M. Schifres and M. Sarazin, *L'Elysée de Mitterrand* (Albin Michel, Paris, 1985).

34 G. Dupeux, *Le Front populaire et les élections de 1936* (Colin, Paris, 1959).

35 *Le Monde*, 11 November 1981.

36 C. Estier and V. Neiertz, *Véridique histoire d'un septennat peu ordinaire* (Grasset, Paris, 1987), pp. 51–4.

37 *L'Humanité*, 18 July 1981.

Chapter 6 The First Socialist Governments: 1981–1985

1 S. Hurtig (ed.), *Alain Savary* (Presses de sciences po, Paris, 2002).

2 C. Gubler and M. Gonod, *Le Grand Secret* (Plon, Paris, 1996).

3 F. Mitterrand, *Ici et maintenant* (Fayard, Paris, 1980), p. 4.

4 Ibid., pp. 171–2.

5 Interim Plan, p. 181.

6 P. Mauroy, *Mémoires, 'Vous mettrez du bleu au ciel'* (Plon, Paris, 2003), p. 18.

7 P. Bergé, *Inventaire Mitterrand* (Stock, Paris, 2001), p. 34.

8 *Le Figaro*, 25 September 1981.

9 Bergé, *Inventaire Mitterrand*, p. 88.

10 Mauroy, *Mémoires*, p. 161.

11 Ibid., p. 132.

12 *Le Nouvel Observateur*, 23 January 1982.

13 Y. Mény, 'Decentralisation in Socialist France', in *West European Politics* (January 1984), pp. 65–79.

14 *Figaro magazine*, 4 February 1983.

15 J. Attali, *Verbatim* (Fayard, Paris, 1995), vol. 1, p. 245.

16 T. Chafer, 'French African Policy', *African Affairs*, 91 (1992), pp. 37–51.

17 See F. Mitterrand, *Aux frontières de l'union française, Indochine-Tunisie* (Juillard, Paris, 1953), p. 23; F. Mitterrand, *Présence française et abandon* (Plon, Paris, 1957), p. 237.
18 J. A. McKesson, 'France and Africa', *French Politics and Society*, 11 (1993).
19 Attali, *Verbatim*, vol. 3, p. 505.
20 Ibid., p. 518.
21 Attali, *Verbatim*, vol. 1, p. 103; H. Simonian, *The Privileged Partnership* (Oxford University Press, Oxford, 1985).
22 *Le Monde*, 1 February 1982.
23 Ibid., 26 November 1982.
24 *France-Soir*, 17 June 1982.
25 P. Bauchard, *La Guerre des deux roses* (Grasset, Paris, 1986), p. 129.
26 C. Salzmann, *Le Bruit de la main gauche* (Laffont, Paris, 1996), pp. 96–9.
27 Bauchard, *La Guerre des deux roses*, p. 143.
28 Attali, *Verbatim*, vol. 1, p. 937.
29 Ibid.; J. Lacouture and P. Rotman, *Mitterrand, le roman du pouvoir* (Seuil, Paris, 1990), pp. 137–40.
30 *Le Monde*, 24 August 1992.
31 *Libération*, 10 May 1984.
32 Attali, *Verbatim*, vol. 1, p. 502.
33 Ibid., p. 503.
34 Ibid., p. 964; *Libération*, 10 May 1984.
35 *Le Monde*, 1 November 1984.
36 Attali, *Verbatim*, vol. 1, pp. 930–3.
37 Ibid., p. 950.
38 Ibid., p. 949.
39 Ibid., p. 1004.
40 *Le Monde*, 5 November 1984.
41 Attali, *Verbatim*, vol. 1, p. 1014.
42 A. Savary, *En toute liberté* (Hachette, Paris, 1985), p. 80.
43 Attali, *Verbatim*, vol. 1, p. 1018.
44 Ibid., pp. 834–5.
45 Lacouture and Rotman, *Mitterrand, le roman du pouvoir*, p. 178.
46 *Le Monde*, 17 September 1985.
47 F.-O. Giesbert, *La Fin d'une époque* (Fayard, Paris, 1993), p. 481; Admiral P. Lacoste, *Un Amiral au secret* (Flammarion, Paris, 1996), p. 147. Lacoste comes close to implicating the President.
48 Attali, *Verbatim*, vol. 1, p. 1319.
49 *Le Nouvel Observateur*, 6 December 1985; P. Savaran, *Mitterrand, les autres jours* (Albin Michel, Paris, 1997), p. 79; *Le Monde*, 6 December 1985.
50 A. Cole and P. Campbell, *French Electoral Systems and Elections* (Gower, Aldershot, 1989), pp. 133–41.

Chapter 7 'Cohabitation': 1986–1988

1 Speech at Verdun-sur-le-Doubs, in *Le Monde*, 'Les Elections législatives de mars 1978' (Dossiers et documents, 1978).
2 *Le Monde*, 16 September 1983.
3 J. Attali, *Verbatim* (Fayard, Paris, 1995), vol. 1, p. 503.
4 J. Lacouture and P. Rotman, *Mitterrand, le roman du pouvoir* (Seuil, Paris, 1990), p. 187.
5 J. Glavany, *Mitterrand, Jospin et nous* (Grasset, Paris, 1998), pp. 196–7.
6 W. Northcutt, *Mitterrand: A Political Biography* (Holmes and Meier, New York, 1992), p. 123.

7 Lacouture and Rotman, *Mitterrand, le roman du pouvoir*, p. 185.

8 Attali, *Verbatim*, vol. 2, p. 16.

9 *Le Monde*, 25 November 1986.

10 10 November 1986.

11 *L'Express*, 14 March 1986.

12 Lacouture and Rotman, *Mitterrand, le roman du pouvoir*, p. 90.

13 P. Favier and M. Martin-Roland, *La Décennie Mitterrand* (Seuil, Paris, 1990), vol. 2, p. 488.

14 Ibid., pp. 491ff.

15 Attali, *Verbatim*, vol 2, p. 57.

16 J.-B. Raimond, *Le Quai d'Orsay à l'épreuve de la cohabitation* (Flammarion, Paris, 1989); Attali, *Verbatim*, vol. 2, p. 67.

17 Raimond, *Le Quai d'Orsay*.

18 Favier and M. Martin-Roland, *La Décennie Mitterrand*, vol. 2, p. 634.

19 *Le Figaro*, 15 October 1987.

20 Favier and M. Martin-Roland, *La Décennie Mitterrand*, vol. 2, p. 645.

21 Ibid., p. 656.

22 J. Lacouture, *François Mitterrand: Une histoire de français* (Seuil, Paris, 1998), vol. 2, p. 254.

23 Favier and Martin-Roland, *La Décennie Mitterrand*, vol. 2, p. 761.

24 Ibid., pp. 711–14.

25 Lacouture and Rotman, *Mitterrand, le roman du pouvoir*, p. 91.

26 Glavany, *Mitterrand, Jospin et nous*, pp. 194–6.

27 Favier and Martin-Roland, *La Décennie Mitterrand*, vol. 2, p. 659.

28 Lacouture and Rotman, *Mitterrand, le roman du pouvoir*, p. 92.

Chapter 8 The Second Term: 1988–1992

1 See *Le Monde*, 2 June 1981; *France Soir*, 22 April 1981.

2 J. Glavany, *Mitterrand, Jospin et nous* (Grasset, Paris, 1998), p. 124.

3 C. Gubler and M. Gonod, *Le Grand Secret* (Plon, Paris, 1996).

4 J. Attali, *Verbatim* (Fayard, Paris, 1995), vol. 1, p. 484.

5 Ibid., p. 492.

6 P. Favier and M. Martin-Roland, *La Décennie Mitterrand* (Seuil, Paris, 1999), vol. 3, p. 739.

7 Attali, *Verbatim*, vol. 1, p. 500.

8 Ibid., p. 499.

9 Favier and Martin-Roland, *La Décennie Mitterrand*, vol. 3, p. 747.

10 Glavany, *Mitterrand, Jospin et nous*, p. 166; Charles Salzmann, *Le Bruit de la main gauche* (Robert Laffont, Paris, 1996), p. 200.

11 F.-O. Giesbert, *Dying Without God* (Arcade, New York, 1998), pp. 70–1.

12 P. Bergé, *Inventaire Mitterrand* (Stock, Paris, 2001), p. 203.

13 *Politis*, 17 November 1994.

14 Glavany, *Mitterrand, Jospin et nous*, p. 188.

15 Ibid., p. 188.

16 Attali, *Verbatim*, vol. 3, p. 17.

17 Ibid., p. 26.

18 Bergé, *Inventaire Mitterrand*.

19 Attali, *Verbatim*, vol. 3, pp. 337, 363.

20 K. H. Jarausch, *The Rush to German Unity* (OUP, New York, 1994); T. Risse 'The Cold War's Endgame and German Reunification', *International Security*, 21 (4), Spring 1997, pp. 159–85.

21 P. Zelikov and C. Rice, *Germany Reunified and Europe Transformed* (Harvard University Press, Cambridge, Mass., 1995), p. 113.
22 J. W. Friend, *The Lynchpin: Franco-German Relations 1950–1990* (Praeger, New York, 1991), p. 82.
23 S. Cohen (ed.,) *Mitterrand et la sortie de la guerre froide* (PUF, Paris, 1998), p. 13.
24 Attali, *Verbatim*, vol. 3, pp. 369ff.
25 F. Elbe and R. Kessler, *A Round Table with Sharp Corners* (Nomos, Baden-Baden, 1996), pp. 112–13.
26 Zelikov and Rice, *Germany Reunified and Europe Transformed*, p. 145.
27 Attali, *Verbatim*, vol. 3, p. 1366; F. Elbe and E. Pond, *Beyond the Wall* (Brookings, Washington, 1993), pp. 192–6.
28 Attali, *Verbatim*, vol. 3, p. 350.
29 Friend, *The Lynchpin*, p. 82.
30 H. Védrine, *Les Mondes de François Mitterrand* (Fayard, Paris, 1996), p. 442; *Le Monde*, 24 November 1989.
31 Favier and Martin-Roland, *La Décennie Mitterrand*, vol. 3, p. 218.
32 Vedrine, *Les Mondes de François Mitterrand*, pp. 435–7.
33 Ibid., p. 554.
34 O. Duhamel and G. Grunberg (eds), *L'Etat de l'opinion 1993* (Seuil, Paris, 1993).
35 Attali, *Verbatim*, vol. 3, p. 401.
36 Cohen (ed.), *Mitterrand et la sortie de la guerre froide*, ch. 3.
37 Védrine, *Les Mondes de François Mitterrand*, p. 616.
38 J.-P. Huchon, *Jours tranquilles à Matignon* (Grasset, Paris, 1993), p. 94.
39 Attali, *Verbatim*, vol. 3, pp. 127–8.
40 *Le Monde*, 27 January 1989; G. Sengès and F. Labrouillère, *Le Piège de Wall Street* (Albin Michel, Paris, 1989).
41 *Le Figaro*, 23 September 1991.
42 Attali, *Verbatim*, vol. 3, p. 187.
43 Ibid., p. 444.
44 Huchon, *Jours tranquilles à Matignon*, p. 10.
45 Attali, *Verbatim*, vol. 3, pp. 551, 129.
46 *Le Monde*, 13 March 1991.
47 Attali, *Verbatim*, vol. 3, p. 562; Favier and Martin-Roland, *La Décennie Mitterrand*, vol. 3, p. 446.
48 J. Alia and C. Clerc, *La Guerre de Mitterrand* (Orban, Paris, 1991), p. 117.
49 Favier and Martin-Roland, *La Décennie Mitterrand*, vol. 3, p. 452.
50 N. Schwarzkopf, *It Doesn't Take a Hero* (Bantam Dell, London, 1993), p. 441.
51 Favier and Martin-Roland, *La Décennie Mitterrand*, vol. 3, pp. 454–5.
52 Attali, *Verbatim*, vol. 3, pp. 620ff; *L'Express*, 11 April 1991.
53 Cohen (ed.), *Mitterrand et la sortie de la guerre froide*, p. 363.
54 Attali, *Verbatim*, vol. 3, p. 759.

Chapter 9 The Last Years: 1991–1996

1 J. Lacouture and P. Rotman, *Mitterrand, le roman du pouvoir* (Seuil, Paris, 1990), p. 203.
2 N. Bazire, *Journal de Matignon* (Plon, Paris, 1995), p. 55.
3 *Le Monde*, 17 May 1991.
4 Ibid.
5 *Le Canard enchaîné*, 1 January 1992.
6 E. Schlema, *Edith Cresson, la femme piégée* (Flammarion, Paris, 1993), p. 187.

7 P. Favier and M. Martin-Roland, *La Décennie Mitterrand* (Seuil, Paris, 1999), vol. 4, p. 22.
8 Ibid., p. 19.
9 Schlema, *Edith Cresson*, p. 140.
10 Ibid., p. 102.
11 *Année politique 1991*, p. 48.
12 Machiavelli, *The Prince* (Penguin, London, 1956), p. 96.
13 *Année politique 1991*, p. 423.
14 *Le Figaro Magazine*, 5 July 1991.
15 Schlema, *Edith Cresson*, p. 201.
16 Ibid., ch. 6.
17 Ibid., p. 176.
18 *Observer*, 16 June 1991.
19 *Le Monde*, 20 June 1991.
20 Schlema, *Edith Cresson*, pp. 203–29.
21 Favier and Martin-Roland, *La Décennie Mitterrand*, vol. 4, p. 51.
22 *Le Monde*, 17 June 1991.
23 *Le Monde*, 23 August 1991.
24 H. Védrine, *Les Mondes de François Mitterrand* (Fayard, Paris, 1996), p. 581.
25 R. Dumas, *Le Fil et la pelote* (Plon, Paris, 1996), p. 276.
26 *Le Monde*, 10 January 1992.
27 Ibid., 19 March 1993.
28 Ibid., 9 March 1993.
29 Favier and Martin-Roland, *La Décennie Mitterrand*, vol. 4, p. 260; L. Adler, *L'Année des adieux* (Flammarion, Paris, 1996), pp. 30, 142.
30 L. Jospin, *L'Invention du possible* (Flammarion, Paris, 1991).
31 Favier and Martin-Roland, *La Décennie Mitterrand*, vol. 3, p. 278.
32 Védrine, *Les Mondes de François Mitterrand*, p. 554.
33 L. Mackenzie, *Peacekeeper: The Road to Sarajevo* (Douglas and McIntyre, Toronto, 1993), p. 195.
34 B. H. Lévy, *Le Lys et la cendre* (Grasset, Paris, 1996), pp. 60–1; M. Braustein, *François Mitterrand à Sarajevo: 28 Juin 1992* (L'Harmattan, Paris, 2001), p. 56.
35 Adler, *L'Année des adieux*, p. 84.
36 *Paris Match*, 9 July 1992.
37 Braustein, *François Mitterrand à Sarajevo*, p. 134.
38 B. Simms, *Unfinest Hour* (Penguin, London, 2001), p. 115.
39 S. Cohen (ed.), *Mitterrand et la sortie de la guerre froide* (PUF, Paris, 1998), ch. 3.
40 Lacouture and Rotman, *Mitterrand, le roman du pouvoir*, p. 256.
41 C. Gubler and M. Gonod, *Le Grand Secret* (Plon, Paris, 1996), p. 117.
42 Ibid., p. 36.
43 See *Paris Match*, 1 June 1996.
44 Gubler and Gonod, *Le Grand Secret*, p. 39.
45 Ibid., p. 65.
46 Ibid., p. 60.
47 Ibid., p. 67.
48 Gubler and Gonod, *Le Grand Secret*, p. 178; C. Salzmann, *Le Bruit de la main gauche* (Robert Laffont, Paris, 1996), p. 233.
49 Ibid., p. 71.
50 Adler, *L'Année des adieux*, p. 31.
51 Lacouture and Rotman, *Mitterrand, le roman du pouvoir*, p. 226; G. Sengès and F. Labouillière, *Le Piège de Wall Street* (Albin Michel, Paris, 1989), pp. 249–75.

52 Lacouture and Rotman, *Mitterrand, le roman du pouvoir*, p. 231.
53 Salzmann, *Le Bruit de la main gauche*, p. 93.
54 *Le Monde*, 17 August 1993; F. Subileau and M.-F. Toinet, *Chemins de l'abstention* (La Découverte, Paris, 1993).
55 *L'Evènement du jeudi*, 10 September 1996.
56 N. Bazire, *Journal du Matignon* (Plon, Paris, 1995), p. 92.
57 E. Balladur, *Deux ans à Matignon* (Plon, Paris, 1995), p. 62.
58 *Le Monde*, Dossiers et documents, 1993.
59 *Le Monde*, 25 March 1993.
60 Ibid., 26 March 1993
61 *L'Année politique, 1993*, p. 16.
62 Bazire, *Journal du Matignon*, p. 102.
63 Salzmann, *Le Bruit de la main gauche*, p. 233.
64 Lacouture and Rotman, *Mitterrand, le roman du pouvoir*, p. 262.
65 Alain Juppé, in ibid.
66 J. Glavany, *Mitterrand, Jospin et nous* (Grasset, Paris, 1998), p. 159.
67 *Le Monde*, 4 May 1993.
68 E. Plenel, *Un Temps de chien* (Stock, Paris, 1994), p. 110; C. Villeneuve, *Les Liaisons dangereuses de Pierre Bérégovoy* (Plon, Paris, 1993).
69 Villeneuve, *Les Liaisons dangereuses de Pierre Bérégovoy*, p. 175.
70 Adler, *L'Année des adieux*, pp. 133, 134.
71 M. Rocard, *Michel Rocard* (Flammarion, Paris, 2001), p. 237; *Le Monde*, 29 April 1994.
72 F. Bazin and J. Macé-Scaron, *Le Rendez-vous manqué* (Grasset, Paris, 1995), p. 271.
73 Balladur, *Deux ans à Matignon*.
74 *Le Figaro*, 1 May 1994.
75 Favier and Martin-Roland, *La Décennie Mitterrand*, vol. 4, p. 548.
76 *Le Monde*, 10 August 1994.
77 *Libération*, 9 January 1996.
78 Lacouture and Rotman, *Mitterrand, le roman du pouvoir*, pp. 262–3.
79 L. Melvern, *Conspiracy to Murder: The Rwandan Genocide* (Verso, London, 2004).
80 P. Péan, *Une Jeunesse française: François Mitterrand 1934–47* (Fayard, Paris, 1994); Adler, *L'Année des adieux*, p. 243.
81 *Le Figaro*, 8 September 1993.
82 *Paris Match*, 29 September 1994.
83 Adler, *L'Année des adieux*, p. 136.
84 E. Wiesel, *Mémoire à deux voix* (Odile Jacob, Paris, 1995). Serge Klarsfeld claims that Mitterrand slowed down the judicial process in Bousquet's case (*Libération*, 12 October 1994).
85 P. Alexandre, *Plaidoyer impossible pour un vieux Président abandonné par les siens* (Albin Michel, Paris, 1994), p. 24.
86 Gubler and Gonod, *Le Grand Secret*, p. 142.
87 *Libération*, 4 March 1993.
88 F.-O. Giesbert, *François Mitterrand, une vie* (Seuil, Paris, 1996), p. 318; G.-M. Benamou, *Le Dernier Mitterrand* (Plon, Paris, 1997).
89 *L'Express*, 13 April 1995.
90 *Libération*, 4 March 1993.
91 Ibid., 4 March 1993; J.-M. Pontaut and J. Dupuis, *Les Oreilles du Président* (Fayard, Paris, 1996).
92 *Le Quotidien de Paris*, 13 September 1994.
93 *Le Monde*, 14 August 1984.
94 Ibid., 6 February 1995.
95 Ibid., 16 May 1995.

96 Glavany, *Mitterrand, Jospin et nous*, p. 249.
97 C. Askolovitch, *Lionel* (Grasset, Paris, 2001), p. 196.
98 Favier and Martin-Roland, *La Décennie Mitterrand*, vol. 4, p. 551.
99 G. Leclerc and F. Muracciole, *Lionel Jospin: l'héritier rebelle* (JC Lattès, Paris, 1996), p. 287.
100 Ibid., p. 299.
101 *Libération*, 9 January 1996, p. 299.
102 *Le Figaro*, 3 March 1995.
103 *Le Monde*, 16 May 1995; Glavany, *Mitterrand, Jospin et nous*, p. 244.
104 Leclerc and Muracciole, *Lionel Jospin: l'héritier rebelle*, p. 294.
105 Ibid., p. 305.
106 F. Mitterrand, *Mémoires interrompus* (Odile Jacob, Paris, 1995).
107 Favier and Martin-Roland, *La Décennie Mitterrand*, vol. 4, p. 617.
108 *L'Evènement du jeudi*, 17 August 1995.
109 M. de Hennezel, *La Mort intime* (Laffont, Paris, 1995).
110 C. Berbier, *Les Derniers Jours de François Mitterrand* (Grasset, Paris, 1995).
111 Wiesel, *Mémoire à deux voix*, p. 53.
112 *L'Evènement du jeudi*, 17 August and 9 September 1995.
113 *Paris Match*, 31 October 1996; *Ici Paris magazine*, no. 2642, 21–27 February 1996.
114 *Le Monde*, 8 January 1996.

Conclusion: 'A Character from a Novel'

1 François Mauriac's description of François Mitterrand.
2 J. Glavany, *Mitterrand, Jospin et nous* (Grasset, Paris, 1998), p. 23.
3 L. Gauthier, *Mitterrand et son armée* (Grasset, Paris, 1999).
4 *L'Evènement du jeudi*, 18 March 1991.
5 C. Salzmann, *Le Bruit de la main gauche* (Robert Laffont, Paris, 1996), p. 217.
6 J.-E. Hallier, *L'Honneur perdu de François Mitterrand* (Rocher, Monaco, 1997), pp. 26–7; Y. Gattaz (head of the CNPF), in *Les Echos*, 8 January 1997.
7 F.-O. Giesbert, *Le Vieil Homme et la mort* (Gallimard, Paris, 1996), pp. 63, 64.
8 Glavany, *Mitterrand, Jospin et nous*, p. 149.
9 D. Benoist, *Mémoires de LUI et de MOI* (Editions du Terroir, Sury-en-Vaux, 2000).
10 H. Vedrine, *Les Mondes de François Mitterrand* (Fayard, Paris, 1996), p. 442.
11 Glavany, *Mitterrand, Jospin et nous*, p. 50.
12 *Le Nouvel Observateur*, May 1997; ('For Mitterrand, morality was for other people').
13 Glavany, *Mitterrand, Jospin et nous*, p. 146.
14 Ibid., p. 98.
15 Ibid., pp. 47ff.
16 For example S. Trano, *Les Amis d'abord* (L'Archipel, Paris, 2000).
17 Ibid.
18 Glavany, *Mitterrand, Jospin et nous*, p. 69.
19 Baltasar Graciàn y Morales, *The Hero* (Dent, London, 1953), p. 70.
20 Salzmann, *Le Bruit de la main gauche*, p. 191; C. Gubler and M. Gonod, *Le Grand Secret* (Plon, Paris, 1996), p. 169.
21 Glavany, *Mitterrand, Jospin et nous*, p. 121.
22 Gubler and Gonod, *Le Grand Secret*, pp. 88–9.
23 Glavany, *Mitterrand, Jospin et nous*, p. 97.
24 A.-M. Mitterrand, *Un Nom dur à porter* (Rocher, Paris, 2003).
25 Salzmann, *Le Bruit de la main gauche*, p. 208.
26 Glavany, *Mitterrand, Jospin et nous*, pp. 143–5, 149, 150.
27 Ibid., p. 96; Savaran, *Mitterrand, les autres jours*, p. 195.

28 Savaran, *Mitterrand, les autres jours*, p. 15.
29 Gubler and Gonod, *Le Grand Secret*, pp. 64–5.
30 Ibid., p. 73.
31 Graciàn y Morales, *The Hero*, p. 155.
32 *L'Unité*, 16 November 1975.
33 Graciàn y Morales, *The Hero*, p. 179.
34 P. Favier and M. Martin-Roland, *La Décennie Mitterrand* (Seuil, Paris, 1999), vol. 4, p. 690.
35 *Le Figaro*, 8 March 1989.
36 *Le Monde*, 24 February 1989.
37 *Paris Match*, 15 November 1988.
38 *Libération*, 6 July 1990.
39 *L'Evènement du jeudi*, 18 March 1991.
40 *Le Figaro*, 20 March 1993.
41 F. Chaslin, *Le Paris de François Mitterrand* (Gallimard, Paris, 1985).

Bibliography

Works by François Mitterrand

Aux frontières de l'union française, Indochine-Tunisie (Juillard, Paris, 1953).
Présence française et abandon (Plon, Paris, 1957).
Le Coup d'état permanent (Plon, Paris, 1964).
Ma Part de vérité (Paris, Fayard, 1969).
Un Socialisme du possible (Seuil, Paris, 1970).
La Rose au poing (Flammarion, Paris, 1975).
Politique 1 (Fayard, Paris, 1977).
Ici et maintenant (Fayard, Paris, 1980).
Politique 2 (Fayard, Paris, 1981).
La Paille et le grain (Flammarion, Paris, 1975).
Mémoires interrompus (Odile Jacob, Paris, 1996).

Other works

Adler, Laure, *L'Année des adieux* (Flammarion, Paris, 1996).
Alia, Josette and Clerc, Christine, *La Guerre de Mitterrand. La dernière grande illusion* (Orban, Paris, 1991).
Arbellot de Vacqueur, Simon, *Eau de Vichy, vin de Malaga* (Editions du Conquistador, Paris, 1952).
Archives nationales and Archives Guy Mollet.
Askolovitch, Claude, *Lionel* (Grasset, Paris, 2001).
Attali, Jacques, *Verbatim* (3 vols) (Fayard, Paris, 1995).
Baker, James A., *The Politics of Diplomacy* (Putnam's, New York, 1995).
Balladur, Edouard, *Deux ans à Matignon* (Plon, Paris, 1995).
Ballet, Marie, *Le Roman familial de François Mitterrand* (Plon, Paris, 1993).
Barril, Cap. Paul, *Guerres secrètes à l'Elysée* (A. Michel, Paris, 1996).
Bayart, Jean-François, 'France-Afrique: Aider moins pour aider mieux', *Politique africaine*, 55 (1992), pp. 141–59.
Bayart, Jean-François, 'Mitterrand et l'Afrique', *Politique africaine*, 91 (1995), pp. 3–100.
Bayart, Jean-François, 'La problématique de la démocratie en Afrique noire "La Baule, et puis après?"', *Politique africaine*, 43 (1991), pp. 5–20.

Bayart, Jean-François, *La Politique africaine de François Mitterrand* (Karthala, Paris, 1984).

Bayart, Jean-François, *L'Etat en Afrique* (Fayard, Paris, 1989).

Bazin, François and J. Macé-Scaron, *Le Rendez-vous manqué* (Grasset, Paris, 1995).

Bazire, Nicolas, *Journal du Matignon* (Plon, Paris, 1995).

Benamou, Georges-Marc, *Jeune homme vous ne savez pas de quoi vous parlez* (Plon, Paris, 2001).

Benamou, Georges-Marc, *Le Dernier Mitterrand* (Plon, Paris, 1997).

Benoist, Daniel, *Mémoires de LUI et de MOI* (Editions du Terroir, Sury-en-Vaux, 2000).

Benot, Y., *Massacres coloniaux, 1944–1950* (La Découverte, Paris, 2001).

Berbier, Christophe, *Les Derniers Jours de François Mitterrand* (Grasset, Paris, 1995).

Bergé, Pierre, *Inventaire Mitterrand* (Stock, Paris, 2001).

Berstein, Serge, Milza, Pierre and Bianco, Jean-Louis, *François Mitterrand: les années du changement 1981–1984* (Perrin, Paris, 2001).

Bocara, Edith, *Mitterrand en toutes lettres* (Belfon, Paris, 1995).

Braustein, Mathieu, *François Mitterrand à Sarajevo: 28 Juin 1992* (L'Harmattan, Paris, 2001).

Brulé, Michel et al. (eds), *Sondages*, 4 (IFOP, Paris, 1965).

Bugeaud, Pierre, *Militant prisonnier de guerre. Une bataille pour l'histoire* (L'Harmattan, Paris, 1990).

Cayrol, Roland, *François Mitterrand, 1945–1967* (FNSP, Paris, 1967).

Chafer, Tony, 'French African Policy; times of change', *African Affairs*, 91 (January 1992), pp. 37–51.

Chaslin, François, *Le Paris de François Mitterrand* (Gallimard, Paris, 1985).

Chevènement, Jean-Pierre, *Les Socialistes, les communistes et les autres* (Aubier Montagne, Paris, 1977).

Chipman, John, *French Power in Africa* (Blackwell, Oxford, 1989).

Christofferson, Thomas, R., *The French Socialists in Power, 1981–1986* (University of Delaware Press, London, 1991).

Clément, Claude, *L'Affaire des fuites* (Olivier Orban, Paris, 1980).

Cohen, Samy (ed.), *Mitterrand et la sortie de la guerre froide* (PUF, Paris, 1998).

Colliard, Sylvie, *La Campagne présidentielle de François Mitterrand en 1974* (PUF, Paris, 1979).

Conan, Eric, *Le Procès Papon. Un journal d'audience* (Gallimard, Paris, 1998).

Coussy, Jean, 'Des objectifs évolutifs', *Politique africaine*, 79 (1994), pp. 19–31.

Dantès, Edmond, *Mitterrand par lui-même* (Grancher, Paris, 1992).

Debray, Régis, *Loués soient nos seigneurs* (Gallimard, Paris, 1996).

Droz, Bernard and Lever, Evelyne, *Histoire de la guerre d'Algérie* (Seuil, Paris, 1982).

Duhamel, Alain, *Portrait d'un artiste* (Flammarion, Paris, 1997).

Duhamel, Eric, *François Mitterrrand, l'unité d'un homme* (Flammarion, Paris, 1998).

Duhamel, Olivier and Grunberg, Gérard, *L'Etat de l'opinion 1993* (Seuil, Paris, 1993).

Dumas, Roland, *Le Fil et la pelote* (Plon, Paris, 1996).

Dumas, Roland, *L'Epreuve, les preuves* (Lafon, Paris, 2003).

Dupeux, Georges, *Le Front populaire et les élections de 1936* (Colin, Paris, 1959).

Duroselle, Jean-Baptiste, *L'Abîme, 1939–45* (Seuil, Paris, 1990).

Einaudi, Jean-Luc, *Pour l'exemple. L'affaire Fernand Iveton* (L'Harmattan, Paris, 1986).

Elbe, F. and Kessler, R., *A Round Table with Sharp Corners* (Nomos, Baden-Baden, 1996).

Estier, Claude, *Journal d'un fédéré* (Stock, Paris, 1977).

Estier, Claude, *De Mitterrand à Jospin: Trente ans de campagnes présidentielles* (Stock, Paris, 1995).

Estier, Claude, *Mitterrand Président. Journal d'une victoire* (Stock, Paris, 1981).

Estier, Claude and Neiertz, Véronique, *Véridique histoire d'un septennat peu ordinaire* (Grasset, Paris, 1987).

Fabius, Laurent, *Les Blessures de la vérité* (Flammarion, Paris, 1995).

Fajon, Etienne, *L'Union est un combat* (Editions sociales, Paris, 1975).

Faux, Emmanuel, Legrand, Thomas and Prez, Gilles, *La Main droite de dieu* (Seuil, Paris, 1994).

Favier, Pierre and Martin-Rolland, Michel, *La Décennie Mitterrand*, 4 vols (Seuil, Paris, 1990).

Foccart, Jacques, *Foccart parle* (Fayard, Paris, 1997).

Forsne, C., *François* (Seuil, Paris, 1997).

François, Jean-Pierre, *Vol d'identité* (Albin Michel, Paris, 2000).

Frears, John, *Parties and Voters in France* (Hurst, London, 1991).

Friend, Julius W., *The Long Presidency: France in the Mitterrand Years 1981–1995* (Westview, Boulder, CO and Oxford, 1998).

Friend, Julius W., *The Lynchpin – Franco/German Relations 1950–1990* (Paeger, New York, 1991).

Gaetner, Gilles, *L'Argent facile* (Stock, Paris, 1992).

Galbraith, J. K., *The Anatomy of Power* (Hamish Hamilton, London, 1984).

Gauthier, Louis, *Mitterrand et son armée* (Grasset, Paris, 1999).

Giesbert, F.-O., *Dying Without God* (Arcade, New York, 1988).

Giesbert, F.-O., *François Mitterrand ou la tentation de l'histoire* (Seuil, Paris, 1977).

Giesbert, F.-O., *François Mitterrand, une vie* (Seuil, Paris, 1996).

Giesbert, F.-O., *Le Vieil Homme et la mort* (Gallimard, Paris, 1996).

Giroud, Françoise, *Le Bon Plaisir* (Mazarine, *sic*, Paris, 1983).

Giscard d'Estaing, Valéry, *Le Pouvoir et la vie* (Compagnie 12, Paris, 1991).

Glavany, J., *Mitterrand, Jospin et nous* (Grasset, Paris, 1998).

Goldey, D. B. and Knapp, A. F., 'Time for a Change: The French Elections of 1981', *Electoral Studies*, 1 (1) (April 1982), pp. 3–42; (August 1982), pp. 169–94.

Görtemaler, M., *Unifying Germany* (St Martin's, London, 1994).

Gow, James, *Triumph of the Lack of Will* (Hurst, London, 1997).

Grémion, Pierre, *Paris/Prague: La Gauche face au renouveau et à la régression tchécoslovaques 1968–1978* (Julliard, Paris, 1985).

Gubler, Claude and Gonod, Michel, *Le Grand Secret* (Plon, Paris, 1996).

Guichard, Marie-Thérèse, *Le Président qui aimait les femmes* (Laffont, Paris, 1993).

Halimi, Serge, *Sisyphe est fatigué, les échecs de la gauche au pouvoir* (Laffont, Paris, 1993).

de Hennezel, Marie, *La Mort intime* (Laffont, Paris, 1995).

Hibou, Béatrice, 'Politique économique de la France en zone franc', *Politique africaine*, 89 (1995), pp. 25–40.

Huchon, Jean-Paul, *Jours tranquilles à Matignon* (Grasset, Paris, 1993).

Hurtig, Serge (ed.), *Alain Savary: politique et honneur* (Presses de sciences po, Paris, 2002).

Jäckel, E., *La France dans l'Europe de Hitler* (Fayard, Paris, 1968).

Jarausch, Konrad, H., *The Rush to German Unity* (Oxford University Press, Oxford, 1994).

Jardin, Pascal, *La Bête et le bon dieu* (Flammarion, Paris, 1980).

Jospin, Lionel, *L'Invention du possible* (Flammarion, Paris, 1991).

Labi, Philippe, *Mitterrand. Le Pouvoir et la guerre* (Ramsay, Paris, 1991).

Laborie, Pierre, *L'Opinion française sous Vichy* (Seuil, Paris, 1990).

Lacoste, Admiral Pierre, *Un Amiral au secret* (Flammarion, Paris, 1997).

Lacouture, Jean, *François Mitterrand, une histoire de français*, 2 vols (Seuil, Paris, 1998).

Lacouture, Jean and Rotman, Patrick, *Mitterrand, le roman du pouvoir* (Seuil, Paris, 2000).

Laïdi, Zaki (ed.), *L'Ordre mondial relâché* (FNSP, Paris, 1993).

Lang, Caroline, *Le Circle des intimes* (La Sirène, Paris, 1996).

Leclerc, Gérard and Muracciole, Florence, *Lionel Jospin: L'héritier rebelle* (JC Lattès, Paris, 1996).

Le Gall, G., 'Le déclin du Pcf', in SOFRES, *L'Opinion publique 1986* (Gallimard, Paris, 1986).

Lemoine, Yves, *Monsieur le Ministre d'État Roland Dumas* (le Félin, Paris, 2002).

Lévy, B. H., *Le Lys et la cendre* (Grasset, Paris, 1996).

Liégeois, Jean-Paul and Bédéï, *Le Feu et l'eau* (Grasset, Paris, 1990).

MacKenzie, Lewis, *Peacekeeper: The Road to Sarajevo* (Douglas and McIntyre, Toronto, 1993).

McKesson, John A., 'France and Africa: The Evolving Saga', *French Politics and Society*, 11(2) (Spring 1993), pp. 55–69.

Malik, Serge, *Histoire secrète de SOS racisme* (Albin Michel, Paris, 1990).

Manceron, P. and Pingaud, B., *François Mitterrand. L'Homme – les idées – le programme* (Flammarion, Paris, 1981).

Marchal, Roland, 'Mitterrand, Djibouti et la Corne de l'Afrique', in *Politique africaine*, 89 (1995), pp. 65–83.

Martinet, Gilles, *Cassandre et les tueurs* (Grasset, Paris, 1986).

Mauroy, Pierre, *Mémoires, 'Vous mettrez du bleu au ciel'* (Plon, Paris, 2003).

Melvern, L., *Conspiracy to Murder: The Rwandan Genocide* (Verso, London, 2004).

Ménière, Laurent, *Bilan de la France 1981–1993* (Pluriel, Paris, 1993).

Mitterrand, Anne-Marie, *Un Nom dur à porter* (Rocher, Paris, 2003).

Mitterrand, Robert, *Frère de quelqu'un* (Laffont, Paris, 1988).

Mossuz, J., *Les Clubs et la politique en France* (Colin, Paris, 1970).

Moulin, Charles, *Mitterrand intime* (Albin Michel, Paris, 1982).

Nay, Catherine, *Le Noir et le rouge* (Grasset, Paris, 1984).

Northcutt, Wayne, *Mitterrand: A Political Biography* (Holmes and Meier, New York, 1992).

Paxton, R. O., *Vichy France: Old Guard and New Order 1940–1944* (Norton, New York, 1972).

Péan, Pierre, *Une Jeunesse française: François Mitterrand 1934–47* (Fayard, Paris, 1994).

Penne, Guy, *Mémoires d'Afrique* (Fayard, Paris, 1999).

Plenel, E. and Rollat, Alain, *Mourir à Ouvéa* (La Découverte, Paris, 1998).

Plenel, Edwy, *La Part d'ombre* (Stock, Paris, 1993).

Plenel, Edwy, *Un Temps de chien* (Stock, Paris, 1994).

Pond, Elizabeth, *Beyond the Wall* (Brookings, Washington, 1993).

Pontaut, Jean-Marie and Dupuis, Jérôme, *Les Oreilles du Président* (Fayard, Paris, 1996).

Raimond, Jean-Baptiste, *Le Quai d'Orsay à l'épreuve de la cohabitation* (Flammarion, Paris, 1989).

Rémond, René, *Le Gouvernement de Vichy* (FNSP, Paris, 1972).

Riker, William, *The Art of Political Manipulation* (Yale University Press, New Haven, 1986).

Risse, T., 'The Cold War's Endgame and German Reunification', *International Security*, 21 (4) (Spring 1997), pp. 159–85.

Rocard, Michel, *Michel Rocard* (Flammarion, Paris, 2001).

Rondin, Jacques, *Le Sacre des notables, la France en décentralisation* (Fayard, Paris, 1985).

Ross, George et al. (eds), *The Mitterrand Experiment* (Polity, Cambridge, 1987).

Roy, Claude, *Moi, je. Essai d'autobiographie* (Gallimard, Paris, 1969).

Salzmann, Charles, *Le Bruit de la main gauche* (Robert Laffont, Paris, 1996).

Savaran, Pascal, *Mitterrand, les autres jours* (Albin Michel, Paris, 1997).

Savary, Alain, *En toute liberté* (Hachette, Paris, 1985).

Schifres, Michel and Sarazin, Michel, *L'Elysée de Mitterrand: secrets de la maison du prince* (Alain Moreau, Paris, 1985).

Schlema, Elizabeth, *Edith Cresson: la femme piégée* (Flammarion, Paris, 1993).

Schwarzkopf, H. Norman, *It Doesn't Take a Hero* (Bantam Dell, London, 1993).

Sengès, Gilles and Labrouillère, François, *Le Piège de Wall Street* (Albin Michel, Paris, 1989).

Simms, Brendan, *Unfinest Hour* (Penguin, London, 2001).

Simonian, Haig, *The Privileged Partnership* (Oxford University Press, Oxford, 1985).

Siriex, Paul-Henri, *Félix Houphouët-Boigny* (Nathan, Paris, 1987).

Smith, Stephan and Glasser, Antoine, *Ces messieurs d'Afrique* (Calmann-Lévy, Paris, 1992).

Smith, Tony, 'Recipe for Disaster', *French Politics and Society*, 14 (3) (Summer 1996).

Subileau, Françoise and Toinet, Marie-France, *Chemins de l'abstention* (La Découverte, Paris, 1994).

Tourancheau, Jean-Marc, *Catherine Langeais, la fiancée des français* (Fayard, Paris, 2003).

Tiersky, Ronald, *François Mitterrand. A Very French President* (Rowman and Littlefield, Lanham, 2003).

Thiolon, J.-R., *Coup d'état* (Plon, Paris, 1960).

Trano, Stéphane, *Mitterrand les amis d'abord* (l'Archipel, Paris, 2006).

Védrine, Hubert, *Les Mondes de François Mitterrand* (Fayard, Paris, 1996).

Verdon, Hugh, *We Landed by Moonlight* (Ian Allen, London, 2071).

Villeneuve, Charles, *Les liaisons dangereuses de François Mitterrand* (Plon, Paris, 1993).

Violet, Bernard, *L'Ami imparfait. Le mystérieux conseiller de François Mitterrand* (Albin Michel, Paris, 1998).

Wauthier, Claude, *Quatre Présidents et l'Afrique* (Seuil, Paris, 1995).

Wiesel, Élie, *Mémoire à deux voix* (Odile Jacob, Paris, 1995).

Williams, P. M., *Crisis and Compromise: Politics in the Fourth Republic* (Longman, London, 1964).

Williams, P. M., *French Politicians and Elections 1951–1969* (Cambridge University Press, Cambridge, 1970).

Williams, P. M., *Wars, Plots and Scandals in Post war France* (Cambridge University Press, Cambridge, 1970).

Archives de France

5AG4/EG66, d2; 5AG4/EG88, d1; 5AG4/EG98, d2, 5AG4/
5AG4/EG89 d2, 5AG4/EG89, d3; 5AG4/EG91, d1, 5AG4/
5AG4/CD174, d3, 5AG4/CD174, d1; 5AG4/J(1)2164; 5AG4
5AG4/EG73, d3; 5AG/5(4)EG96, d3, 5AG4/EG87, d1; 5AG4/

Index